From the President's Pen

AN ILLUSTRATED GUIDE TO PRESIDENTIAL AUTOGRAPHS

by

LARRY F. VRZALIK

and

MICHAEL MINOR

introduction by

Senator Ralph W. Yarborough

STATE HOUSE PRESS

1991

Library of Congress Cataloging-in-Publication Data

Vrzalik, Larry F., 1955-
From the president's pen : an illustrated guide to presidential
autographs / by Larry F. Vrzalik and Michael Minor ;
introduction by Ralph W. Yarborough.
p. cm.
ISBN 0-938349-34-1 (cloth) — ISBN 0-938349-59-7 (pbk.)
ISBN 0-938349-61-9 (lim. ed.)
1. Presidents — United States — Autographs.
2. Autographs — Collectors and collecting — United States.
I. Minor, Michael, 1946- . II. Title.

Z42.3.P7V79 1990
973'.092'2 — dc20
[B]

90 — 19634

Printed in the United States of America

STATE HOUSE PRESS
P.O. Box 15247 ● Austin, Texas 78761

Dedications

Dedicated to my mother, Millie Vrzalik.

L.V.

Dedicated to the loving memory of my mother, Lillian Ervin Minor.

M.M.

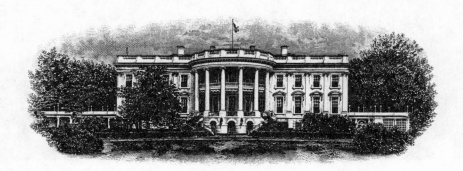

Best Wishes to Michael Manr — Jimmy Carter

Post presidential signed and inscribed photograph of Jimmy Carter and co-author, Michael Minor. 1987.

TABLE OF CONTENTS

PREFACE

The purpose of the authors in writing *From the Presidents' Pen* is to provide autograph collectors with a study guide to the authentic philographic material of the presidents of the United States, including scores of illustrations of previously unpublished presidential autographs, some of which are historically significant. Biographical sketches of the presidents, many containing little known anecdotes about the presidents, emphasize their humanity as well as their major accomplishments.

Our book also contains a price guide to presidential autographs and a section highlighting the history of autograph collecting, detailing how to start and assemble a valuable autograph collection.

The philographic material of recent presidents has been emphasized because of the confusion about their authentic material, particularly John F. Kennedy's, Lyndon B. Johnson's, and Richard M. Nixon's. In other cases, especially with those presidents from World War I to the present, the biographical sketches have been written in more depth because of the greater impact these chief executives have had on our lives today.

Heading each section is a brief synopsis of the basic facts about each president, his dates of birth and death, the dates of his term of office, his political affiliation, and the major events of his presidential administration.

A Recommended Reading List of many fine and classic works on autograph collecting is included in Appendix A, as well as a list of the names and addresses of autograph collector organizations and publications in Appendix B.

From the Presidents' Pen additionally contains a monograph on the handwriting and signature of Lyndon B. Johnson entitled "Lyndon B. Johnson: The Surprising Modern Presidential 'Button Gwinett.' " The monograph is the first and only study ever done on the philographic material of our 36th president. The Johnson study has been included because, ironically, the authentic autographic material of Lyndon B. Johnson may be the scarcest of all the presidents, particularly in holographic material.

We gratefully acknowledge the help and encouragement of many of our colleagues and customers, whom we regard as friends. We especially acknowledge the friendship and aid of the late Conway Barker, who helped us in the beginning. Our thanks and appreciation also to Senator Ralph Yarborough, a great statesman, jurist, scholar, bibliophile, and autograph collector, who read our manuscript and graciously consented to write the introduction for our book. Finally, we extend special thanks to our friends and publishers, Tom Munnerlyn and Deborah Brothers, for putting up with us.

LARRY F. VRZALIK
MICHAEL MINOR
Kaufman, Texas
August, 1990

INTRODUCTION

RUMINATIONS OF A WOULD-BE PRESIDENTIAL AUTOGRAPH COLLECTOR

. . . is a strange title for an introduction to a serious presidential autograph text by two experts on presidential autographs, Mike Minor and Larry Vrzalik, who together have collected and studied presidential autographs for over thirty years.

I am not an expert on presidential autographs, but my two friends have urged me to write a brief introduction because of my own collection and because I have observed two presidents, John F. Kennedy and Lyndon B. Johnson, autographing books and photographs on several occasions in the White House.

My involvement in presidential autographs goes back to my earliest days. I was born in 1903 in a small town of five hundred people on the banks of the Neches River deep in East Texas, a town of strong southern heritage. I personally knew many Confederate veterans who resided there and I absorbed every word as they exchanged their war experiences. My favorite was a Virginian who had charged with Pickett's Brigade at Gettysburg where his company was decimated from sixty-three at the morning roll call to only four who answered the evening roll call. Heady stuff for a young boy. I longed as only a child can for just one memento of that tragic period — a Confederate button, a discharge paper, or anything indigenous to the Confederacy. At last I became the proud owner of a pair of faded Confederate stamps and felt I had touched a star!

As I became older and my experience broadened, my interest centered on the American Revolution with its glories and its heroes, and I began to yearn for something written by a signer of the Declaration of Independence. I decided that, in order to possess something that was part of the American record, I should look to presidential autographs, symbols of our history from the American Revolution into the present and even the future.

My democratic heroes, Thomas Jefferson, Andrew Jackson, Woodrow Wilson and Franklin D. Roosevelt were beyond my means, but Herbert Hoover's autographs were in abundant supply. Soon I had a number of Hoover letters, but since I was a strong Democrat in a strong Democratic area, I never mentioned it to anyone. Campaigning for Harry Truman, I received a thank-you note which possibly had a printed signature. When Harry Truman left the White House, however, he seemed to answer everything with a letter, even birthday greetings, and soon I had more Truman letters than Hoover letters. Whether many of the Hoover and Truman letters were actually signed by them I still do not know, but considering myself a man of the people, letters from these common-man presidents had a special appeal to me.

To return to the reason I was asked to write this introduction, I can comment only on what I saw or experienced concerning the genuine signatures of Kennedy and Johnson on letters, photographs or books.

The authors of this book contend that Kennedy rarely ever personally signed a book, photograph or letter, as he had several secretaries and an autopen to do most of the signing. They argue that every Kennedy signature on a letter, photograph or book is subject to challenge and can be accepted as a genuinely personal signature only when observed by witnesses.

I personally watched John F. Kennedy sign a stack of letters and photographs in the White House on an occasion resulting from my efforts to obtain his aid for my Cold War GI Bill for educating veterans. I had first introduced the bill in the United States Senate in 1958, when both Kennedy and Johnson were senators who had aided me in passing the bill in the Senate, but it had been blocked in the House at the urging of President Eisenhower and the Pentagon.

After Kennedy became president, I proposed the same bill only to hear from him, "Yes Ralph, but I am president now." Finally, in the third year of his presidency, he granted me another opportunity to present it, and I was hoping that he would relent and approve my bill.

When I came into the White House room where the appeal was to be made, his personal secretary, Mrs. Lincoln, was waiting with a stack of papers, including photographs, for his signature. I saw immediately that this was a working session and that his main business was signing papers and photographs. Having served with Kennedy on the Senate Labor and Public Welfare Committee for four years, I was familiar with his habits and knew he would continue working and would listen with only half an ear to my often-heard pleas. In the course of the meeting, Mrs. Lincoln placed a number of papers and photographs before him, with a brief statement of who or what was involved, and brought a pillow to put under his right elbow on the desk. As he was signing the photographs, I was aware that this brilliant man knew I wanted one but wouldn't ask for it. I thought perhaps, before bidding me a kind adieu, he would present me one with a nice inscription as a sop to his repeating "Yes Ralph, but I am president now," concerning my GI bill.

I wasn't willing to scrap my bill in exchange for an autographed photograph, but I thought he would be reelected the following year and there would be plenty of time for both the bill and the photograph in his second term. I left his office without the photograph or the bill, but with an indelible and cherished memory of that smiling, charming man saying "Ralph, we are friends."

Then he was gone. I still have no autographed photograph of John F. Kennedy, and I believe the authors are correct in their opinion as to the scarcity of genuine autographed material—he was such a dynamic president he could not take time to hold autograph parties. Then too, he was killed after serving only thirty-four months of his vigorous presidency. I have read that Kennedy's plans for the future after the presidency included writing or teaching, which would have increased the availability of signatures, but the opportunity never came for him to do either.

President Lyndon B. Johnson, of course, was the antithesis of John F. Kennedy. He was the shrewdest politician I have ever known. Although he was generous to a fault with books which had been written about him, as well as photographs and objects which he showered on other people without waiting to be asked , the authors of this book point to his similar use of secretaries and autopens and to his seldom taking time to autograph items personally. They also describe his gifts of books, photographs, and other objects to augment support for his objectives. I often observed these strategies being used. As I sought to get his support for my Cold War GI Bill, he would look up and smile, as though he had read Kennedy's tapes, and intone "Yes, Ralph, but I am president now."

On visits with President Johnson at the Ranch or the White House, to make yet another appeal for my GI Bill, he would shower me with books or photographs autographed in my presence. Knowing the interest of every senator, he was aware of my love of books and my book collection. I doubt that he took much time for signing many of the books and gifts he pressed upon others. A dynamo in action, the process was simply too slow; his bevy of secretaries and the autopen did that work for him. It is my opinion that the authors are correct in estimating that there is no large body of books, letters, or photographs genuinely autographed by Johnson. Caveat emptor, let the buyer beware, would be the safest rule for the buyer in search of genuine material autographed by Johnson. Although he served as president for sixty-two months, he was so extremely active that I do not think he allocated much time for autograph parties.

RALPH W. YARBOROUGH

n.b. With the growing opposition to the war in Viet Nam, I was able to steer my Cold War Viet Nam GI Bill to passage in 1966, when President Johnson had an elaborate signing ceremony. I had the great personal satisfaction of knowing that, by the mid 70's, over 8,200,000 veterans had received benefits under the Bill.

RWY

Autograph Collecting, Past and Present

Autograph collecting is almost as old as recorded history; Cicero is reported to have treasured a letter of Julius Caesar! More recently, Queen Victoria was an avid collector, and among her prizes was a letter from the aged James Madison, who wrote her with palsied difficulty. Two of our presidents, Franklin D. Roosevelt and John F. Kennedy, have been autograph collectors. A letter from the Washington-Lafayette correspondence was given by President Kennedy to French President Charles De Gaulle as a state gift.

Autographs have weathered all economic storms; they continued to escalate in value in the midst of the Great Depression as well as during the more recent stock market crash. During the last ten years, however, fine quality documents have escalated in price at an average of 15 to 20 percent a year. Paradoxically, the worse the economy the better the document market—fine autographs offer collectors and investors a relatively risk-free investment. For example, thirty years ago a document signed by Thomas Jefferson as president and James Madison as secretary of state was sold by a major dealer for $38.50. Ten years ago the same document sold for $1,500. Today the document is worth approximately $5,000. Many collectors now have valuable "blue chip" investment portfolios of autographs, and investors are driving the prices still higher with no end in sight.

The number of autograph collectors has increased during the last ten years from approximately five thousand to approximately fifteen thousand, and the number is steadily increasing.

Fine quality items in all specialties are desirable, and among the most avidly collected fields are presidents, scientists, vintage movie figures, literary giants, major historical figures, and aviation greats.

When acquiring a letter or document, its content, condition, rarity and, of course, authenticity should be considered. The best insurance when buying autographs is to buy from established, knowledgeable, and reputable dealers who offer unqualified money-back guarantees of authenticity. In terms of value, it is generally better to purchase one $1,000 item than ten $100 items. Happily, an interesting and valuable autograph collection can still be assembled for the price of a postage stamp. Collectors can acquire a valuable collection within a few years by writing celebrities and obtaining their autographs by mail. The value of their collections will be as valuable as the time and effort they put into them. A celebrity's autograph or signed photograph is not nearly so valuable as a well-written, well-thought-out letter. Not all celebrities will respond—or if they do it might be with a secretarial or autopen signature. For example, all letters and autographs from incumbent presidents (and, in some instances, former presidents) should not be considered genuine until *proven* genuine. However, a large percentage, 50 percent or more, of the celebrities one writes to ask for an autograph will respond. Letters to a celebrity should always include a stamped, self-addressed return envelope. Various publications which are available through autograph collector organizations contain the addresses of thousands of celebrities.

Autographs can quite easily be cared for if a few simple but basic rules are followed. Never, ever, for any reason whatsoever, should adhesive tape or glue be applied to autographs, nor should they be kept in sleeves or album pages which have an adhesive backing. The adhesive backing used in some photograph albums becomes permanently affixed to the photograph or autograph, causing irreversible damage. Repairs should be made only by an expert. If properly done, framing can enhance both the value and appearance of an autograph, but if improperly done it can damage or destroy the autograph. Only archival, acid-free materials should be used in framing autographs, and no glue or tape should be used on the autograph in the framing process. Framed items should not be hung where direct sunlight can touch them, as sunlight will cause the ink to fade and the document or photograph to become brittle, eventually destroying it.

In the past few years, interior decorators have discovered that attractively framed autographs make interesting accent, display, and conversation pieces, and a number of autograph galleries specializing in framed material have sprung up. The acquisition of more and more items in this fashion has been a factor in the continued rise in prices for autographic material.

As in any field, there is no substitute for knowledge, and one should educate oneself about autograph collecting. A number of fine books on the subject have been written and are listed in the Recommended Reading List.

1. GEORGE WASHINGTON

February 22, 1732 - December 14, 1799

First President
April 30, 1789 - March 4, 1797

Federalist

Highlights in office:
Bill of Rights; U.S. neutrality
maintained in Anglo-French War;
Whiskey Rebellion; Jay's Treaty.

George Washington was from a land-poor Virginia family. His father died when he was eleven, and his formal education was sporadic at best. He is the only one of our first six presidents who did not attend college. When he was fourteen George wanted to run away to sea, probably to get away from his shrewish and tyrannical mother, Mary Ball Washington, whose children all escaped from home at early ages. Mrs. Washington, seemingly resentful of her famous son's success, falsely and publicly complained that he neglected her. To Washington's extreme embarrassment she applied to Congress for financial aid. She also refused to participate in any event honoring him, including his presidential inauguration.

As a youth, Washington experienced a number of close calls with death. Before he was thirty he suffered from smallpox, pleurisy, malaria, and dysentery. While returning from his famous expedition to the French Fort Le Boeuf, he fell off his raft into icy river water and almost drowned. During the same trip an Indian, standing less than fifty feet away, shot at him but missed.

In 1753, when Virginia was threatened with French attack, Washington was commissioned a lieutenant colonel of the militia. His ill-advised attack on a French scouting party became one of the precipitating events of the French and Indian War. He showed great valor and courage at the battle known as "Braddock's Defeat" in 1755, during which four bullets punctured his coat and two horses were shot out from under him. By his leadership about a third of the British-American troops escaped with their lives. Consequently he was promoted to full colonel at the age of twenty-three, given command of all Virginia forces in the French and Indian War, and for three years skillfully defended the Virginia frontier from Indian and French attack. These combat actions were the extent of his military experience when he was named commander in chief of the American forces during the revolutionary war.

Biographers and historians have made much of the fact that Washington turned down a salary as commander in chief and asked only that his expenses be paid, but the fact of the matter is that Washington made a very shrewd business decision. Had he accepted the $500 a month salary, or its equivalent, he would have received a total of approximately $50,000 for all his war service; however, during the eight year period his "expenses" totaled almost $500,000! Among his expenses were such items as new carriages and imported wines for his headquarters.

Washington fell in love with but was spurned by several young ladies before he was twenty-five, and at least two marriage proposals are known to have been rejected. The love of his life was a married woman, Sally Fairfax, who was one of the daughters-in-law of a wealthy and powerful Virginia family. Washington corresponded with Sally throughout his life, and it is to her that he wrote his final letter shortly before he died. She was then a destitute sixty-eight year old widow living in London.

Washington eventually married Martha Custis, a widow with two small children, who was one of the wealthiest

1

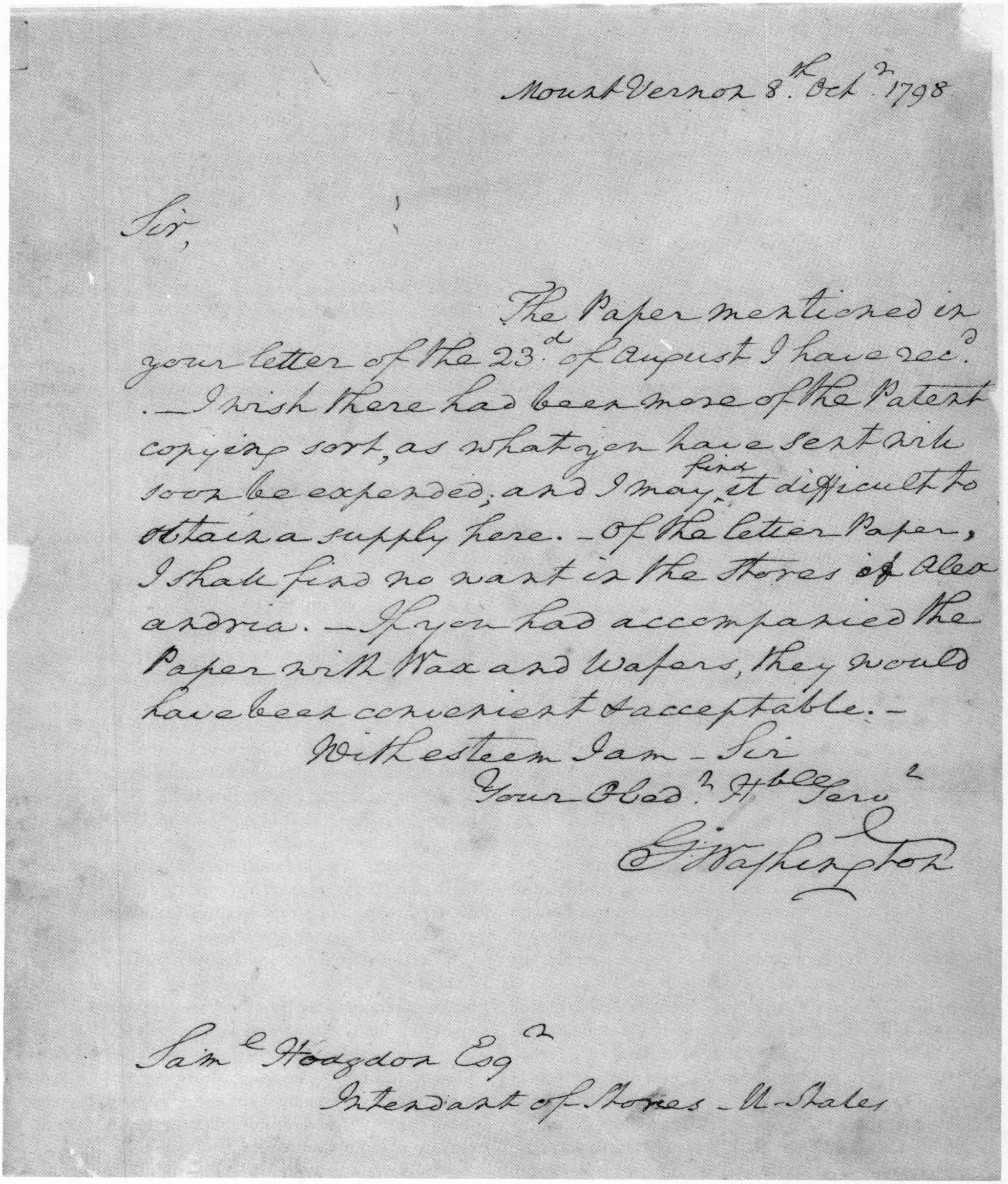

Mount Vernon 8th Octr 1798.

Sir,

The Paper mentioned in your letter of the 23d of August I have recd. — I wish there had been more of the Patent copying sort, as what you have sent will soon be expended, and I may find it difficult to obtain a supply here. — Of the Letter Paper, I shall find no want in the Stores of Alexandria. — If you had accompanied the Paper with Wax and Wafers, they would have been convenient & acceptable. —

With esteem I am — Sir
Your Obedt Hbl Serv
G Washington

Saml Hodgdon Esqr
Intendant of Stores — U. States

Post presidential Washington Autograph Letter Signed., 1798

women in Virginia. George capably managed and expanded Martha's vast holdings, and at the time of his death they were one of the wealthiest couples in America. George was also an affectionate and over-indulgent stepfather to Martha's children. Inasmuch as Martha burned all of Washington's letters to her after his death, little is known about their personal relationship. It was not exactly a love match, but it is certain that they developed a deep respect and attachment for each other.

Although contemporary accounts on his height are conflicting, Washington was between six feet two inches and six feet three and one-half inches. His face was deeply pockmarked from small pox, and by the time he was in his late fifties he had lost all his teeth. Throughout the rest of his life he engaged in a never-ending and frustrating search for dentures which would fit him. It is his poorly fitting dentures which give Washington's portraits their tight-lipped, unsmiling appearance—he was in fact simply trying to keep his teeth from falling out!

Although Washington was known for his calm and courteous disposition, when provoked he had a raging temper and could swear quite colorfully. Once, while he was commander in chief, two drunk soldiers brawling outside his tent so enraged him that he charged outside and knocked them out cold with his massive fists.

Washington died at his famous home, Mount Vernon, on December 14, 1799, two months before his sixty-eighth birthday. He had become chilled two days earlier while riding fifteen miles through hail and snow to inspect his farms. He awoke in the night with a chill, and although he could speak and breath only with difficulty, he refused to allow his wife to get out of bed to call a servant for fear she would catch cold. His condition, further weakened by the ministrations of his physicians, which included bleeding him, probably turned into pneumonia. Shortly before his death he placed the fingers of his left hand on his right wrist and counted his pulse. His last words were: "Tis well."

Autographs of Washington are more scarce than are complete letters or documents bearing his signature—most people had the good sense not to cut the signatures off of the complete documents.

Although all of his handwriting was quite attractive and graceful, Washington's early handwriting and signatures are more ornate and florid than his later, plainer, more flowing script. The transition was complete by the time Washington was thirty years old, and his handwriting and signature varied little thereafter. His revolutionary correspondence, for which he employed a number of secretaries, including Alexander Hamilton, is avidly sought. Washington personally wrote his private letters during the revolutionary period and thereafter. Although he employed secretaries to write most of his official correspondence, he personally signed much of it. Like many of his contemporaries, Washington's spelling and punctuation were subject to whim.

In terms of content, although Washington's letters generally lack the substance and strong opinions of the letters of John Adams and Thomas Jefferson, he nevertheless wrote a good letter. He used gracefully turned phrases and usually conveyed his thoughts plainly and succinctly. The letters with the most interesting content generally date from the revolutionary war period, and thus are the most avidly sought. Most are Ls.S. instead of A.Ls.S.

Land surveys done by the youthful Washington are quite desirable and have become both scarce and expensive. Washington is also obtainable in various types of financial documents, signed lottery tickets and vouchers from his pre-revolutionary period.

Revolutionary war discharges, all personally signed by Washington, are particularly desirable items. They were cherished by the recipients, usually being kept in the family Bible. Most are very worn and faded. A pristine example of a revolutionary war discharge signed by Washington is extremely rare and highly desirable.

A large number of Washington's letters and documents from all periods concern real estate and financial matters. The "Father of our Country", almost always short of cash, was extremely interested in all details of his lands and personal finances.

Although the number of Washington's letters and documents is plentiful, the great demand far exceeds the supply. Many documents and letters are being absorbed by institutions, never again to appear on the market. Because of Washington's popularity, he has been a favorite subject for forgers. Holographic bank checks of Washington have been widely forged, and all such examples should be carefully scrutinized. Fortunately, however, Washington's handwriting is difficult to duplicate. Washington forgeries, like almost all other forgeries, are smaller than his normal handwriting and, when closely examined, do not have the graceful flow of his authentic holographs. Washington's presidential documents are rare, and many of those extant have light or faded signatures.

2. JOHN ADAMS

October 30, 1735 - July 4, 1826

Second President
March 4, 1797 - March 4, 1801

Federalist

Highlights in office:
Department of the Navy established;
Alien and Sedition Acts;
peace treaty with France.

John Adams was the first president to occupy the White House, which was still unfinished when he and his family moved in on November 1, 1800, with less than five months remaining in his term. Adding to the gloom of his defeat for reelection by Jefferson in December, 1800, was the dampness in the White House walls, still so wet that seven cords of wood had to be burned to dry them out.

Adams was a Harvard graduate, a schoolteacher, and a brilliant lawyer who had successfully and courageously defended a group of British redcoat soldiers prior to the revolution. He was also a forceful revolutionary essayist, a member of the Massachusetts legislature and a delegate to the Continental Congress. He served as envoy to France and Holland, as minister to Great Britain, and as the first vice president of the United States.

John Adams' administration focused on diplomatic relations with France where the Directoire, the ruling group, refused to receive the American envoy and suspended commercial relations with the U.S., a contretemps which resulted in the "X-Y-Z Affair." Adams' sending of a peace mission to France was probably instrumental in his defeat for reelection.

A short, plump man only five feet seven inches tall, Adams was called "His Rotundity" by his critics. He had an irascible personality and a sharp tongue with which he delivered strong opinions. Although a fierce and uncompromising patriot who rendered exceptionally selfless services to the United States, he was more remarkable as a political philosopher than as a politician.

Adams died on July 4, 1826, at his Braintree home in

Massachusetts on the fiftieth anniversary of the Declaration of Independence, a document for which he was in large measure responsible. He lived to be older than any other president — 90 years, 147 days — and his last words were "Thomas Jefferson still lives." Jefferson had in fact died a few hours earlier on the same day.

Although John Adams, with Herbert Hoover, was probably the most prolific presidential correspondent, his letters and documents are among the most expensive and most avidly sought of all the presidents. Adams was the only president who held only one term until his son, John Quincy Adams, the sixth president, was also defeated for reelection. John Adams' presidential-signed documents are particularly rare and expensive, and pristine examples with choice dark signatures are very scarce since Adams' signatures tend to be rather faded or, equally undesirable, signed with an uneven ink-flow in which some letters are faint and others dark. Ink from quill pens apparently did not adhere evenly to vellum documents, frequently causing the signatures to have a mottled and unattractive appearance.

Adams' signature changed markedly during his life. His early signatures were quite small and are most frequently found in the form of legal documents written while he was a practicing attorney. These early legal documents are often signed with a simple "J. Adams." Adams' signature reached its zenith in both size and attractiveness during his presidential term, and his post-presidential signatures again diminished in size. His advanced-age signatures and holographs were small and palsied and had

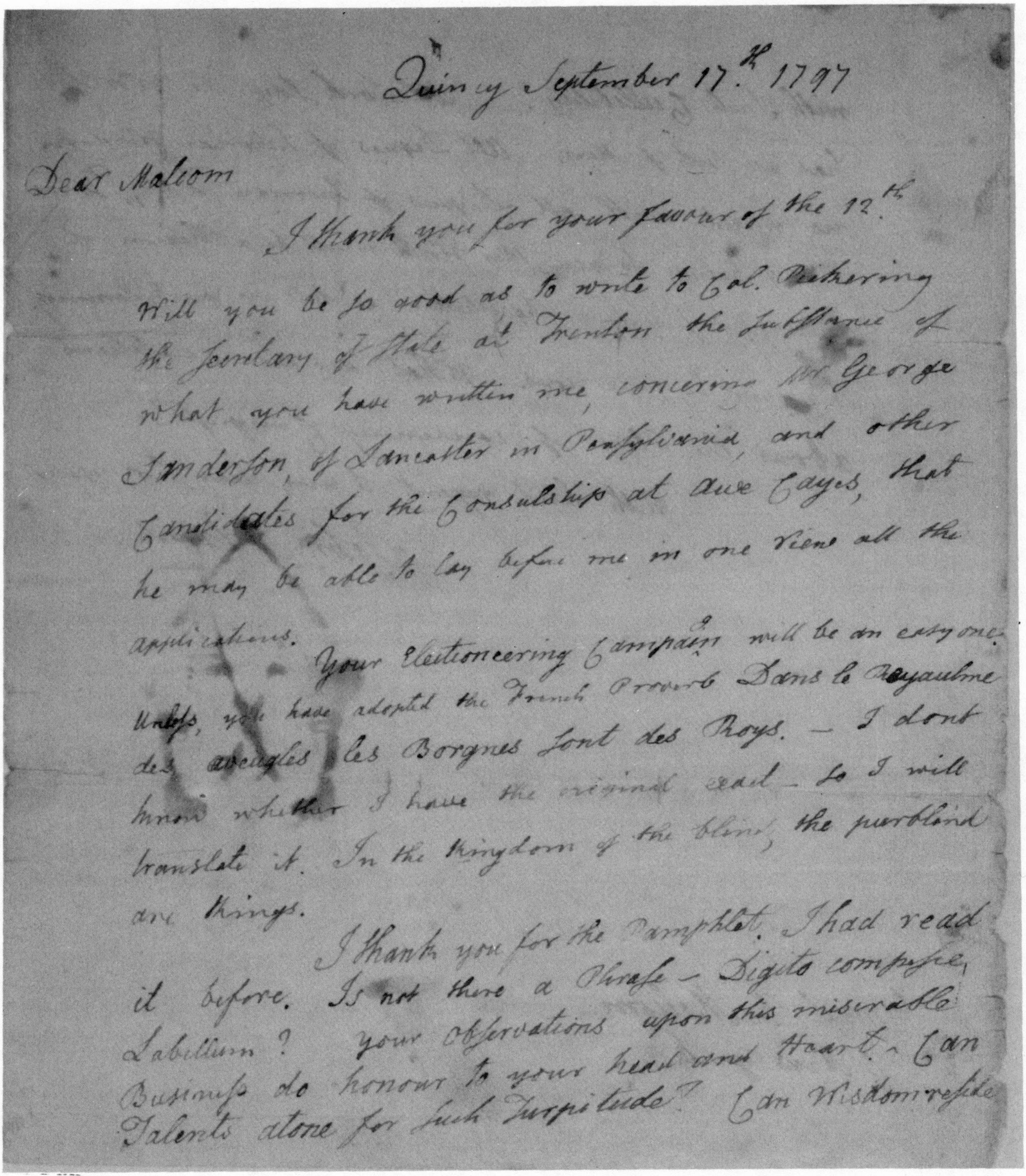

Quincy September 17th 1797

Dear Malcom

I thank you for your favour of the 12th

Will you be so good as to write to Col. Pickering the Secretary of State at Trenton the substance of what you have written me, concerning Mr George Sanderson, of Lancaster in Pensylvania, and other Candidates for the Consulship at Aux Cayes, that he may be able to lay before me in one view all the applications.

Your Electioneering Campaign will be an easy one. Unless you have adopted the French Proverb Dans le Royaume des aveugles les Borgnes sont des Roys. — I dont know whether I have the original exact. So I will translate it. In the kingdom of the blind, the purblind are kings.

I thank you for the Pamphlet. I had read it before. Is not there a Phrase — Digito compesce Labellum? Your observations upon this miserable Business do honour to your head and Heart. Can Talents atone for such Turpitude? Can Wisdom reside

---

John Adams presidential Autograph Letter Signed written to his private secretary, Samuel B. Malcom (who was a son-in-law of General Philip Schuyler and a brother-in-law of Alexander Hamilton), mentioning, in part: "What are the speculations about the place of convening Congress?" (reduced 82%)

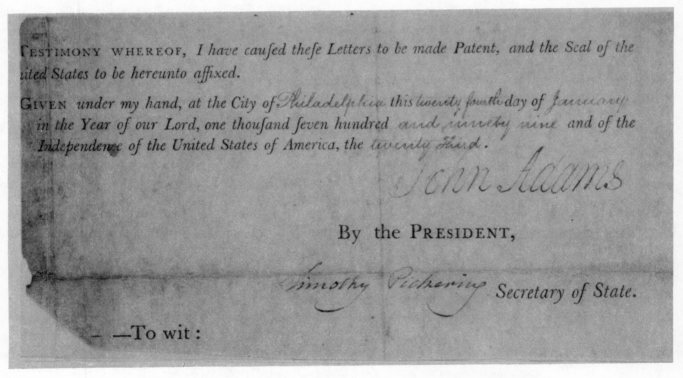

with such Gullibility? Mr Lock says the World has all sorts of Men. All Degrees of human Wisdom are mixed with all Degrees of human Folly. To me and I believe, to you, this World would be a Region of Torment, if such a Recollection existed in our Memories. This must be, entre nous. What are the Speculations about the Place of convening Congress?

With kind regard, I am, dear Sir, your

John Adams

Verso of John Adams presidential Autograph Letter Signed, 1747.

TESTIMONY WHEREOF, I have caused these Letters to be made Patent, and the Seal of the united States to be hereunto affixed.

GIVEN under my hand, at the City of *Philadelphia* this *twenty fourth* day of *January* in the Year of our Lord, one thousand seven hundred *and ninety nine* and of the Independence of the United States of America, the *twenty third*.

John Adams

By the PRESIDENT,

Timothy Pickering Secretary of State.

— —To wit :

Lower portion of John Adams presidential Document Signed, 1799. (reduced 82%)

the appearance of being printed rather than written, no doubt due to the arthritic condition in his hands.

John Adams wrote extremely interesting letters, many laced with vitriol, self-pity, self-righteousness, his philosophy of life, and his views about contemporaries and events of the day. He stated his views in the strongest possible terms, frequently using Latin words and phrases and references to the classics, all of which add to the desirability of his letters. In summary, John Adams was possibly the most skilled and most interesting letter writer of all the presidents, and he is certainly one of the most expensive.

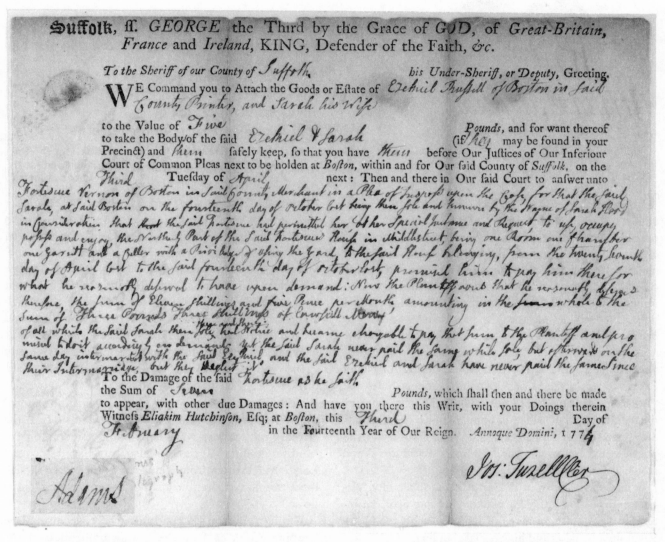

Early partially printed Autograph Document Signed, of attorney John Adams, 1774. (reduced 82%)

3. THOMAS JEFFERSON

April 13, 1743 - July 4, 1826

Third President
March 4, 1801 - March 4, 1809

Democrat-Republican

Highlights in office:
Louisiana Purchase; reinstated rights of free
speech and press; avoided American
involvement in Napoleonic Wars.

Thomas Jefferson was the most versatile and broadly educated of all our presidents. Of his contemporaries, possibly only Benjamin Franklin rivaled him as a scholar, inventor and philosopher, but even Franklin could not match Jefferson in architectural and farming skills, musical abilities, and medical knowledge. Jefferson is also remembered for his lifetime concerns regarding personal liberty. He is among the few presidents who had no driving ambition for high office or politics, preferring the academic atmosphere of the philosopher. A toast President Kennedy gave at a White House dinner for Nobel Prize winners perhaps best sums up Thomas Jefferson: "We have assembled here this evening the most extraordinary collection of talent, of human knowledge, that has ever been gathered together at the White House, with the possible exception of when Thomas Jefferson dined alone."

Jefferson was born in 1743 in Albemarle County, Virginia. From his father, a planter and surveyor, he inherited five thousand acres of land; from his mother, a Randolph, he inherited high social standing.

Jefferson became a prosperous colonial lawyer and, at age twenty-six, was a member of the Virginia House of Burgesses. At age thirty-three he authored the Declaration of Independence. He later became governor of Virginia, minister to France, and secretary of state under Washington. As a reluctant candidate for president in 1796 he came within three votes of victory; through a technicality in the Constitution he became vice president, even though he was an opponent of President-elect Adams. In 1800 this constitutional defect caused a more serious problem. Republican electors, attempting to name both a president and vice president from their own party, cast a tie vote between Jefferson and Aaron Burr, and the House of Representatives settled the tie. Alexander Hamilton disliked both Jefferson and Burr, but he nevertheless urged Jefferson's election. Although Hamilton was no longer a cabinet member he still retained great influence with congress and had a loyal following.

When Jefferson assumed the presidency, the crisis with France had passed. He cut military and defense expenditures, reduced the budget, and eliminated the unpopular Whiskey Tax while at the same time reducing the national debt by a third. He sent an American fleet to fight the Barbary pirates who were harassing commerce on the Mediterranean. Jefferson also purchased the vast Louisiana Territory from Napoleon in 1803, even though there was no constitutional authority empowering him to do so.

During Jefferson's second term, he concentrated on keeping America from becoming embroiled in the Napoleonic Wars. Both England and France were interfering with the neutrality of American merchantmen, and Jefferson tried to solve the problem with an embargo on shipping which was both ineffective and unpopular.

Jefferson was over six feet two inches tall with a fair, freckled complexion, carrot-red hair and hazel eyes. He preferred informality and comfortable clothes, and once scandalized the British ambassador when he received him wearing a worn brown coat and carpet slippers.

Jefferson suffered most of his life from severe migraine headaches. While president, one migraine lasted six weeks without relief. Jefferson bathed his feet every morning in cold water because he thought this practice would prevent colds. During the eight years of his presidency he depleted his personal fortune, largely in official entertaining, and ran up a personal wine bill of $10,835. He kept a pet mockingbird in his White House study and taught the bird to sit on his shoulder and take food from his lips.

Jefferson's inventions included a letter-copying press, a revolving chair, a pedometer, a revolving music stand and a hemp machine.

As a young man, Jefferson led a somewhat scandalous personal life. He attempted to seduce the wife of one his friends and pursued an unhappy relationship with another Virginia lass before he married the young widow Martha Skelton. Their ten years of marriage were happy ones. Martha died at thirty-three, worn out from child bearing. On her death bed Jefferson promised Martha he would

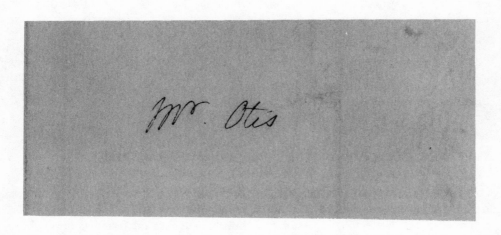

Third person presidential Autograph Letter Signed with integral address leaf, all in Jefferson's hand.

never remarry, a promise he honored although he had other relationships, including one with a married woman, the beautiful Maria Cosway, while he was minister to France. Jefferson's primary involvement, however, was with an octoroon slave named Sally Hemings, a lovely creature with long, straight dark hair and an olive complexion. One of the 135 slaves bequeathed to Jefferson by his father-in-law, she was actually the half-sister of Jefferson's wife, as she had been born out of an illicit union between Jefferson's father-in-law and one of his mulatto

contemporaries, and it was used against him by his critics and the newspapers while he was president.

Like John Adams, Thomas Jefferson also died on July 4, 1826, the fiftieth anniversary of the signing of The Declaration of Independence.

As the philosophic father of the American Revolution, Jefferson's letters are among the most avidly sought and expensive of all the presidents. Large quantities of his material continue to be absorbed by institutions.

So eclectic were Jefferson's interests and so vast was his

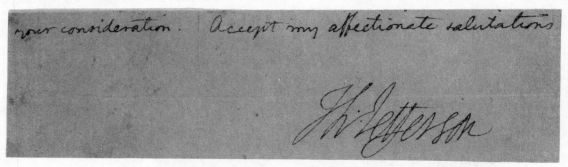

Concluding portion of Jefferson Autograph Letter Signed

slaves. At the age of fifteen, Sally Hemings accompanied Jefferson's daughter on the voyage to join Jefferson in Paris, and she probably became Jefferson's concubine soon thereafter. Under French law Sally was free, and before she would agree to return to America with Jefferson she made him promise to free any children she might bear him before the children were twenty-one. She subsequently bore five children, some, if not all, fathered by Jefferson. Visitors to Monticello reported the uncanny resemblance between Jefferson and some of his slaves; the resemblance between Jefferson and one of his black slave-sons was reportedly so strong that from a distance it was impossible to tell them apart. Jefferson's involvement with Sally Hemings was common knowledge among his

knowledge that the content of his letters quite literally ranged the spectrum of man's knowledge. He wrote well-informed letters on farming, horticulture, zoology, architecture, medicine, philosophy, religion, law, politics, mathematics, astronomy, music, and science.

Jefferson's letters were formal, correct, polished, eloquent and erudite. Interesting idiosyncrasies were his habit of seldom beginning a sentence with a capital letter, and his frequently writing letters in the formal, third-person style. Jefferson's penmanship was small, rounded, and devoid of ornamentation. His signatures are proportionately so much larger than his script that his A.Ls.S. are sometimes mistaken for Ls.S.

While Jefferson was minister to France he wrote fluent letters in French. Some of his official communiques to Washington are in code or cipher. Jefferson is readily available in presidential documents, many of which were co-signed by his secretary of state, James Madison. He is scarce in clipped signatures, partially because he normally responded to requests for his autograph with an A.L.S.

Autographic material of Jefferson is in great demand and the price continues to escalate steadily with no end in sight.

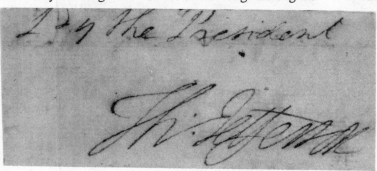

Jefferson signature from a presidential document.

4. JAMES MADISON

March 16, 1751 - June 28, 1836

Fourth President
March 4, 1809 - March 4, 1817

Democrat-Republican

Highlights in office:
War of 1812; White House burned;
Second U.S. Bank chartered;
protective tariff instituted.

James Madison, the "Father of the Constitution," was the smallest of our presidents, at five feet four inches and weighing only ninety-five pounds. His popular nickname was "Jemmy". He was reared in Orange County, Virginia. A graduate of Princeton and a revolutionary activist, he was too frail and sickly to enlist in the Continental Army. Madison was always plagued with ill health and did not think he would live long. He was elected to the Virginia legislature at age twenty-five and later became a delegate to the Continental Congress and a leading figure at the Constitutional Convention. He was co-author of the Federalist Papers, a member of the House of Representatives, organizer of the Democratic-Republican party, and Thomas Jefferson's secretary of state. Madison was Jefferson's personal choice to succeed him, and in 1808 he won an easy victory over the Federalist candidate Charles C. Pinckney.

Before Madison took office, the Embargo Act was repealed and, during the first year of his administration, the United States prohibited trade with both Great Britain and France. In 1810 Congress authorized trade with both countries but directed the president that, should either country recognize America's neutrality, trade should be curtailed with the other. Napoleon pretended to comply and Madison proclaimed a policy of passive non-intercourse with Great Britain. The congressional "War Hawks," including Henry Clay and John C. Calhoun, pressured the president into more militant action.

British impressment of American seamen and their seizure of ships' cargos forced Madison to bow to congres-

sional pressure, and on June 1, 1812, he asked Congress to declare war. The country was unprepared for war, however, and its forces were defeated in the early battles. The nation experienced its ultimate humiliation when British troops captured the city of Washington and burned the White House. Later the tide turned with American naval and military victories, climaxed by General Andrew Jackson's brilliant triumph at New Orleans which, ironically, occurred two weeks after the signing of the Treaty of Ghent ending the war. A great surge of nationalism resulted, so thoroughly repudiating the Federalists who had opposed the war that the Federalists ceased to exist as a national party.

Madison retired to Montpelier, his estate in Orange County. In retirement he spoke out against the disruptive states' rights influences that threatened his beloved union.

Madison remained a bachelor until he was forty-three, when his friend Aaron Burr introduced him to a lively and charming widow named Dolley Todd. Theirs was a long and happy union, and Dolley became a distinct asset to her husband and one of the most famous of all first ladies.

James Madison is the only president to face enemy gunfire while in office. When the British invaded Washington "Jemmy" personally took command of an artillery battery, but soon escaped when it became apparent defeat was imminent.

After Madison's death in 1836, a note he had written was opened which stated: "The advice nearest to my heart and deepest in my convictions is that the Union of the States be cherished and perpetuated."

Madison post presidential Autograph Letter Signed regarding the sale of land.

James Madison, wrote a small, plain, unembellished and legible script. He signed his name in full on official documents and correspondence, but on personal correspondence he frequently signed himself "J. Madison." Madison's letters tend to be somewhat terse, formal, dull, and generally lack the grace and interest of his presidential predecessors. Like John Adams, in his later years Madison was troubled by arthritis which caused his holographs to have the appearance of tremulous printing, since the letters within the words were disconnected.

Like his predecessors and the other Founding Fathers, the great bulk of Madison's letters and papers have been

absorbed by institutions. For this reason, both Madison's A.Ls.S. and Ls.S. are scarce and expensive. However, Madison's Ds.S. are quite plentiful, particularly in the form of the numerous land grants which resulted from the Louisiana Purchase. Even more fortuitous is that Madison's land grants were co-signed by his secretary of state, James Monroe, who also co-signed military commissions when he was Madison's secretary of war. As with most of the early presidents, Madison is also scarce in cut signatures. He is relatively common in franking signatures, many of which date from his tenure as secretary of state.

A recent upsurge in interest in Madison has caused the price of his material, particularly his letters, to substantially rise in price.

5. JAMES MONROE

April 28, 1758 - July 4, 1831

Fifth President
March 4, 1817 - March 4, 1825

Democrat-Republican

Highlights in office:
Monroe Doctrine; acquisition of
Florida; Missouri Compromise.

James Monroe is one of the "Virginia Dynasty," the fourth of five presidents from the Old Dominion. He is known for the Monroe Doctrine and the "Era of Good Feelings," a period almost devoid of political strife. According to legend, Monroe would have received a unanimous electoral vote when he was reelected in 1820, but one elector voted for John Quincy Adams so that Washington would continue to hold the distinction of having received the only unanimous electoral vote.

In actual fact, Monroe's political career was far less placid than his presidency. As a diplomat in Europe he angered both Presidents Washington and Jefferson, and he offended Madison in 1808 by offering himself as a rival presidential candidate. Although he had a good record as Madison's secretary of state and secretary of war, he was not the universal favorite for the presidential nomination of 1816. With the Federalist party in a state of collapse, however, Monroe swept to an easy victory of 183 to 34 over Rufus King. In his reelection in 1820 he was virtually unopposed and carried the electoral college 231 to 1.

Monroe was a college dropout. He volunteered to fight in the revolutionary army, rising to the rank of major, then studied law under Thomas Jefferson and served as a Virginia assemblyman, U.S. senator, ambassador to France, governor of Virginia, then secretary of state and secretary of war under Madison, serving simultaneously in both posts during the War of 1812.

A well-built man who was six feet tall, Monroe was said to bear a striking resemblance to George Washington. As one contemporary described him: "He is tall and well formed. His dress plain and in the old style....His manner was frank and dignified. From the frank, honest expression of his eye I think he well deserves the encomium passed upon him by the great Jefferson...."

During the revolution, Monroe served as aide to the alcoholic General Stirling. Legend has it that Stirling taught his young aide to drink; all his life Monroe was a heavy drinker although not regarded as a problem drinker.

When Monroe was twenty-eight he married Elizabeth Kortwright, the beautiful daughter of a wealthy New York merchant, with whom he had two daughters. In personal matters Monroe was dominated by his elegant wife and daughters, notorious and affected snobs who put on airs. They spent money so extravagantly that Monroe died almost destitute. As first lady, Mrs. Monroe immediately decreed that she would neither make nor return social calls, a heresy to the congressional ladies who, in retaliation, boycotted Mrs. Monroe's "at-homes." So strained did relations become between the ladies that President Monroe referred the matter to his secretary of state, John Quincy Adams. In his diary Adams blamed Mrs. Monroe for having raised "this senseless war of protocol."

As president, Monroe chose an unusually strong cabinet, naming John C. Calhoun, a southerner, as secretary of state.

Early in his administration he undertook a national good-will tour which, at Boston, was called the beginning of an "Era of Good Feelings." The name thereafter became associated with his administration.

The Missouri Compromise occurred under Monroe. It paired the entry of Missouri, a slave state, with Maine, a

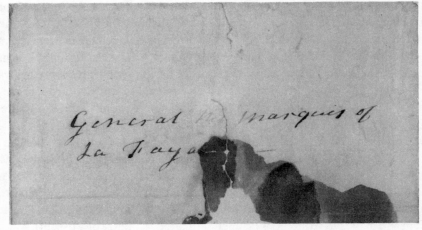

Washington June 10. 1823

Dear Sir

Mr Haines, a citizen of New York, very respectable for his talents, & sound in his political principles, intends to compose a work on our form of government, & has inti:mated a desire to communicate with you on the subject. Well knowing the deep interest, which you take, in all the concerns of our country, & particularly in what relates to the principles of our government, in support of which you fought, & bled, in our re:volutionary struggle, I have not hesitated, to for:ward Mr Haines's object, by giving him this let:ter of introduction to you. I avail myself of the opportunity, of renewing to you the assurance of my great respect, & of the constant & sincere re:gard of dear Sir yours —

James Monroe

Monroe presidential letter of introduction to the famous Revolutionary War patriot Lafayette.

General the Marquis of
La Fayette

Address cover to LaFayette in Monroe's hand.

14

free state, and forever barred slavery north and west of Missouri.

In foreign affairs Monroe promulgated the doctrine that bears his name in response to the threat of attempts by conservative European governments to assist Spain in winning back her former Latin American colonies. Monroe did not formally recognize the young Latin American republics until 1822, after determining that Congress would fund diplomatic missions, because he and Secretary of State John Quincy Adams wanted to avoid trouble with Spain until it ceded the Floridas, which it did in 1821. Monroe subsequently stated: "The American continents are henceforth not to be considered as subjects for future colonization by any European powers."

Monroe died in New York City on July 4, 1831, the third founding father to die on the anniversary of the Declaration of Independence.

James Monroe wrote a heavy, angular, unembellished hand. He usually signed his name in full but on occasion abbreviated his first name to "Jas.," particularly on pre-presidential documents. On rare occasions he signed himself "J. Monroe." His autographic material is more common than for any of his predecessors, and is par-

ticularly plentiful in signed documents. Monroe probably signed more land grants than any other president, both as Madison's secretary of state and later as president with John Quincy Adams as his secretary of state.

Like the man himself, Monroe's letters are courteous but direct and to the point. Although they are formal and written in the somewhat stilted phraseology of the nineteenth century, his letters exude honesty, sincerity, and good will. Jefferson once said: "Monroe is so honest that if you turned his soul inside out there would not be a spot on it." It was no accident that Monroe's administration became known as the "Era of Good Feelings." Happily for collectors, he is more common in A.Ls.S. than in Ls.S. One peculiarity of his A.Ls.S. is that his handwriting is often noticeably larger at the end of the documents than at the beginning. His signatures are larger than his writing, but not disproportionately so.

As had Jefferson and Madison before him, Monroe suffered extreme financial hardship in his post-presidential years, and he died a virtual pauper. Many of his post-presidential letters are in regard to his pathetic financial plight.

Concluding portion of a Monroe Autograph Letter Signed.

6. JOHN QUINCY ADAMS

July 11, 1767 - February 23, 1848

Sixth President
March 4, 1825 - March 4, 1829

Democrat-Republican

Highlights in office:
Erie Canal; Baltimore and Ohio
Railroad; joint occupation with
England of the Oregon country.

John Quincy Adams is the only president who was the son of a president. He seems to have been born and bred to fight for liberty, for as a boy he watched the Battle of Bunker Hill from atop Penn's Hill near his family's farm.

The young Adams received much of his early training while aide and companion to his father, John Adams. He was a Harvard graduate and a Boston lawyer who later served as diplomatic representative to Holland, Prussia, and Russia. He also served as U.S. senator, minister to England, and secretary of state under Monroe. He was the actual author of the Monroe Doctrine, and one of our greatest and most skilled secretaries of state.

When he was thirty, he married Louisa Catherine Johnson in London, the lovely daughter of an American diplomat. Despite major difficulties, the marriage lasted over fifty years. Many years later his wife wrote: "As it regards women, the Adams family are one and peculiarly harsh and severe in their characters. There seems to exist no sympathy, no tenderness for the weakness of the sex." The Adams' had three sons; their eldest, George Washington Adams, a would-be poet who suffered from hallucinations, committed suicide at age twenty-eight by jumping off a river boat and drowning.

When Adams ran for the presidency as the candidate of the North, neither he nor the other three candidates, Andrew Jackson, William H. Crawford, and Henry Clay, received a majority of the electoral votes. The election was decided by the House of Representatives, and Adams was elected when Clay, who favored a program similar to Adams', threw his crucial support to his fellow New Englander.

As soon as he became president, Adams appointed Henry Clay as his secretary of state. Jackson and his angry followers charged that a "corrupt bargain" had taken place, and they immediately began their successful campaign to defeat Adams in 1828.

In Adams' first annual message to Congress, he proclaimed a remarkable national program even more commendable in light of the congressional hostility he faced. He proposed that the federal government unite the various sections of the country with a network of highways and canals, and also that the government develop and conserve the public domain by using funds from the sale of public lands. In 1828 Adams broke ground for the 185 mile Chesapeake Ohio Canal. He also recommended that the U.S. take the lead in the development of the arts and sciences by establishing a national university. Additionally, he recommended that the government finance scientific expeditions and erect a national observatory, a recommendation which technically may have been the inception of our space program. Adams' opponents labeled his proposals unconstitutional.

As president, Adams had the habit of slipping down to the Potomac River at 5 a.m. on warm mornings and swimming nude in the river. A lady reporter, Ann Royalle, who had been unsuccessful in her attempts to interview the president, surprised him in the buff during one of his swims, sat on his clothes, and refused to leave until he

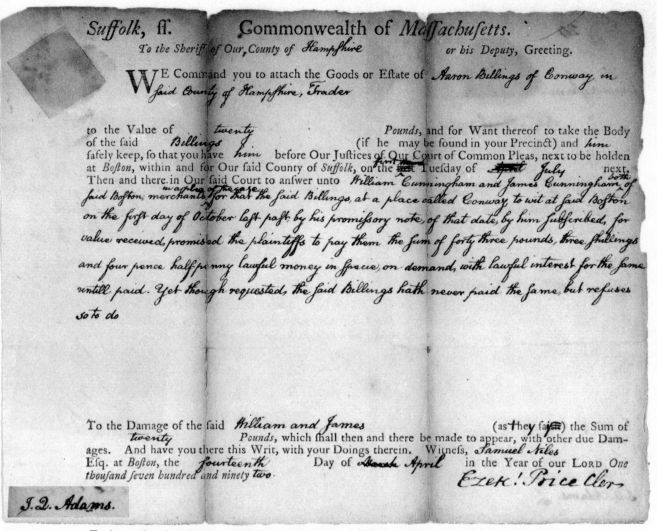

Early partly printed Autograph Document Signed of attorney John Quincy Adams, 1792.

agreed to give her the long-sought interview—to which he hastily acquiesced.

The campaign of 1828 was an ordeal that Adams did not suffer gladly. Jacksonian followers accused him of public plunder and corruption. After his overwhelming and ignominious defeat, like his father he did not remain in Washington for the inauguration of his successor. He returned to Massachusetts where he expected to spend the rest of his life in retirement, as had his father; however, in 1830 the Plymouth district in his home state unexpectedly elected him to the House of Representatives where, for the remaining eighteen years of his life, he served with honor and distinction. He emerged as a powerful leader of the anti-slavery and anti-sectional forces. In 1836 southern congressmen passed a gag rule providing that the House automatically table anti-slavery petitions. Adams tirelessly fought the rule, and eight years later obtained its repeal. He became known as "Old Man Eloquent," and

died from complications following a stroke in the speaker's room in the U.S. House of Representatives where he had tirelessly fought the forces of slavery.

John Quincy Adams was a linguist and diarist, and he holds the distinction of being the only president to be a published poet. Full poems written entirely in Adams's handwriting and signed by him are highly desirable and are both scarce and expensive. More common are stanzas from his poems written in autograph albums. He also knew and practiced shorthand.

Adams wrote a small, neat, meticulous and legible hand which, unlike his father's, varied little throughout his life, although his old-age handwriting, like his father's, became quite tremulous. Adams' signature was small and identical to his writing in both size and appearance. With equal frequency he signed his name in full and with initials on both letters and documents of all periods. Happily, he is more common in A.Ls.S. than in Ls.S. With the exception

Quincy 30. August 1802. For value received I promise to pay John Quincy Adams or order the sum of four thousand six hundred and sixteen dollars and thirty seven cents, on demand, with interest untill paid.

John Adams

4616 : 37.

Unique promissory note entirely in the hand of John Quincy Adams, signed by his father, John Adams. Documents signed by both father and son are extremely rare and desirable. John Adams used the proceeds of the loan to pay off debts probably incurred while he was president and to pay off "lands."

Boston 26 February 1873

Dear Sir

I have nothing left at hand for an autograph of John Adams but the inclosed note, the body of which was written by John Quincy Adams, and the signature is crossed

If that will do, you are welcome to it. If not, please destroy it.

Yrs ~

Charles Francis Adams

of his writing during his diplomatic career, both domestic and foreign when many of his letters were prepared for his signature by a secretary, he personally wrote all his letters. Adams is common in Ds.S. and franks. Although scarce and costly, he is also obtainable in copies of signed congressional speeches and in signed engravings of his likeness. In his old age he was the first president to be photographed, but no signed photographs of him are known to exist.

For the most part, Adams did not write interesting letters. His poetical turn of phrase did not carry over to his letters, which were usually written in the formal, dull, legalese phraseology of the day. However, when provoked, which was not particularly difficult to do, Adams could and did write fiery letters, of excellent content, which did credit to those of his father.

Autograph Letter Signed of Charles Francis Adams sending the promissary note of his father and grandfather.

7. ANDREW JACKSON

March 15, 1767 - June 8, 1845

Seventh President
March 4, 1829 - March 4, 1837

Democrat

Highlights in office:
Nullification crisis; opposed the
Bank of the United States.

Andrew Jackson was the first president who considered himself to be the personal representative of the common man—the first "peoples' president." He aroused great passions, both for and against him. His supporters virtually deified him while his opponents with equal energy vilified him. Thomas Jefferson said of him in 1824: "I feel much alarmed at the prospect of seeing General Jackson president. He is one of the most unfit men I know for such a place."

Jackson was born March 15, 1767, in the frontier region known as "The Waxhaws" along the border between North and South Carolina, and both states claim the honor of being his birth place. His formal education was sketchy and sporadic, and he became a volunteer with the revolutionary forces when he was fourteen years old. He was a gambler, cock fighter and brawler before becoming a lawyer and public prosecutor in Tennessee Territory. He was elected to the House of Representatives and the U.S. Senate, appointed a superior court judge, speculated in land, slaves and race horses, became a major general of volunteers in the War of 1812, and was the hero of the Battle of New Orleans. He was also the defeated presidential candidate in the bitterly contested presidential election of 1824.

Jackson married Rachel Donelson before her divorce from her previous husband was final, a fact which neither Jackson nor Rachel knew. Their error was an innocent one, and when Jackson learned the divorce had not been finalized until after his marriage to Rachel, they immediately had another marriage ceremony performed. In the bitter presidential election of 1828 Jackson was called an adulterer and Rachel a bigamist, and Jackson fought numerous duels defending his wife's honor. During the presidential campaign Rachel became deeply depressed by all the scurrilous charges and probably suffered a nervous breakdown as a result. Sadly, she died shortly after her husband was elected but before he was inaugurated. During the vicious campaign Jackson was also called a murderer, duelist and gambler. In one bit of gutter journalism his mother was described as a "common Prostitute, brought to this country by British Soldiers. She afterward married a mulatto man, with whom she had several children, one of whom is General Jackson."

In Jackson's first annual message to Congress he recommended elimination of the electoral college. He also believed that government offices should rotate among deserving applicants, the most deserving of whom, of course, were his supporters, a practice which became known as the "spoils system".

Jackson's polarization of national politics caused two political parties to evolve. The Democrats, emerging out of the Democratic-Republican party, supported Jackson, while the National Republicans, or Whigs, opposed him.

Whig leaders, such as Henry Clay and Daniel Webster, proclaimed themselves defenders against Jackson's usurpation of the "popular liberties," and hostile cartoonists portrayed him as "King Andrew I." Regarding his opponents, Jackson said in 1837: "I have only two regrets: that I have not shot Henry Clay or hanged John C. Calhoun."

Unlike previous presidents, Jackson did not defer to Congress in policy-making matters; he used both his veto

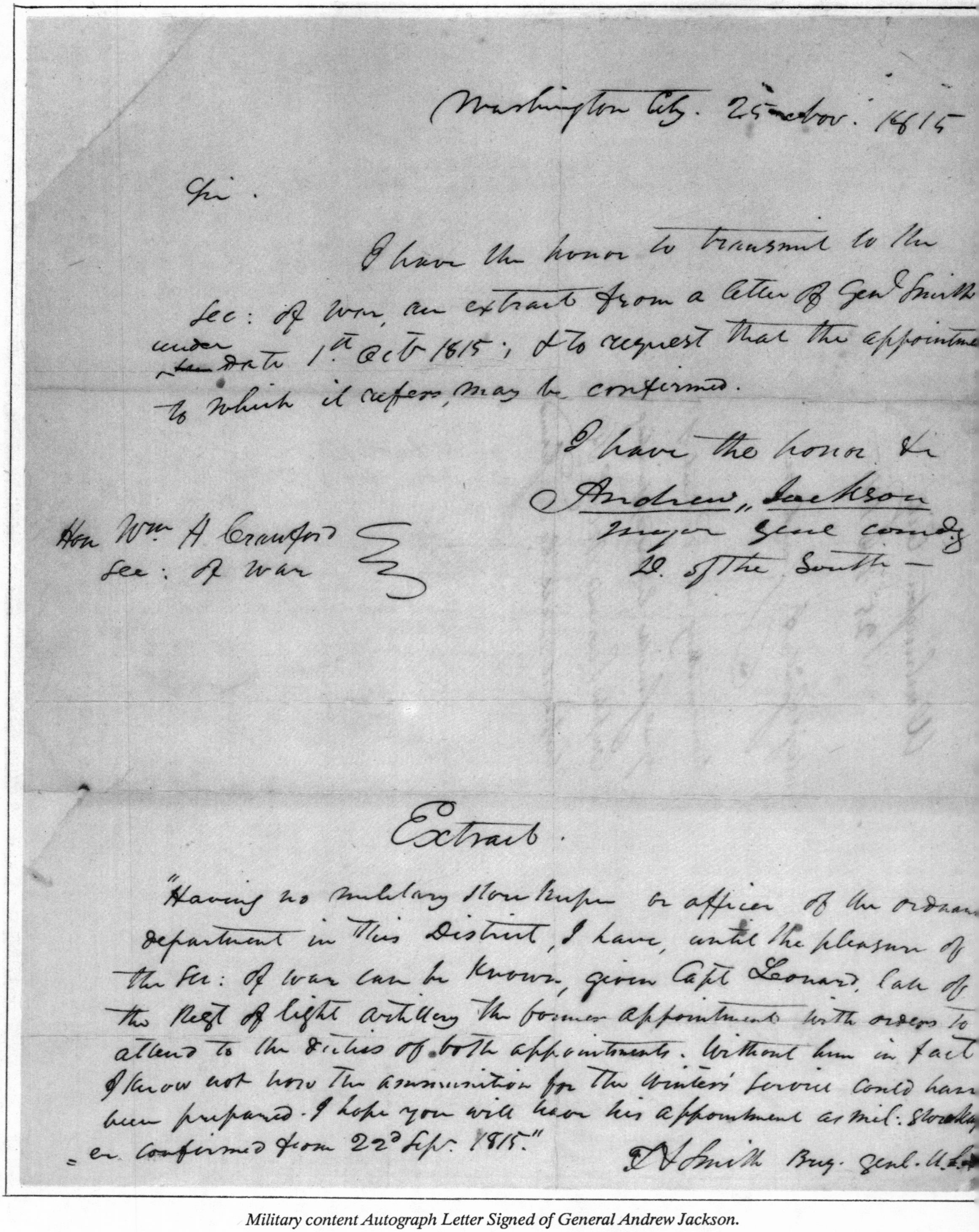

Washington City. 25ᵗʰ Novᵇʳ. 1815

Sir.

I have the honor to transmit to the Sec: of War, an extract from a letter of Genˡ Smith under date 1ˢᵗ Octᵇ 1815; & to request that the appointment to which it refers, may be confirmed.

I have the honor &c

Andrew Jackson
Major Genˡ comdg
D. of the South —

Hon Wᵐ A Crawford
Sec: of War

Extract.

"Having no military store keeper or officer of the ordnance department in this District, I have, until the pleasure of the Sec: of War can be known, given Capt Leonard, late of the Regt of light Artillery the former appointment with orders to attend to the duties of both appointments. Without him in fact I know not how the ammunition for the winter's service could have been prepared. I hope you will have his appointment as mil: Store keeper confirmed from 22ᵈ Sep: 1815."

T A Smith Brig: Genˡ U.S.

Military content Autograph Letter Signed of General Andrew Jackson.

20

power and his position as party leader to carry out his policies.

The greatest party battle centered around Jackson's battle with the Second Bank of the United States. Although the bank was a private corporation, it was in effect a government-sponsored monopoly which threw its power against Jackson when he did not support its practices. The fight for the recharter of the bank was led by Webster and Clay, who had represented the bank as private attorneys. Jackson vetoed the recharter bill, charging the bank with undue economic privilege. He told Martin Van Buren: "The bank is trying to kill me, but I will kill it."

In another major crisis, Jackson met the challenge of the anti-tariff forces head-on. Their leader was his nemesis, John C. Calhoun. When South Carolina attempted to nullify the tariff, Jackson ordered federal troops to Charleston and threatened to hang Calhoun. Violence seemed imminent, but at the last minute a compromise was engineered by Henry Clay. The tariffs were slightly lowered and South Carolina dropped nullification.

In January, 1832, the Senate rejected Jackson's nomination of Martin Van Buren as minister to England. Jackson, at dinner when he received the word, jumped to his feet and thundered: "By the Eternal I'll smash them." And so he did; he chose Van Buren as his vice-presidential running mate in 1836. As Jackson's hand-picked successor, Martin Van Buren became the eighth president in 1837.

Andrew Jackson wrote a bold, plain, rather large, angular and somewhat crude hand. At first glance, Jackson's letters appear to have no beginning and no end, since he had the idiosyncrasy of completely filling a page, leaving no margins and little or no space at the top or bottom of the page. The signatures of Jackson's A.Ls.S. are usually little, if any, larger than the body of the text, and have the appearance of an A.D.S. or a page from a manuscript, rather than a letter. Throughout his adult life his handwriting and signature changed little. He always signed his name in full. On some items, particularly Ds.S., he had the habit of running his signature almost off the edge of the paper, with the last few letters of his last name being quite cramped in order to fit them into the little remaining space.

Jackson's early signatures employed a slightly variant capital "A" for "Andrew" than did his later signatures after approximately 1805. The initial loop in his early signatures curved to the left and below the line, somewhat like an inverted fish hook. Jackson's signature was the boldest of the presidents', and on presidential documents it is sometimes an amazing six inches in length.

As one might expect, "Old Hickory" was capable of writing a good letter. As a result of little formal education his spelling was poor, but he nonetheless wrote intelligent letters of often fiery content. He expressed his feelings and opinions bluntly and with great force and candor, but he could also write quite charming and even gentle letters to his wife, relatives and friends. Although he employed a secretary to write his presidential letters, he wrote most of his personal letters himself. While Jackson's autographic material is not considered to be rare, the demand far exceeds the supply and his material has become quite expensive, particularly letters with good content.

During his second term, Jackson quit signing land grants personally. With few exceptions, after Andrew Jackson's second term almost all land grants were signed by secretaries who, in most cases, also signed their own names below those of the presidents and who, in some cases, made efforts to imitate the presidents' signatures. In several instances presidential sons served as presidential secretaries. Any land grant authentically signed by a president after Andrew Jackson's second term should be considered a great rarity and would be quite costly. We have seen only two during the past thirty-five years—both of which were signed by President John Tyler, likely in error.

Although Jackson studied law and became a distinguished lawyer and jurist, his letters were never models of grammar or spelling, with which he took great license, but they more than compensate in substance what they lack in form. Jackson ranks among the best letter writers of all the presidents.

Presidential signature of Andrew Jackson.

8. MARTIN VAN BUREN

December 5, 1782 - July 24, 1862

Eighth President
March 4, 1837 - March 4, 1841

Democrat

Highlights in office:
Panic of 1837; Seminole
Indian Wars; independent
subtreasury established.

Unlike almost all of his predecessors, Martin Van Buren was neither a Founding Father nor a war hero. He was the first true politician to become president, and he was also the first president born under the United States flag. His greatest single misfortune was that his single term coincided with a severe economic depression, causing his critics to dub him "Martin Van Ruin."

Van Buren was born of Dutch parents in Kinderhook, New York, and he is the only president who spoke English as a second language. As a youth he was a helper in his father's tavern, but became a lawyer and quickly climbed the political ladder, soon becoming a county judge then a state senator. He organized the "Albany Regency," one of the first political machines in the United States. At age thirty-eight Van Buren became U.S. senator, then governor of New York, secretary of state, minister to England, and vice president under Jackson.

Much of Van Buren's inaugural address was devoted to establishing the contention that the "American Experiment" was a noble example to the rest of the world. Less than three months later, however, the panic of 1837 began, plunging the country into what may have been the worst depression in its history. Van Buren's continued use of the deflationary policies of Jackson only worsened the depression.

The slavery question was beginning to be of great concern and importance during the administration of Van Buren, who opposed slavery and blocked the annexation of Texas, a slave area.

Because he was a professional politician, Van Buren was largely regarded by his contemporaries as an "operator," and he was known as "The Red Fox of Kinderhook" and "The Little Magician." David Crockett, who was one of his critics, said of Van Buren: "He could take a piece of meat on one side of his mouth, a piece of bread on the other, and cabbage in the middle, and chew and swallow each severally while never mixing them together."

Van Buren was defeated for reelection by the Whig candidate, William Henry Harrison, in 1840. In 1844, Van Buren tried unsuccessfully to obtain the Democratic presidential nomination. In 1848 he ran for president on the "Free Soil" ticket but polled only 10 percent of the popular vote.

When Van Buren left office he said: "As to the presidency, the two happiest days of my life were those of my entrance upon the office and my surrender of it."

Van Buren's wife of twelve years, Hannah Hoes Van Buren, a cousin whom he called "Jannetje" in their Dutch language, bore him five sons. She died when he was thirty-six and he never remarried. Van Buren burned all their letters and almost nothing is known of his wife; in his autobiography he made not a single mention of her. Like Jackson, Van Buren was a widower when be became president. For the first part of his term, he and his four bachelor sons occupied the only womanless White House. Later, in 1838, his eldest son Abraham married Angelica Singleton, an attractive young relative by marriage of Dolley Madison who had performed the introduction. Angelica served as White House hostess during the remainder of Van Buren's term.

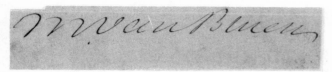

Typical signature of Van Buren

Early signature of Van Buren.

Only about five feet six inches tall, yet trim and erect, Van Buren was a natty dresser. His refined tastes became a campaign issue, and the accusation of using gold flatware in the White House contributed to his defeat for reelection.

With the exception of presidential-date material, which is relatively rare because of his single term, Van Buren is common in Ds.S. and A.Ls.S. His letters, written in a bold hand, are virtually illegible and often ramble on for several pages. Unlike Kennedy, whose adult handwriting was always illegible, Van Buren was capable of writing legible, even attractively penned epistles, but they are rare. There seems to be no middle ground—his letters are either almost totally illegible or legibly and attractively written, although the latter are decidedly rare. Ironically, Van

Buren's legible letters are sometimes mistaken for Ls.S. or secretarially written epistles.

In terms of content, Van Buren's letters are decidedly dull. He was a master of saying absolutely nothing in a flowery fashion and taking several virtually illegible pages to do so. One might assume that his almost totally illegible penmanship was deliberate and possibly an attempt at obfuscation. After all, he could not be held accountable for that which was indecipherable.

Van Buren's A.Ls.S are common, especially those dating from his post-presidential period. He used both octavo and quarto-size stationery. He is also relatively common in clipped signatures and franks. His signed photographs, which were taken in old age, are extremely rare and expensive, and most are c.d.v.'s.

Martin Van Buren Autograph Letter Signed as president.

9. WILLIAM HENRY HARRISON

February 9, 1773 - April 4, 1841

Ninth President
March 4, 1841 - April 4, 1841

Whig

Highlights in office:
Did not make a single major decision
while in office; Amistad Mutiny;
Claims Convention signed with Peru.

At sixty-eight years of age, William Henry Harrison was the second-oldest man to be sworn-in as president and is the only president to be the grandfather of a president. He served the shortest presidential term, dying after exactly one month in office. His inaugural address was the longest of any president, lasting almost two hours during which he wore no hat or coat in the freezing Washington winter. He caught a cold which turned into the pneumonia from which he died. He was the first president to die in office.

When Harrison was twenty-three he eloped with Anna Tuthill Symmes, daughter of a prominent frontier judge who had been a member of the Continental Congress. They had ten children. Harrison is perhaps best remembered for the famous "log cabin and hard cider" campaign of 1840 and for the fact that during his brief term as president he did not make a single major decision. It is doubtful that Harrison would have been a strong president—in his inaugural address he stressed that he would bow to the judgment of Congress.

Notwithstanding Harrison's homespun presidential campaign, he was descended from a prominent and aristocratic Virginia family. His father, Benjamin Harrison, was a signer of the Declaration of Independence and a governor of Virginia. Harrison studied medicine under another signer, Dr. Benjamin Rush, but abruptly switched to a military career and served as aide-de-camp to General "Mad Anthony" Wayne. He became a renowned Indian fighter and won famous victories over Tecumseh and the British at the Battles of Tippecanoe and Thames, breaking the Indians' power in the Northwest. He was the first governor of the Indiana Territory and a major general in the War of 1812. Later he became a member of the U.S. House of Representatives and a U.S. senator. Harrison served briefly as U.S. minister to Columbia, a disastrous position from which he was recalled by President John Quincy Adams. His last public office prior to being elevated to the presidency was, ironically, in a lucrative position as county clerk in the court of Hamilton County, Ohio, a position he held in an effort to pay off the massive personal debts which resulted from his high living on his three thousand acre estate in Ohio.

Scarce early full signature of William Henry Harrison.

Last page of an 1836 Document Signed by William Henry Harrison as County Clerk of Hamilton County, Ohio.

Harrison's autographic material is not common in any form for any date but, with the important exception of presidential items, his autographic material is not terribly expensive.

Harrison wrote a small, plain but legible hand. His early handwriting was somewhat meticulous but attractive. His signature changed markedly in both form and appearance during his life. The earliest and most common form of his signature is the early "Wm. H. Harrison," the form he signed on the small, oblong, octavo military vouchers written during his service as aide-de-camp to General Wayne (1794-96) and which are both A.Ds.S. and Ds.S. Shortly before the dawn of the nineteenth century, Harrison changed the form of his signature to a bold, often florid "Willm. Henry Harrison." Sometime after the War of 1812, Harrison yet again changed the form of his signature to his initials "W.H. Harrison," and this form appears on his few presidential documents and letters that are known to exist.

Harrison died only thirty-one days after becoming president. He was ill approximately half of his brief term and signed very little, making his presidential material the scarcest and most costly of any president. There are only approximately a dozen presidential Ds.S. known to exist,

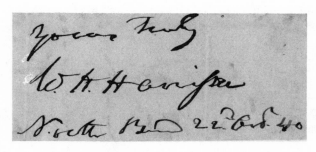

Close of William Henry Harrison Autograph Letter Signed eighteen days before he was elected president on November 10, 1840. Signed with his "presidential type" signature.

Early military Autograph Documents Signed of William Henry Harrison. Written while serving as aide-de-camp to General "Mad" Anthony Wayne.

which include a partial D.S. and a handful of presidential A.Ls.S, probably the most famous and important of which was written to Henry Clay on March 13, 1841 in which President Harrison tells Senator Henry Clay that "you use the privilege of a friend to lecture me and I will take the same liberty with you—you are too imperious." Harrison goes on to tell Clay he values counsel but that he must at times make decisions adverse to Clay's "suggestions."

Most of Harrison's letters concerned mundane matters such as real estate, finances, family, or routine military matters. On occasion Harrison did write good letters, many of which had military content. Once Harrison warmed to a subject he tended to be verbose, and many of his letters are several pages in length, foreshadowing his record-setting and fatal inaugural address.

10. JOHN TYLER

March 29, 1790 - January 18, 1862

Tenth President
April 4, 1845 - March 4, 1849

Whig

Highlights in office:
Webster-Ashburton Treaty;
annexation of Texas.

John Tyler was the first vice president to succeed to the presidency upon the death of the president, causing him to be labeled "His Accidency" by his detractors.

The son of a prominent Virginia family, Tyler studied law under Edmund Randolph, a former U.S. attorney general, and was admitted to the bar when he was nineteen. At twenty-one he was elected to the Virginia House of Delegates while his father was governor of Virginia. Later he was elected to both the U.S. House of Representatives and the U.S. Senate, as well as to the governorship of Virginia.

As president, Tyler vetoed nine bills—more than any previous one-term president—which precipitated another nickname for him: "Old Veto." As a result of his veto of a tariff bill, he became the first president to face a serious impeachment attempt. A committee headed by Representative John Quincy Adams reported to Congress that the president had misused his veto powers, but the resolution failed to pass. Earlier, when Tyler had vetoed a bill creating a U.S. bank with branches in several states, his entire cabinet, except Secretary of State Daniel Webster, resigned and the Whigs expelled Tyler from their party. Consequently, he became a president without a party.

It is not surprising that when Charles Dickens visited President Tyler in the White House he wrote: "He looked somewhat worn and anxious, and well he might, being at war with everybody."

Tyler was not renominated by his party and retired to his Virginia estate where he spent his time siring children, of which he had more than any other president—eight by

his first wife and seven by his second. All his children by his second wife were born after he left the White House. Tyler's children, not surprisingly, lived over the greatest span of time—there was an amazing 132 years between the birth of his first child in 1815 to the death of his last child in 1947.

In 1861 when the first southern states seceded, Tyler headed an unsuccessful peace commission. He sided with the southern cause and, when he died in 1862, was serving as a member of the Confederate House of Representatives.

Happily for collectors, John Tyler personally handled most of his correspondence throughout his career, and his A.Ls.S are therefore far less scarce than are his Ls.S. His handwriting tended to be small, neat and legible. Although he did on rare occasions write letters of interesting content with almost the touch of a poet in his phraseology, most of his letters concern mundane matters and tend to

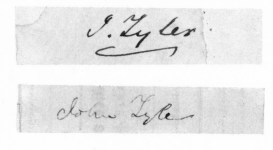

Signatures of John Tyler.

Pre-presidential Autograph Letter Signed of John Tyler.

be uninteresting. Except while president, when his letters were terse and direct, Tyler generally wrote lengthy letters which frequently were several pages in length. An interesting idiosyncrasy of Tyler's was his occasionally omitting the salutation and dating his letters after his signature, causing his letters to appear to be A.Ds.S.

Regarding his signature, one can almost determine the period during which an example was written because of certain characteristics. Tyler's signature reached its zenith in size while he was president. On correspondence he normally signed "J. Tyler," while on official documents he signed his full name since he, like most of the earlier presidents, was required by law to do so. During his pre-presidential and congressional periods, he signed his name in full but with a tiny signature which was scarcely, if at all, larger than the text. After leaving the presidency, Tyler continued to sign his name in full, generally small in size but with a plain paraph or line beneath his signature.

Tyler is relatively common in franks, and he frequently illegally franked his wife's letters—as did a number of other presidents.

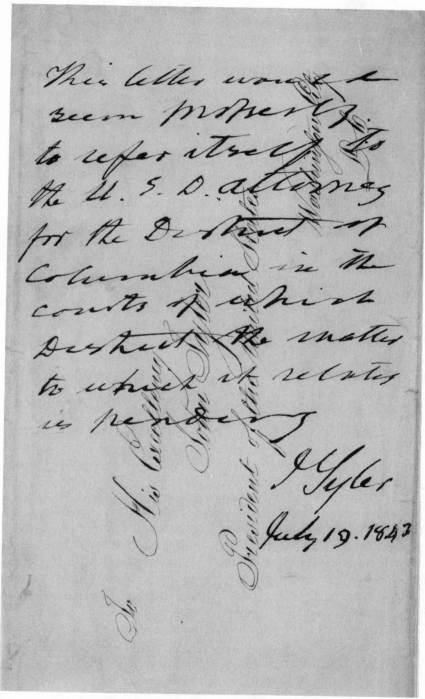

Presidential Autograph Document Signed of John Tyler
written on an envelope addressed to him.

11. JAMES KNOX POLK

November 2, 1795 - June 15, 1849

Eleventh President
March 4, 1845 - March 4, 1849

Democrat

Highlights in office:
Mexican-American War;
49th parallel treaty.

"**W**ho is James K. Polk?" was the Whig campaign slogan in 1844. The Whigs were soon to find out. James K. Polk was the first "dark horse" president, the last Jacksonian president, and the last strong president before the Civil War.

Polk was the son of a prominent Tennessee planter. He became a lawyer and, by age twenty-seven, was a state legislator. A devout follower of Andrew Jackson, he became known as "Young Hickory." He became a congressman, speaker of the U.S. House of Representatives, and governor of Tennessee. He was defeated for the vice-presidential nomination in 1840.

In 1844, Polk's presidential nomination was personally engineered by former President Andrew Jackson. The main campaign issue was expansionism.

Legend has it that his romance with his future wife, Sarah Childress, was encouraged by Andrew Jackson. Sarah agreed to marry Polk, who was serving as chief clerk of the Tennessee House of Representatives, on the condition that he run for the state legislature. He ran and won, and he and Sarah were married on New Year's Day in 1824. During twenty-five years of marriage, including the period of his presidency, Sarah worked tirelessly at his side as his secretary and his only confidant. Mrs. Polk was probably the first politically influential first lady.

During his presidential administration President and Mrs. Polk, who had no children, toiled together twelve to fourteen hours a day. They banned both dancing and alcohol from the White House. Polk's last words were addressed to his wife: "I love you, Sarah, for all eternity, I love you."

Polk successfully supervised the war with Mexico, as a result of which Mexico ceded New Mexico and California to the U.S. in return for $15 million. He also successfully negotiated settlement of the Oregon Territory dispute with Great Britain. His administration was one of the most successful in history; during a single four-year term he fulfilled every campaign promise, a feat which has never been duplicated.

Polk was a "workaholic" and had no levity in his life. He was so worn out by the ordeal of the presidency that he died only three months after leaving office. He literally worked himself to death, dying of exhaustion and diarrhea.

Polk wrote a small, angular and somewhat feminine-appearing hand. His signature was the most ornate and ostentatious of all the presidents, with an elaborate paraph beneath his signature. He normally wrote his signature "James K. Polk" but, on occasion apparently as a time saving device, signed with his initials, "J.K. Polk," with an attenuated paraph. His early signatures are usually quite small.

Because he was largely unknown before becoming president, few of his early documents and letters were saved, and since he served but a single term as president and died soon thereafter at the early age of fifty-three, his autographic material is among the scarcest of the presidents. For all these reasons, Polk is expensive in all forms of autographic material. His letters and documents are among the most attractive and spectacular in appearance of any president.

As a letter writer Polk does not receive high marks.

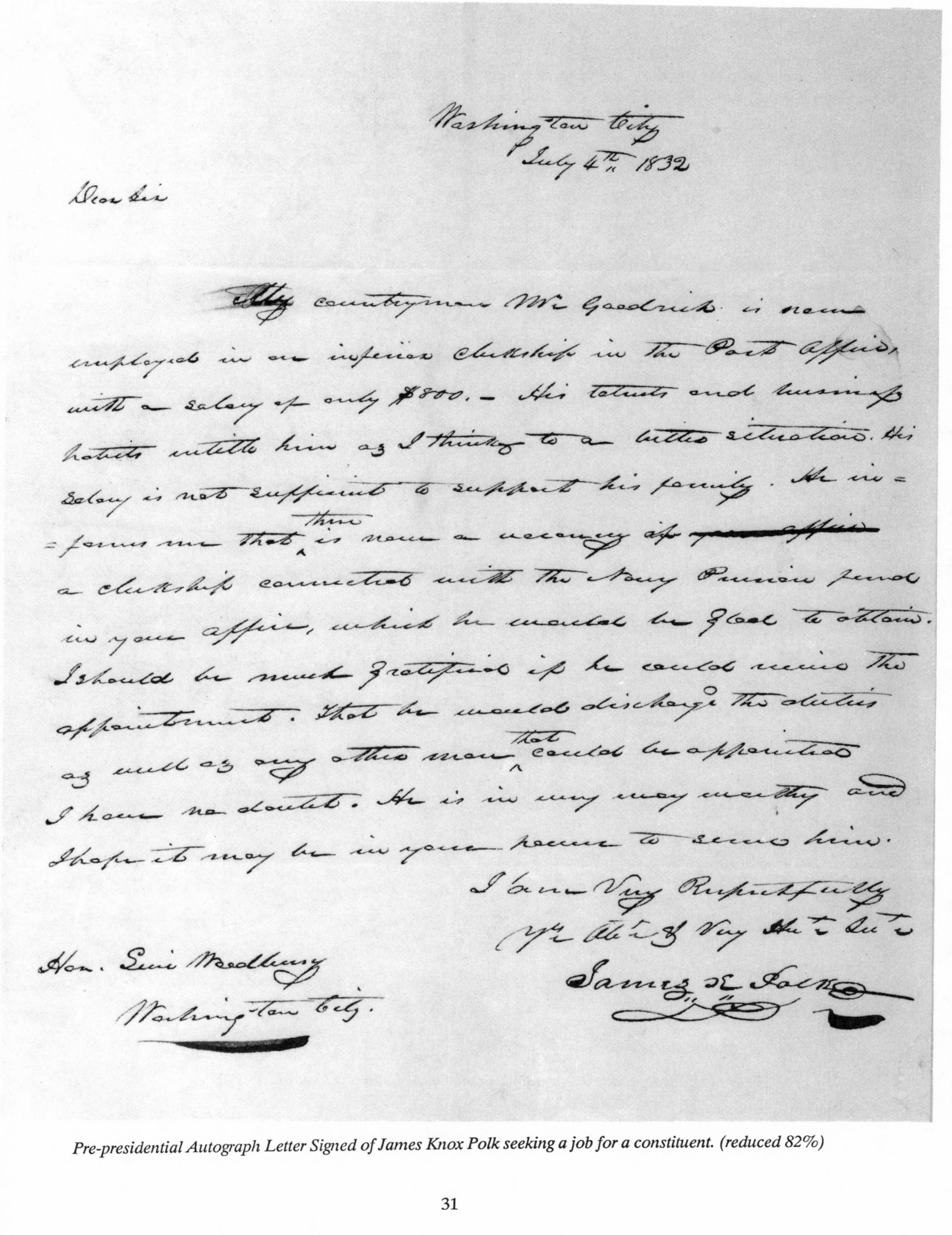

Washington City
July 4th 1832

Dear Sir

My countryman Mr. Goodrich is now employed in an inferior clerkship in the Post Office, with a salary of only $800. — His talents and business habits entitle him as I think to a better situation. His salary is not sufficient to support his family. He informs me that there is now a vacancy in a clerkship connected with the Navy Pension fund in your office, which he would be glad to obtain. I should be much gratified if he could receive the appointment. That he would discharge the duties as well as any other man that could be appointed I have no doubt. He is in every way worthy and I hope it may be in your power to serve him.

I am Very Respectfully
Yr Obt & Very Humbl Sevt

James K. Polk

Hon. Levi Woodbury
Washington City.

Pre-presidential Autograph Letter Signed of James Knox Polk seeking a job for a constituent. (reduced 82%)

31

Although he was capable of writing a letter of important content, so detailed was he that his letters, frequently more than one page long, come across as more belabored than anything else.

Early legal document entirely in the hand of attorney James Knox Polk.

12. ZACHARY TAYLOR

November 24, 1784 - July 9, 1850

Twelfth President
March 4, 1849 - July 9, 1850

Whig

Highlights in office:
Treaty with Hawaiian Islands;
Clayton-Bulwer Treaty; Clay Compromise.

The Mexican War made Zachary Taylor president. In 1845 he was an obscure old soldier of almost forty years service. By 1848 he was "Old Rough and Ready," the hero of the Mexican War.

Zachary Taylor, a second cousin of James Madison, had little formal education. He was commissioned an army lieutenant at the age of twenty-three and became a career army officer and Indian fighter. He was later promoted to brigadier general and became the leading commander of the Mexican War, from which he emerged as a national hero.

Taylor was stocky in build, five feet eight inches tall, weighed about 170 pounds, and had a large head and unusually short legs. He was noted for the sloppiness of his military dress—for comfort he preferred uniforms two sizes too large—and for his colorful cursing and his addiction to tobacco chewing. However, his fiercely loyal troops loved him and gave him the nickname "Old Rough & Ready."

In 1848, the Whigs nominated Taylor for president—despite his hatred of politics and politicians. He had never even voted. When Taylor's presidential nomination was being discussed he said: "The idea that I should become president seems to me too visionary to require a serious answer. It has never entered my head, nor is it likely to enter the head of any sane person."

He was several days late learning of his presidential nomination because he refused to pay the ten cents postage due on his formal letter of notification. In the campaign Taylor said nothing and made no campaign appearances, relying on the split in the Democratic ranks to elect him. He said privately: "I'm a Whig—but not an ultra-Whig."

Taylor's wife, Margaret, was opposed to his running for president. She fervently prayed for his defeat because she thought he was too old and that the office would kill him. Unfortunately, her worst fears were realized.

One of Taylor's daughters married Lieutenant Jefferson Davis, who was later president of the Confederacy. The Taylors strongly opposed the match, but Davis married the daughter despite the objections of her parents. She died tragically three months later of malaria. Years

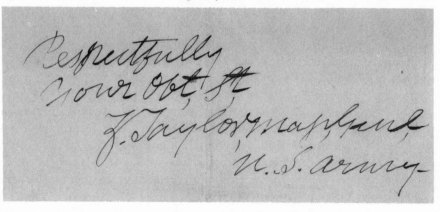

Close of an Autograph Letter Signed of Zachary Taylor as General.

Close of an Autograph Letter Signed from Zachary Taylor to his brother. (reduced 82%)

later, Davis made peace with his former in-laws, and he and his second wife were frequent guests at the Taylor White House. Taylor's only son, Richard, later became a general in the Confederacy.

Taylor was the last president to own slaves and the last nationally minded southerner until Woodrow Wilson.

Although Taylor basically agreed with Whig tenets as to legislative leadership, he was not a puppet to Whig congressional leaders. To the chagrin of his party he often acted as if he were above parties and politics.

The cauldron of the slavery issue continued to boil ever more fiercely during Taylor's administration. Traditionally, states could decide whether or not they wanted slavery when they drafted new state constitutions. For this reason, and in an effort to end slavery in new areas, Taylor urged settlers in New Mexico and California to draft constitutions and apply for statehood status, bypassing the territorial stage. Since neither state was likely to permit slavery, southerners were furious, as were the members of Congress because they felt the president had usurped their policy-making prerogatives. Taylor's anti-slavery solution also ignored both southern demands for a more stringent slave law and northern protests against the slave market operating in the District of Columbia.

President Taylor had a tension-filled and acrimonious conference in February, 1850, with southern secession leaders. He told them he would personally lead the army if necessary to enforce the laws, and further told the group that persons "taken in rebellion against the Union I will hang . . . with less reluctance than I hung deserters and spies in Mexico." He never wavered in this resolve, but died before the great "Compromise of 1850." It is ap-

parent that Taylor intended to be a strong president and that his common sense instincts were sound.

On July 4, 1850, Taylor attended ceremonies at the Washington Monument. He sat in boiling heat and listened to an interminable speech by George Washington's grandson by marriage, "Little-Wash" Custis. After returning to the White House he cooled off by eating large quantities of cherries washed down with iced milk. His doctor pleaded with him to stop, to no avail, and that night he was stricken with violent cramps. He died five days later of coronary thrombosis following an acute attack of gastro-enteritis.

Taylor died only sixteen months after becoming president, thus making his presidency the third shortest on record, following those of William Henry Harrison and James A. Garfield.

Zachary Taylor, like Polk, is one of the rarest of all presidents in all forms of autographic material. He, too, came to national prominence late in life, and few of his early letters or documents were saved.

Most of Taylor's pre-presidential letters are on mundane subjects and concern military matters, many of which are Ls.S. Many of his personal letters concern his plantation and farming or family matters. Occasionally, however, fine military-content letters do appear. Although polite and invariably gracious, Taylor's letters are to the point and rarely more than one page in length. Taylor's handwriting and signature are perhaps the boldest of all the presidents. He favored a broad-nibbed pen and, consequently, wrote a heavy, angular hand which, like the man, was totally devoid of ornamentation. Taylor always signed himself "Z. Taylor" even on official presidential documents. An interesting characteristic of most of Taylor's pre-presidential signatures is that he connected his rank and title to the "r" in "Taylor," *e.g.,* "Z. Taylor-Col." or "Z. TaylorMajr. Gen." A full signature of Taylor's is virtually unobtainable and the authors have never seen one, although they must exist.

Taylor is particularly rare in presidential-date A.Ls.S. because his son-in-law, "Perfect" Bliss, in an effort to improve Old Rough and Ready's literary form and grammar, drafted virtually all his presidential letters. Another contributing factor to the rarity of Taylor's material is the destruction of all of his papers when his house was burned by Union troops during the Civil War. The authors once owned a letter from Taylor's daughter, Betty Taylor Bliss, describing the destruction of his home and making it plain that her sympathies did not lie with the federal troops.

Franking signature of Zachery Taylor.

Signature of Taylor clipped from a presidential document.

13. MILLARD FILLMORE

January 7, 1800 - March 8, 1874

Thirteenth President
July 9, 1850 - March 4, 1853

Whig

Highlights in office:
Compromise of 1850;
Fugitive Slave Act.

Millard Fillmore was one of the "accidental" presidents, being the second vice president to become president upon the death of a president. Though he was not an ordinary man, neither was he extraordinary, thus making him an eminently forgettable president.

He was born in a log cabin, and at the age of fourteen was apprenticed to a wool carder. Not until he was nineteen did he begin his formal education. He first became a clerk in a law office and then a practicing attorney. As an associate of Whig politician Thurlow Weed, Fillmore held state office for eight years. He was elected to the New York assembly and, later, the U.S. House of Representatives, where he served as chairman of the Ways and Means Committee. He was defeated as a candidate for governor of New York but was subsequently elected state comptroller. In 1848 the Whigs nominated Fillmore for the vice presidency in an effort to balance the ticket headed by Zachary Taylor.

As a young man Fillmore fell in love with his school teacher, Abigail Powers, whom he eventually married after a long, seven year courtship during which Fillmore established a successful law practice. They had an unusually happy marriage. Abigail Fillmore is best remembered for establishing the White House Library with a modest congressional appropriation of $250. Abigail died shortly after Fillmore left the White House but before they left Washington. Five years later, at age fifty-eight, Fillmore married a wealthy widow, Caroline Carmichael McIntosh.

Fortuitously, it has been virtually forgotten that one of the most-heated controversies of Fillmore's brief term concerned the guano reserves off the coast of Peru. The fowl excrement was a valuable component of fertilizer and was the basis of a dispute between the Peruvian government and American businessmen. So heated did the controversy become that Fillmore intervened and negotiated a special treaty.

When Fillmore suddenly and unexpectedly became president in July, 1850, it augured a political shift in the national administration. Taylor's entire cabinet resigned and Fillmore appointed Daniel Webster as his secretary of state, thereby proclaiming his alliance with the moderate Whigs who favored the Compromise of 1850.

Stephen A. Douglas' effective congressional strategy, combined with Fillmore's pressure from the White House, was sufficient to secure congressional approval of the Compromise of 1850, but in a few short years it became painfully apparent that the compromise served merely as an uneasy truce rather than a settlement of the slavery issue.

The militant northern Whig faction refused to forgive Fillmore for having signed the Fugitive Slave Act, and they were instrumental in depriving him of the presidential nomination in his own right in 1852.

Although the Whig party disintegrated before the Civil War, Fillmore refused to join the Republican Party. Instead, in 1856, he accepted the presidential nomination of the American, or Know-Nothing, party. The Know-Nothings sought national unity by means of a dubious appeal to the patriotism—in reality to the ethnic prejudices—of native-born Americans. It was thus a party with only one idea, and that a particularly narrow-minded and prejudi-

Close of Autograph Letter Signed by Millard Fillmore as president with postscript signed with initials.

Post-presidential Autograph Letter Signed of Millard Fillmore.

cial one. Fillmore ran third behind the Democratic and Republican candidates and was never again a serious presidential contender. Before the Civil War he spearheaded a movement to send the slaves back to Africa as a solution to the slavery problem. Throughout the Civil War, Fillmore opposed Lincoln's policies but, paradoxically, during Reconstruction he supported Johnson.

Fillmore was well-liked and respected by his contemporaries. John Quincy Adams said of him: "Whether to the nation or to the state, no service can or ever will be rendered by a more able or a more faithful public servant." Despite this encomium, Fillmore's lack of presidential diplomatic accomplishments, and his presidential candidacy in 1856 on the Know-Nothing ticket, have not enhanced his reputation among historians.

Excepting presidential-date material, Fillmore is common in most forms of autographic material, including free franks, Ds.S, A.Ls.S., and signed books from his library. He was one of the first presidents to sign photographs, although these are old-age post-presidential examples and are rare and extremely expensive.

Fillmore lived twenty-one years after leaving the White House and carried on a voluminous correspondence. He wrote an attractive, legible, rather embellished hand and signature and preferred a fine-nibbed pen. His signature was written both with his initial and in full. Signatures with his initial "M. Fillmore" on free franks are quite common. Many of Fillmore's early documents date from his term as comptroller of New York, and he is also obtainable in ornate and quite attractive signed bonds.

As Fillmore was president only two years and eight months, his presidential-date material is scarce in all forms, particularly A.Ls.S. Most of his presidential letters are Ls.S; conversely, most letters from all other periods are A.Ls.S.

The content of Fillmore's letters was generally routine and uninspired, being couched in a legalese tone. He seemed reticent about expressing his strong feelings on paper. For this reason, important or interesting-content Fillmore letters are extremely rare. Routine-content Fillmore letters are among the most plentiful and inexpensive of the presidential series.

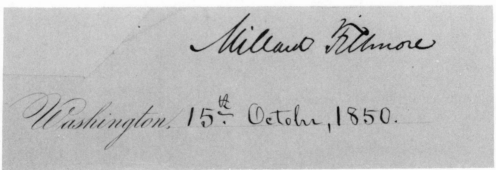

Presidential signature of Millard Fillmore.

Post presidential Autograph Note Signed of Fillmore.

14. FRANKLIN PIERCE

November 23, 1804 - October 8, 1869

Fourteenth President of the United States
March 4, 1853 - March 4, 1857

Democrat

Highlights in office:
Trade and diplomatic relations
opened with Japan; Gadsden
Purchase; Kansas-Nebraska Bill.

Franklin Pierce, the son of a New Hampshire governor, was one of our most handsome and tragic presidents. By the time he was twenty-five he was a prosperous lawyer and a state legislator. He also served in the U.S. House of Representatives and, at age thirty-three, became one of the youngest members of the U.S. Senate. However, largely at the insistence of his wife, who hated politics and politicians, he resigned from the Senate and returned to private law practice, refusing nominations both for governor of New Hampshire and reappointment to the U.S. Senate, and also declining Polk's offer to become his attorney general. However, despite his wife's strenuous objections, he volunteered for the army during the Mexican War and became a brigadier general. During Pierce's 1852 presidential campaign, the Whigs, with some truth, charged that he was "the hero of many a well-fought bottle" and also that he had been guilty of cowardice during the Mexican War. The truth is that as Pierce rode to the front during his first and only major engagement, his horse, frightened by exploding shells, bucked and drove the saddle horn sharply into his groin. As a result Pierce fainted, fell from his horse, and injured his knee.

Pierce's mentally fragile and religiously fanatic wife, Jane, fainted when she was told her husband had been nominated for president. During the campaign she ardently prayed for her husband's defeat. While Pierce was president-elect, he, his wife, and their only surviving son, "Benny", were involved in a train accident. Benny was killed and decapitated before his parents' eyes—to their abject horror, they saw the child's head roll down the aisle

of the train. Neither ever recovered from this tragedy, which forever ended Jane Pierce's life as a functioning member of society. She blamed Benny's death on Pierce's involvement in politics, and Pierce also blamed himself for the tragedy. As a sad result, Pierce was a weak, guilt-ridden and vacillating president, one of the least effective in our history even though he served during a critical time of growing sectional differences when decisive leadership was desperately needed. Due largely to his son's tragic death and his wife's mental and emotional collapse, Pierce was unable to provide strong leadership, allowing the country to drift toward civil war.

Like Fillmore, Pierce's autographic material is plentiful, except of presidential date. He is also obtainable in signed photographs made after he left office, although they are extremely rare and expensive. Rare but also obtainable are signed books from Pierce's library. His A.Ls.S. are more common than his Ls.S. Pierce's holographs almost appear to have been printed, as most of the letters within the words were disconnected. He preferred fine-nibbed pens.

Pierce's handwriting was attractive but is difficult to read and, in some cases, is indecipherable. His signature, one of the most ornate of the presidential series, varied from time to time as "Franklin Pierce," "Frank Pierce," "F. Pierce," or "Fr. Pierce."

As Pierce served only one term, his presidential letters are not common. Although his letters in general are uninteresting, albeit unfailingly polite and well-written, he was definitely capable of writing a good letter, particularly

Signature of Franklin Pierce.

Concord
Wednesday Mar 7,

My dear Stephen,

I was glad to receive your note this morning, but sorry to hear of the illness of faithful Mary Caldwell. Ellen, I hope, may be able to remain until Mary shall be about again. Give my kind regards to them both. My appointments were quite complete for a drive with the horses to Lowell today, but

Recto of post presidential Autograph Letter Signed of Franklin Pierce on monogrammed stationery.

when he held strong views on a particular topic. He was prone to write on the front and back of a single page, making display difficult. He favored the octavo double stationery popular during his time.

Pierce's franks are scarce although he frequently illegally franked his wife's letters, which were normally written to her relatives.

Perhaps the most desirable type of Pierce's presidential documents are those co-signed by Jefferson Davis, who served as his secretary of war.

Verso of Pierce Autograph Letter Signed.

15. JAMES BUCHANAN

April 23, 1791 - June 1, 1868

Fifteenth President of the United States
March 4, 1857 - March 4, 1861

Democrat

Highlights in office:
Dred Scott decision; Harper's Ferry
raid; Pony Express begun; southern
states seceded from the Union.

On his fourth try, in 1856 at age sixty-five, James Buchanan finally won the Democratic presidential nomination. A prosperous lawyer who had turned to public service, he had been a member of the Pennsylvania state legislature, congressman, ambassador to Russia, U.S. senator, secretary of state, and ambassador to Britain.

Buchanan was heavy-set and about six feet tall. He always held his head tilted due to an eye defect (one eye was nearsighted and one was farsighted). In 1819 Buchanan became engaged to Ann Caroline Coleman, daughter of millionaire Robert Coleman. Miss Coleman mysteriously broke the engagement in early December and, while visiting in Philadelphia, she suddenly died, reportedly by suicide. Buchanan was inconsolable. His letter of condolence to her family was returned unopened. He kept Caroline's letters all his life, tied with silk ribbon, but directed the executor of his estate to burn them after his death. He never spoke of the affair, the true details of which will never be known. This tragedy permanently scarred him and, although he enjoyed the company of women, he is the only president who never married. His beautiful and charming niece, Harriet Lane, a violet-eyed blond, served as her uncle's official White House hostess. The popular tune "Listen to the Mockingbird" was dedicated to her.

Some recently discovered and previously unpublished correspondence between Buchanan and Alabama U.S. Senator William R. King (who became Franklin Pierce's vice president but who died approximately one month later) suggests that the two men were lovers. It is a fact that Buchanan and King shared living quarters in Washington, D.C., for almost a quarter-century and neither ever married. Buchanan was regarded as "old maidish" by his contemporaries. Mrs. Varina Jefferson Davis wrote: "The first thought that one had in looking at him was, how very clean he was."

As president, Buchanan's pro-southern bias in the bitter slavery controversy made him so unpopular that he did not seek reelection.

Buchanan's signature is the second most ornate of the presidential series, following that of James K. Polk, and changed little throughout his adult life. He signed his full name. He wrote one of the most attractive hands of all the presidents, small, neat, beautifully written and feminine-appearing. Like Jefferson, Buchanan's signature was much larger than his handwriting, which at first glance gives his A.Ls.S. the appearance of Ls.S.

Buchanan is more common in A.Ls.S. than Ls.S. and, except for presidential-date A.Ls.S., his material is easily obtainable for all periods and is moderately priced. Although his letters were somewhat stilted and formal, Buchanan must be classified as an interesting correspondent, compared to many of the presidents. His innate conservatism caused him to limit most of his letters to one page, thus lending themselves to convenient display.

Buchanan is common in Ds.S. and routine letters, and his franks are also obtainable and affordable. Although Buchanan is obtainable in signed photographs and signed books from his personal library (some of which were also

Pre-presidential Autograph Note Signed of James Buchanan.

signed by his niece, Harriet Lane Johnson), he is rare and expensive in these formats, particularly in photographs which, like those of his predecessors, were taken in old age and few of which, signed or otherwise, are known to exist.

Signature of James Buchanan.

16. ABRAHAM LINCOLN

February 12, 1809 - April 15, 1865

Sixteenth President
March 4, 1861 - April 15, 1865

Republican

Highlights in office:
Civil War; Emancipation
Proclamation; Homestead Act.

Lincoln was born in a crude log cabin in Kentucky, the son of a poor illiterate farmer, Thomas Lincoln, who moved his family first to Indiana and then to Illinois. After working several years as an itinerant laborer, Lincoln moved to New Salem, Illinois, where he first obtained a job as a clerk in a general store and eventually became the postmaster. Lincoln had very little schooling, but he had a brilliant mind and read every book he could beg, borrow, or buy. He eventually obtained a set of *Blackstone's Commentaries* in a barrel of goods he accepted in trade for supplies from the general store. Thus began a brilliant legal career. After an initial defeat, Lincoln served four terms in the Illinois legislature and, later, a single term in Congress during which he introduced a major bill that would have abolished slavery in the District of Columbia.

Two of Lincoln's most pronounced personality traits were his sparkling sense of humor, which tended to be somewhat bawdy, and his ever-present melancholia. All his life he had precognitive dreams, including one about his own assassination which he related to his cabinet shortly before the event. Lincoln admitted that: "I have all my life been a fatalist. What is to be, will be, or rather, I have found all my life as Hamlet says, 'There is a divinity that shapes our ends, rough hew them how we will.' " Lincoln also suffered from a severe inferiority complex, which may have stemmed, at least in part, from the fact that his mother, Nancy Hanks, was illegitimate. Ironically, Lincoln privately attributed his intelligence through his mother's line to her unknown but reputedly well-born father. The circumstances surrounding his mother's birth, and his abject poverty, combined to incubate in Lincoln a

burning desire to excel and achieve. Equally important, they gave Lincoln the deep sense of compassion for humanity for which he has become deservedly immortal.

Lincoln's melancholia worsened with time, particularly after the deaths of two of his children, the deteriorating mental condition of his wife, the pressures of the Civil War, and the ever-present financial problems caused by his wife's compulsive and excessive spending.

Lincoln's wit and logic are evidenced by the following quotes: "If slavery is not wrong, nothing is wrong"; "Republicans are for both the man and the dollar, but in case of conflict, the man before the dollar"; "Men are not flattered by being shown that there has been a difference of purpose between the Almighty and them"; "I protest, now and forever, against the counterfeit logic which presumes because I do not want a Negro woman for a slave I necessarily want her for a wife. My understanding is that I do not have to have her for either."

During the height of the Civil War, Lincoln's secretary of the treasury, Salmon P. Chase, proposed at a cabinet meeting that the motto "In God We Trust" be placed on all U.S. coins and currency. Lincoln humorously replied that, given the near-bankrupt condition of the federal treasury, a more appropriate injunction would be that of the apostle Paul to the cripple at the Gate Beautiful: "Silver and gold have I none. Such as I have, give I thee."

Lincoln material is perhaps in the greatest demand of all the presidents and, with Washington's and Jefferson's, is among the most expensive of any president. His material is not rare in terms of numbers, but the demand far exceeds the supply, particularly in good-content

Autograph Letter Signed of Abraham Lincoln written shortly before he was nominated for president.

material which is steadily being absorbed by institutions, never to reappear on the market. Because he became nationally prominent rather late in life and there was no reason at the time to save it, Lincoln's pre-presidential material is a great deal scarcer than his presidential material. His early material is most commonly encountered in the form of legal briefs, generally signed with one of his firm names: "Stuart & Lincoln," "Logan & Lincoln" or "Lincoln and Herndon." His pre-presidential letters and legal briefs were usually written on blue quarto stationery.

Lincoln, one of the acknowledged masters of the English language, is also rightfully acknowledged for his brevity. He did not waste words, expressing himself perfectly and clearly with a few, well-chosen ones. The brevity of his letters increased after he became president, and he introduced the first personalized presidential

Rare full signature of Abraham Lincoln clipped from an official presidential document.

stationery, octavo sheets imprinted "Executive Mansion, Washington," with a printed line for the date. Lincoln probably wrote the most beautifully phrased letters of any president. Letters with important content are extremely scarce, in terms of numbers, as well as prohibitively expensive. He is common in presidential-date documents and in endorsements on letters or petitions to him. He is, however, the most widely and easily forged of the presidents, particularly his endorsements. At least one well-known forger made a virtual career of cleverly forging Lincoln endorsements on actual letters or petitions written to him.

Lincoln wrote a small, plain, attractive and quite distinctive hand. He always signed himself "A. Lincoln" except on official presidential documents which law required he sign in full. These documents, great numbers of which were military commissions, are virtually the only source of his desirable full signature. There are perhaps only a handful of his full signatures known to exist on other than official presidential documents.

Lincoln is also obtainable in signed photographs, although he is the most expensive of the presidents in this format. His signed photographs have also been forged, so any photograph purported to be signed by Lincoln should be authenticated by an expert.

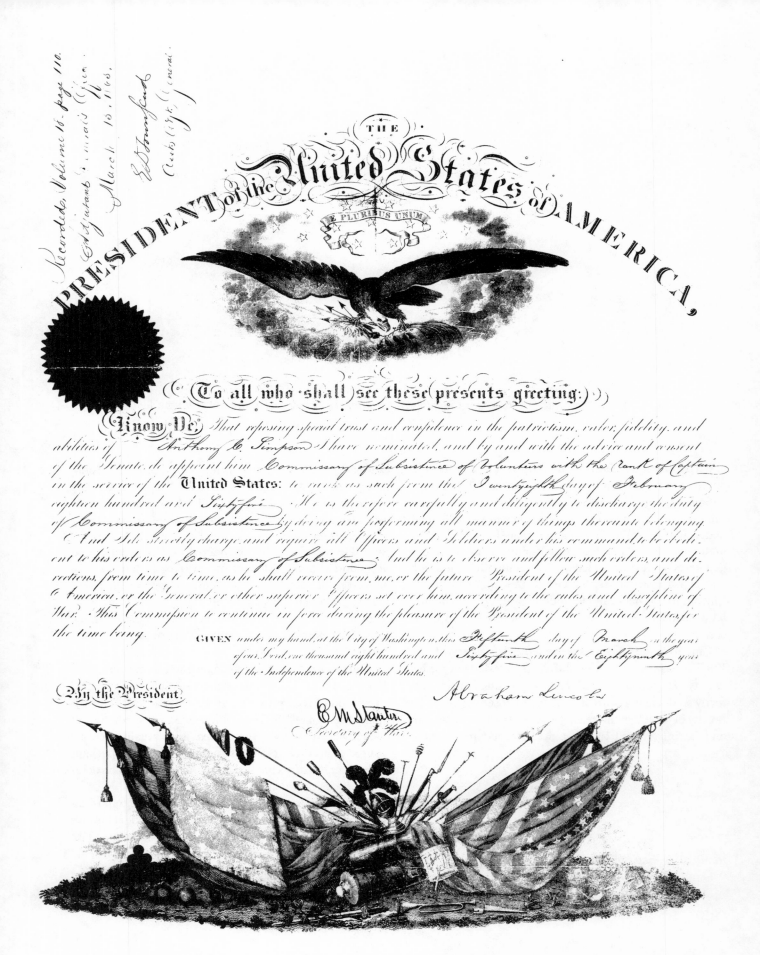

Folio Document Signed by Lincoln as president with his rare full signature. (reduced 50 %)

17. ANDREW JOHNSON

December 29, 1808 - July 31, 1875

Seventeenth President
April 15, 1865 - March 4, 1869

Republican (A Democrat but nominated
for vice president by the Republicans)

Highlights in office:
13th and 14th amendments;
Reconstruction Acts;
purchase of Alaska from Russia.

Andrew Johnson had as humble a beginning and even less formal education than Lincoln. At the age of twelve he was apprenticed to a tailor, but he ran away and worked at transient jobs. Later he opened a tailor shop in Greeneville, Tennessee. At age eighteen he married a woman who taught him to read and write—he even misspelled his own name on his marriage license, leaving the "n" out of "Johnson." He became active in the local debating society, was elected alderman, mayor, and to the Tennessee legislature. At the age of thirty-five he was elected to Congress, and then became governor of Tennessee and U.S. senator. He was the only southern senator to remain loyal to the Union during the Civil War. Lincoln appointed him military governor of Tennessee after Union troops took over the state.

In 1864, the Republicans placed Johnson, a Democrat and a pro-Union southerner, on the ticket with Lincoln in order to appeal to the broadest possible voter base. In later terminology Johnson might have been labeled a Populist. He favored free education and a Homestead Bill to give men without capital the chance to own land. He disliked slavery because it threatened the livelihood of poor whites.

After Lincoln's assassination, Republican leaders were shocked to find a "stranger in their midst" in the person of Johnson, for his basic differences with the Republican party were insuperable. He was a Democrat, only nominally heading the Republican party, as well as a southerner attempting to deal with men like Thaddeus

Stevens, of Pennsylvania, to whom southerners were anathemas. It is not surprising that these forces combined in an attempt to impeach Johnson. After a lengthy Senate trial he was acquitted by only one vote.

Even Johnson's harshest critics admitted he was a strong and tenacious opponent. His temper was legendary. When told of the impeachment proceedings against him he retorted: "Let them impeach and be damned!" After his acquittal he hoped to be nominated for the presidency—this time by the Democrats!

Shortly before he died Johnson was returned to the Senate by Tennessee, thus becoming the only former president to serve in that body. When he entered the senate chamber he received a standing ovation from both the galleries and the Senate members, and fresh flowers had been placed on his desk. He died only four months later.

About the time Johnson became president he injured his arm or hand. Because of this injury he ordered a steel stamp to be made of his signature, and thus became the first president to use a stamped signature. Johnson was also the only president until John F. Kennedy to employ secretaries to sign his name for him while president on documents other than land grants. Johnson's son acted as his presidential secretary and signed letters and franked envelopes for his father. Johnson had the franking privilege as a member of Congress, as president, and as former president. His rare post-presidential franks are both quaint and charming, and he usually signed them

I hereby authorize and direct the Secretary of State to affix the Seal of the United States to the Envelope of my Letter to the King of Sweden & Norway.

(Credence of Mr McGinnis)

dated this day, and signed by me; and for so doing this shall be his warrant.

Andrew Johnson

Washington, December 21, 1866.

Document Signed by Andrew Johnson as president.

Signature of Andrew Johnson shown actual size.

"Free, Andrew Johnson, Ex. Pres. U.S." His franks of all dates are scarce and quite expensive. Johnson is also available in signed photographs, primarily c.d.v.'s, which are also very expensive. In all his photographs Johnson has a stern, even fierce expression, and in general looks as if he had been weaned on a pickle.

Although Johnson apparently disliked writing letters because of his injury, those he did write frequently expressed his strong, acrid opinions and prejudices, and often were several pages long. Such letters are avidly sought and highly desirable. Johnson was indeed capable of writing a good letter. Although he continued to sign warrants and pardons personally, almost all his military commissions and other routine presidential documents were signed with his steel-stamped signature. Nonetheless, Johnson is much more abundant in signed documents than in letters. No presidential A.Ls.S., in the technical sense, are known to exist by the authors. All known presidential letters are Ls.S. Although scarce, he is available in brief, presidential-date notes normally written in pencil on letters or envelopes addressed to him. These A.Ns.S. do not constitute presidential A.Ls.S. but, as a practical matter, they are as close as one is likely to come to a presidential A.L.S.

One obvious reason for the scarcity of Johnson's A.Ls.S. was that he did not write with ease, due, no doubt to his late and rudimentary education. Johnson wrote a laborious, plain and somewhat crabbed hand although his penmanship is quite legible and remained virtually unchanged throughout his life. He normally signed "Andrew Johnson" in full, although he did on occasion sign himself "A. Johnson" and "And. Johnson," the latter form being quite rare. Johnson's signature was usually a modest size, but he occasionally signed documents with huge, bold, full signatures, sometimes measuring almost six inches.

Variant signatures of Andrew Johnson.

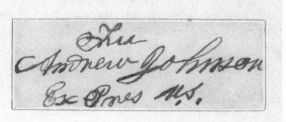

Left: Rare and charming post presidential franking signature of Andrew Johnson, mounted below a c.d.v.

18. ULYSSES S. GRANT

August 27, 1822 - July 23, 1885

Eighteenth President
March 4, 1869 - March 4, 1877

Republican

Highlights in office:
15th Amendment; Justice Department created;
Credit Mobilier scandal; panic of 1873;
Sioux Indian Wars and Custer's Defeat.

The son of a tanner and a farmer's daughter, Ulysses S. Grant, one of our greatest and toughest military generals, became one of our most mediocre presidents. One of his obituaries states, probably with accuracy, that the greatest mistake of his life was his acceptance of the presidency. Although Grant was personally fearless, he could not stand the sight of blood. Even the sight of rare meat made him queasy and, if he ate meat at all, it had to be almost charred. During the Civil War Grant would often break-fast on a cucumber soaked in vinegar, and he smoked up to twenty cigars a day, probably inducing the throat cancer which subsequently killed him.

Unlike Lincoln, he could not tolerate swearing or off-color stories or jokes. Once a man looked around the room and prefaced a risque story with "I see there are no ladies present" but Grant quickly interrupted him, saying "Ah, but there are gentlemen present." He could not stand to see animals abused. An extremely devoted family man, he was totally loyal to—and dependent on—his plain, plump, cross-eyed wife, Julia. She was the only woman he ever loved, and they remained happily married for the thirty-seven years until his death. She was the sister of his West Point roommate, Frederick Dent, who was later his military and presidential aide.

Against his will, Grant was sent to West Point by his father and was graduated near the bottom of his class. He received a commission and became a career army officer but was forced to resign because of his heavy drinking. Grant once said: "A military life had no charms for me, and I had not the faintest idea of staying in the Army even

if I should be graduated, which I did not expect." After unsuccessful farming and real estate ventures, Grant returned in disgrace, at age thirty-eight, to clerk in his brother's store. The Civil War rescued Grant from his failures. Commissioned a colonel of volunteers, through a combination of military genius and luck he became the commanding general of all Union armies.

Like several of our other general-presidents, prior to becoming president Grant's own political views were obscure—but he definitely was not the typical Republican. In 1856 he had voted for the Democrat, Buchanan. Although Grant's popularity and prestige were so great he was twice overwhelmingly elected president, and probably could have been elected to a consecutive third term, his administrations were weak to the point of disaster. Grant was personally honest, but he was politically naive and made many bad appointments. His enemies joked that "unconditional surrender" meant turning his presidential power over to the Republican Senate bosses. There was great scandal and corruption during his administration, and his secretary of war was impeached for accepting a bribe.

After leaving the White House Grant and his family embarked on a two-year world tour during which they were treated like royalty. When Grant returned home, he became involved in a disastrous financial venture which left him $16 million in debt. Fighting against time and suffering from painful throat cancer, Grant wrote his best-selling memoirs so he could leave his family financial-ly secure. He completed his memoirs only seven days

United States Marshal's Office,

Northern District of Illinois,

1868

Chicago, Ill. Ap.º 6ᵗ 1868

Dear Dent,

I am just in receipt of a letter from Mr. Welch, of Phila showing that Richard has taken my mares from his place! I am anxious to hear that they all arrived home safely and are now doing well. I wish you would get a complete halter for the Colt and tell Richard to wean it whilst it can get pasture in the lot about the house. It ought to run out during the day every day when the weather is not bad.

The number of stalls in my stable are not sufficient for all the horses and the colt. To remedy this get Webster to have a stall built for the colt either in the carriage house or other convenient place. To make room the Barouche carriage may be stored with the Quartermaster.

I am just on my way from St. Louis and Springfield. Will go home tonight. Julia and the children are all well.

Yours Truly

U. S. Grant

Pre-presidential Autograph Letter Signed of Ulysses S. Grant to his brother-in-law and West Point classmate, General Frederick T. Dent.

Autograph Document Signed of General Ulysses S. Grant, being a field order directive for Generals Butler and Meade, to fire a hundred gun salute in honor of the "second great victory" of the Union at Fishers Hill. Grant mentions this field order in his memoirs.

prior to his death, and they were published posthumously.

Grant was the first president to change his name. His original name "Ulysses Hiram Grant" was erroneously changed to "Ulysses S. Grant" by West Point and, for reasons known only to Grant, he chose to retain the error. Only one example of Grant's "Hiram" signature is known by the authors to exist, although early in his West Point career he also signed himself "Cadet U.H. Grant" before he settled on "Ulysses S. Grant."

Grant wrote a relatively small, plain hand, usually in haste, and some of his letters, usually on octavo-size stationery, are quite difficult to decipher, particularly during the war and presidential periods. One characteristic of his handwriting is that his capital "D's" and "W's" look quite similar. Grant had the habit of completely filling the page, particularly on one-page letters, which often necessitated his signing with a tiny, crabbed signature which give his letters an unbalanced and unattractive appearance. Grant's signature varied greatly, ranging from a diminutive two inches to well over five inches in size.

Grant seems almost always to have handled his correspondence personally so that, happily, his A.Ls.S. are more common than his Ls.S. Grant material is in demand by both Civil War and presidential collectors and his material is obtainable in most forms. He was the first president to introduce the Executive Mansion card to autograph for collectors although, to the knowledge of the authors, only one or two such examples are known to exist. Grant's war-date material is substantially more expensive than his presidential material and is obtainable both in letters and military field orders, which are technically A.Ds.S. He is also available in signed c.d.v.'s and cabinet photographs as well as in signed engravings. He is also relatively common in presidential Ds.S.

Since Grant's memoirs were published posthumously,

there are no signed copies. Grant dedicated his memoirs to American soldiers and sailors, and the dedication page contains a facsimile of his handwritten dedication often mistaken by collectors as being authentically written by Grant.

As a letter writer Grant was surprisingly good. He was terse and to the point, but expressed himself well. Many of his war-date letters and field orders have important and interesting content. His letters of presidential and post-presidential date often have interesting content in which Grant forcefully states his opinions. Grant's letters to his wife and children are particularly charming and usually have quite good content.

Grant is the first president whose signed photographs and engravings are relatively common and affordable. Photographs from the Civil War period show him in military uniform and are c.d.v.'s, while his post-war photographs are cabinet-size and show him in business suits. Handsome engravings, usually 8vo in size, are obtainable and date from presidential and post-presidential eras, many signed in purple ink. Grant's photographs usually bear only a signature, although he did on occasion inscribe them to certain individuals.

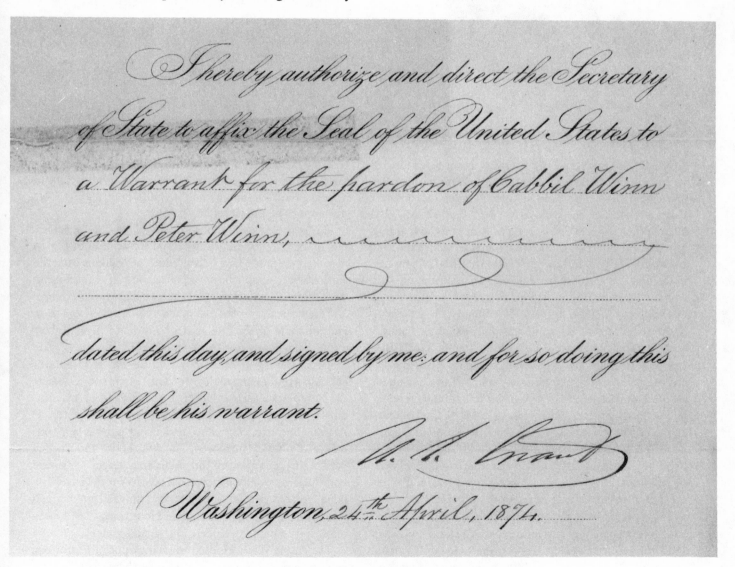

Grant presidential Document Signed

19. RUTHERFORD B. HAYES

October 4, 1822 - January 17, 1893

Nineteenth President
March 4, 1877 - March 4, 1881

Republican

Highlights in office:
Removal of all federal troops
from the South; Civil Service
reform; railroad strikes.

Rutherford Birchard Hayes was the son of New England parents who emigrated to Ohio in 1822. His father died before he was born, and two brothers and a sister died at very young ages. Hayes was left with only his mother and one sister, Fanny, to whom he formed an extraordinarily close attachment and who addressed him almost as a lover. When she married he refused to attend the wedding or to establish a law practice in Columbus where she and her husband lived. Instead, he established his law practice in the smaller and less profitable town of Fremont. His wife, Lucy Webb, resembled his sister. When Fanny died in childbirth in 1856 he told his wife: "You are Sister Fanny to me now." He named his only daughter Fanny.

With financial assistance from his uncle, Sardis Birchard, he studied law at Harvard, became a prosperous attorney, and later served as city solicitor of Cincinnati. At the outbreak of the Civil War he was commissioned a major of volunteers. Hayes saw a great deal of military action and was wounded five times. At the end of the war he held the brevet rank of major general, and for the rest of his life he retained a fondness for sentimental regimental reunions. After the war Hayes served a term in Congress and two terms as governor of Ohio. He was known as a competent but lackluster reformer.

Hayes became the Republican presidential nominee in 1876 in what became the most tortuous and controversial presidential election in the nation's history. Although he ran 250,000 votes behind Democratic nominee Samuel J. Tilden, the electoral college count was disputed. At the last minute on the very eve of the inauguration, Hayes was awarded all of the nineteen contested electors, giving him a razor-thin victory by a single electoral vote, from which rose his nickname of "Rutherfraud." Many concessions, including the end of Reconstruction, were necessary to appease the Democrats and the South before Hayes was declared to be the victor.

Hayes took office under the worst possible auspices. His immediate announcement that he would not seek a second term made him a "lame duck" president from the start. The Republican bosses assumed he would be as tractable as Grant in allowing them to dispense patronage and continue their graft but, much to their surprise, Hayes ignored their advice. He wrote in his diary: "I shall show a grit that will astonish those who predict weakness." He ignored the spoilsmen in selecting his high-caliber cabinet. He challenged the very heart of the spoils system, the New York Customs House, by dismissing its two principals, one of whom was future president Chester A. Arthur, because they continued using federal appointments for political purposes. The issue in this and ensuing battles was the power of the presidency versus legislative and local-government power—Hayes won decisively on behalf of the presidency. He also showed great good sense in reconciling the South and in vetoing the California-inspired bill to exclude Chinese nationals.

The Hayes White House, which introduced Easter-egg rolling on the White House lawn, was the personification of gentility and domesticity. The family was Methodist of the missionary persuasion, and in the White House the president and first lady held daily morning prayer meet-

Post presidential Autograph Letter Signed of Hayes.

Autograph Letter Signed of Hayes as president on an Executive Mansion card.

ings after breakfast. For intimate family entertainment their favorite pastime was old fashioned, Sunday night hymn-singing, in which the vice president, cabinet, and members of Congress often participated. All alcoholic beverages were banned from the White House, giving rise to Mrs. Hayes' nickname of "Lemonade Lucy." The liquorless White House prompted Hayes' witty secretary of state, William Evarts, to remark that at White House receptions "the water flowed like wine." When Hayes left office he was genuinely esteemed and he wrote: "Nobody ever left the Presidency with less regret, less disappointment, fewer heartburnings, or more general content with the result of his term . . . than I do." After leaving the White House he kept himself moderately active, although he was devastated by Lucy's death in 1889, a tragedy from which he never recovered. Shortly before his own death in 1893, he wrote that he wanted only to rest quietly beside her. His wish was soon fulfilled.

Hayes' handwriting is quite difficult to read, and his words have the paradoxical characteristic of strokes which slant both to the left and right, a quality which gives them an unattractive overall appearance as well as contributing to their general illegibility. He is particularly common in signed documents from his gubernatorial and presidential terms, and from various organizations such as the veterans, of which he was an officer. Hayes normally signed with his initials "R.B. Hayes," although on documents and occasionally on letters he signed "Rutherford B. Hayes." His full signature "Rutherford Birchard Hayes" is extremely rare with only the one example, illustrated, known to the authors.

Like several other presidents, Hayes kept a diary most of his adult life.

Rare full signature of Rutherford Birchard Hayes.

His A.Ls.S. are more common than his Ls.S. Although large numbers of Hayes' letters have been and continue to be absorbed by his presidential library (the first presidential library), his routine letters are still relatively common although now moderately expensive. In general his letters were somewhat dull and uninspired, with a legal tone, and they tended to be only one page in length. Hayes was capable of writing candid letters of good content, although they are rare and expensive. He is obtainable in franks, in signed Executive Mansion cards, Ds.S., A.Ls.S., signed c.d.v.'s normally from his military service, and cabinet photos. His signed photographs are expensive.

SPIEGEL GROVE, FREMONT, O.
2 JULY, 1889.

The friends who have sent telegraphic messages, letters, floral tributes and newspaper articles, tokens of their regard for Mrs. Hayes, and of sympathy with me and my family, are so numerous that I can not, by the use of the pen alone, within the time it ought to be done, suitably express to all of them my gratitude and thanks.

I therefore beg them to excuse me for sending in this form my assurance of the fullest appreciation of their kindness, and of my lasting and heartfelt obligation to each of them.

Post presidential Autograph Letter Signed on bottom of a printed acknowledgment of a sympathy letter on the death of his wife, Lucy Webb Hayes.

20. JAMES A. GARFIELD

November 19, 1831 - September 19, 1881

Twentieth President
March 4, 1881 - September 19, 1881

Republican

Highlights in office:
Post Office Department scandal;
Red Cross organized.

James A. Garfield was the last president to be born in a log cabin, "so politically perfect a mansion," in 1831 at Orange, Ohio, where his parents had moved from New England. His mother was widowed when he was two. As a youth Garfield did many kinds of work, from chopping wood to steering a canal boat, in order to support the family and to pay for his education. He was a tall, broad-shouldered man with an athletic build.

Garfield was a multi-faceted man of great talent, bearing a close resemblance to Jefferson in that respect. He graduated first in his class at Williams College, and eventually became the president of Ohio's Hiram College, where he was also a professor of Latin and Greek. He was our first left-handed president, with the interesting and well-documented ability to write simultaneously in Latin with one hand and Greek with the other.

The only ordained minister ever to become president, he was a lay minister and evangelist of the Disciples of Christ, a denomination opposed to both war and slavery. He became a lawyer, then state senator, a general in the Civil War, and subsequently served eight terms in the U.S. House of Representatives.

Like Kennedy, Garfield was able to absorb information extremely rapidly. He mastered the elements of soldiering and applied them so efficiently that he left the army, after less than three years, with the rank of major general.

He married a childhood playmate and former pupil, Lucretia Rudolph, whom he called "Crete." She was a scholarly woman, usually described as plain, who personally instructed her children and who designed the family mansion. Although the Garfield's marriage was

initially rocky, they later enjoyed a stable relationship despite the constant presence of Garfield's mother, who accompanied them even to the White House where she became the first presidential mother to see her son inaugurated. When Garfield was shot his mother said: "How could anybody be so cold-hearted as to want to kill my baby?"

In the 1880 Republican convention, Garfield was a compromise choice selected over the other candidates, former-president Grant, James G. Blaine and John Sherman. His Democratic opponent was the Civil War hero, General Winfield Scott Hancock. Although Garfield won by only ten thousand popular votes, he decisively won the electoral vote.

Garfield was the second president to be assassinated. The 199 days of his presidential term make it the second shortest period of time served by any president.

We can only speculate how good a president Garfield might have been. His political contemporaries, including ex-president Hayes, did not expect him to be a strong president, but he demonstrated considerable grit during his brief term. He refused to knuckle under to the arrogant Republican "Stalwarts" of New York, and he won battles against their two Senate leaders, Roscoe Conkling and Thomas Platt. He also ordered his attorney general to investigate fraud in post office contracts even though the results would be damaging to the Republicans.

The politics of the era stimulated corruption, fraud, hysteria and violence, and Garfield became the victim of the system that created him. Four months after his inauguration he was shot twice, once in the back, by a

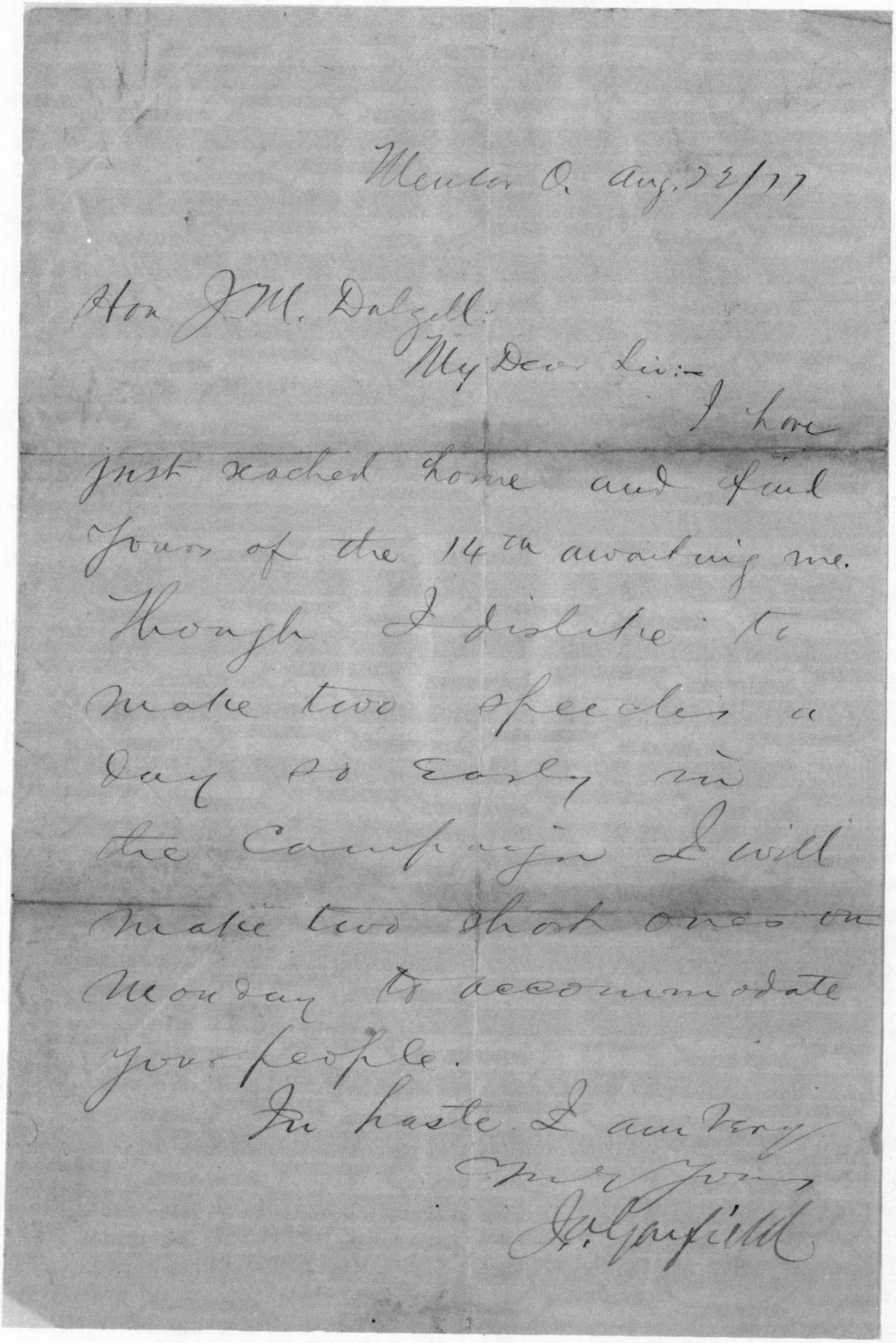

Mentor O. Aug 23/??

Hon J. M. Dalzell:

My Dear Sir:—

I have just reached home and find yours of the 14th awaiting me. Though I dislike to make two speeches a day so early in the campaign I will make two short ones on Monday to accommodate your people.

In haste I am very truly yours,

J A Garfield

Pre-presidential Manuscript Letter Signed by James A. Garfield.

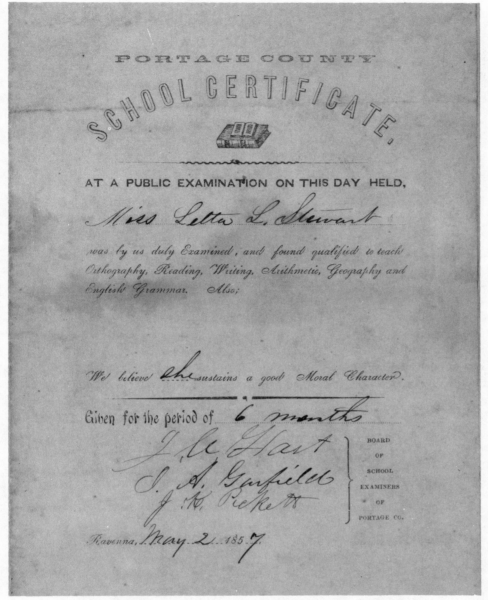

One of the earliest known signatures of Garfield, a Document Signed as a twenty-five years old college professor.

secretary of war, Robert Todd Lincoln, son of Abraham Lincoln, and asked him to relate all the details of his father's assassination. He listened intently to Lincoln's account for over an hour. (By a strange quirk of fate, Robert Todd Lincoln was with both Garfield and, later, McKinley when they were shot.)

Garfield wrote a bold, flowing hand with the interesting characteristics of connecting many of his words and often failing to cross small case "t's," particularly in the middle of words. He almost always signed his name with his initials "J.A. Garfield," except during his brief presidential term when he used his full signature on official documents and various other items, including a small number of extremely rare Executive Mansion cards. Paradoxically, as president he also continued signing his name with his initials on unofficial documents. An interesting fact about Garfield's full presidential signature is that, after becoming president, he changed the form of his middle initial "A" from his usual rounded style to a cursive style. To the knowledge of the authors, the relatively few known examples of Garfield's extremely rare full signature were all signed while he was president.

Garfield's letters are dull for the most part, and usually concern routine personal and political matters, patronage, and his finances. Good-content Garfield letters are quite rare. Like many of the late nineteenth century presidents he favored octavo-size stationery. He

disappointed office seeker, a deranged lawyer named Charles J. Guiteau. Ironically, Garfield was probably killed by his doctors rather than Guiteau, because the bullet in his back lodged in a muscle and did not do any vital harm. The fatal damage was done by the well-intentioned but deadly probing of his doctors in a vain effort to find and extract the bullet. The wound became infected and Garfield died of blood poisoning.

As did Lincoln, Garfield had a premonition of his death. Two days before he was shot he sent for his

From Mollie Garfield, **EXECUTIVE MANSION, WASHINGTON**

James A. Garfield.
June 28, 1881.

*Rare Executive Mansion card signed by President James
A. Garfield (courtesy of Bob Erickson).*

A.Ls.S. Although Garfield is obtainable in A.Ls.S. he is much more common in Ls.S.

Since Garfield was active as president for only four months before being assassinated, anything signed by him as president is rare and expensive. After being shot he signed only three items: one official extradition paper, one brief letter to his mother, and a card he signed for his physician to demonstrate his strength. The few presidential, pre-assassination items which do appear are normally seal authorizations or the sender's copy of telegrams. Only a handful of presidential-date letters are known to exist.

employed secretaries to write his letters during much of his congressional career as well as during his presidential campaign. Joseph Stanley Brown, his secretary (and later his son-in-law) who worked for him during the presidential campaign, imitated his handwriting style very closely, even to the point of connecting words. Consequently, Garfield's campaign-date letters should be closely scrutinized, since these campaign-date Ls.S appear to be

Garfield is abundant in pre-presidential franks and Ls.S., but somewhat scarce in A.Ls.S. He is scarce but obtainable in S.P.'s, both c.d.v.'s and cabinet-size. He is the second rarest of all presidents, following Harrison, in signed presidential-date material. Garfield is scarce but obtainable in early documents from his school teaching days, usually in the form of report cards or teacher certifications.

Envelope adressed to his wife by Garfield, incorporating his signature, with a note added later by his wife, Lucretia.

21. CHESTER A. ARTHUR

October 5, 1830 - November 18, 1886

Twenty-First Presidents
September 19, 1881 - March 4, 1885

Republican

Highlights in office:
Pendleton Act of 1883; corrected the abuses
of the spoils system; Chinese Exclusion Act;
First Labor Day Celebration.

Chester Alan Arthur is an enigma among our presidents. There is perhaps less hard information about his personal life than any other president. The son of the Reverend William Arthur, a Baptist preacher from County Antrim, Ireland, his official birth date is October 5, 1830. His political opponents charged that he was born in Canada rather than Vermont, and some recent historians agree — he was probably born in Canada in 1829 and, if so, would have been ineligible to serve as president. This could possibly explain why Arthur ordered all his personal papers destroyed after his death. Their destruction left a great void which probably can never be filled.

Arthur, a Phi Beta Kappa graduate of Union College, was first a school teacher in Vermont and later studied law. As a lawyer he practiced in New York City and became active in New York Republican politics. Interestingly, he handled several cases championing Negro rights, including an 1853 case in which he argued that in fugitive slave cases the fugitive slaves transported through New York State were thereby freed. During the Civil War he was appointed quartermaster general of New York. He then became chairman of the state's Republican party and was appointed collector of the port of New York, a lucrative political plum which gave him control of over a thousand job appointments and employees, all of whom were expected to contribute both time and money to party activities.

President Hayes made bitter enemies of the New York political bosses when he instituted civil service reforms which forced Arthur to resign. Arthur and the "Stalwarts"

tried to nominate Grant for a third term, but Garfield was nominated as a compromise candidate. In the interest of harmony and to placate New York political boss Roscoe Conkling, Arthur, the "Gentleman Boss," was nominated for vice president, although he was Garfield's second choice. Many reform-minded Republicans bitterly opposed the choice and tried to devise a means to vote for Garfield without voting for Arthur.

Arthur is the classic example of the political boss who was ennobled by the presidency. Although he kept bad company, there is no evidence that he was personally dishonest. In the minds of the electorate, however, he was guilty by association. In any event, as president Arthur effaced his previous image and left a surprisingly good record. He continued Garfield's prosecution of post office frauds and, to the utter horror of the Republicans and other critics, he undertook civil service reforms and broke with Conkling. His administration saw the passage of the Pendleton Act which established the Civil Service Commission. He also vetoed legislation he considered undesirable, and supported the Tariff of 1883. He was defeated for renomination by James G. Blaine, who was subsequently defeated by Cleveland.

Little is known about Arthur's personal life, and still less is known about his wife. He married a socially prominent beauty named Nell Herndon who died of pneumonia at age forty-two shortly before her husband's vice-presidential nomination. Her death left Arthur inconsolable and he gave orders that her room should remain forever untouched. He never remarried and,

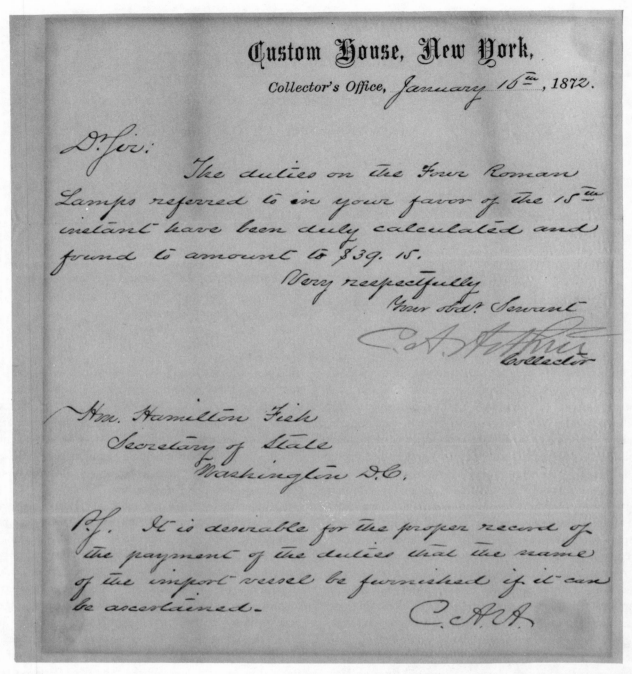

Manuscript Letter Signed by Chester A. Arthur as collector of the Port of New York from which position he was fired by President Hayes. (reduced 82%)

while president, had fresh flowers placed daily before a small, silver-framed photograph of his wife.

Arthur was a six feet two inch bon vivant, an elegant dresser who ordered as many as twenty-five pairs of custom-made trousers at one time. As a gourmand, he loved fine wines and good food and often spent two or three hours or more at the dinner table.

He was appalled by the hodgepodge of White House furniture which greeted him after he became president, and he refused to move in until twenty-four wagon loads of furniture, some of it priceless, had been auctioned off and the White House totally refurbished and redecorated by his friend Louis Comfort Tiffany. Arthur was criticized

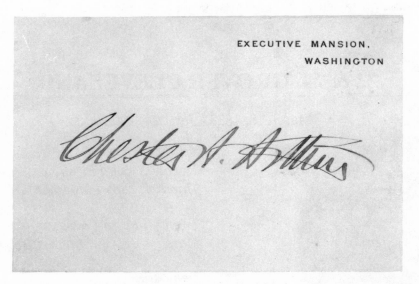

EXECUTIVE MANSION,
WASHINGTON

Presidential signature of Chester A. Arthur on an Executive Mansion card.

for his elegant living; Congressman Joe Cannon said: "Arthur was defeated by his trousers."

Arthur demonstrated as president that he was above party factions and, at times, even the party itself. The well-kept secret he had known since a year after becoming president—that he was suffering from a fatal kidney disease—was probably an instrumental factor in his independence. He only stayed in the running for renomination as president in 1884 so as not to be regarded as a lame duck. He was not renominated, however, and died only twenty months after leaving the White House.

Arthur wrote a bold, attractive, somewhat florid hand and, like Garfield, connected many of his words. He favored a broad-nibbed pen which made his writing appear quite bold and heavy. He used octavo-size stationery, often with double sheets, and completely filled the pages with his large script. His letters were normally terse and to the point but rather uninteresting. Arthur signed his name both as "C.A. Arthur" and "Chester A. Arthur." His signature is one of the largest and boldest of the presidential series. He introduced the octavo

engraved vignettes of the White House which he selectively signed for collectors. He is available also in signed Executive Mansion cards.

Arthur's material is perhaps the scarcest of any post-Civil War president. He was not nationally prominent before becoming president, served less than a single term, and died less than two years after leaving office. Because of his large handwriting and signature and his preference for small octavo stationery, Arthur's letters, particularly his A.Ls.S., are often several pages in length. His Ls.S. are more plentiful than his A.Ls.S. He is available in signed documents from his periods as port collector and president, and occasionally early legal documents are offered. His signed photographs are both rare and expensive. Arthur was the first president to utilize the typewriter, and many of his presidential letters were typewritten for him.

Fewer of Chester A. Arthur's letters survive than perhaps those of any other president, making it difficult to pass judgment on him as a correspondent and letter writer. His post-presidential letters are especially scarce.

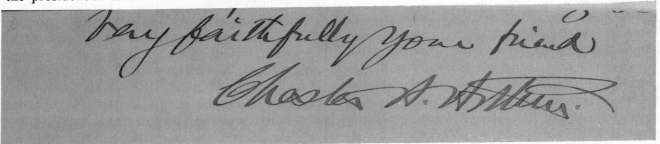

Close of an Autograph Letter Signed. Note how Arthur connected many of his words.

22 & 24. GROVER CLEVELAND

March 18, 1837 - June 24, 1908

Twenty-Second President
March 4, 1885 - March 4, 1889

Twenty-Fourth President
March 4, 1893 - March 4, 1897

Democrat

Highlights in office:
Interstate Commerce Act passed;
Pullman Strike; panic of 1893.

Stephen Grover Cleveland was the first Democrat to be elected president since James Buchanan almost thirty years before. The only incumbent president to be defeated and then reelected, he thus became the only president to serve two non-consecutive terms. He was a bachelor when elected president, and was the first and only president to marry in the White House.

One of the nine children of Richard F. Cleveland, a Presbyterian minister, Cleveland was born in New Jersey but was reared in upstate New York. He clerked in Clinton, in Buffalo, and in the New York City Institution for the Blind. He was admitted to the bar in Buffalo and soon became known for the single-mindedness with which he faced all tasks. Active in Democratic politics, he was appointed assistant district attorney of Erie County and was later elected sheriff of the county. While sheriff, he personally assumed his statutory duty as executioner of condemned prisoners, thus becoming our only president to be a hangman.

After leaving the sheriff's office, Cleveland practiced law for seven years and then, at the age of forty-four, began to run for political office as a reform candidate. Within less than four years he was elected mayor of Buffalo, governor of New York, and president of the United States.

Cleveland was elected president in 1884 after one of the dirtiest but most colorful campaigns in American history, with one of the narrowest margins of victory for any president. The fact that Cleveland had fathered an il-

legitimate child, whose paternity he publicly acknowledged, became a campaign issue. The Republicans coined a catchy campaign slogan about Cleveland's illegitimate child: "Maw, Maw, where's my Paw," and the Democrats answered with their slogan: "Gone to the White House, haw, haw, haw!"

A forty-seven year old bachelor at the time of his election, during the second year of his first term Cleveland married Frances Folsom, the beautiful twenty-one year old daughter of his former law partner. When his law partner died, Cleveland became administrator of his estate and the unofficial guardian of his future wife. Cleveland had known Frances all her life and had purchased her first baby buggy. During her youth, she called him "Uncle Cleve" and he called her "Frank." With her mother's permission he sent her flowers and letters while she was in college. In a remark to one of his sisters, which she did not understand at the time, he said he was "waiting for his wife to grow up." Cleveland personally hand-wrote all his wedding invitations, and John Philip Sousa conducted the Marine Band for the occasion. The Cleveland's second child, Esther, became the first and only child of a president to be born in the White House.

As president, Cleveland vigorously pursued a policy barring special favors to any economic group, including Civil War veterans and drought-stricken Texas farmers. In a veto message he wrote: "Federal aid in such cases encourages the expectation of paternal care on the part of

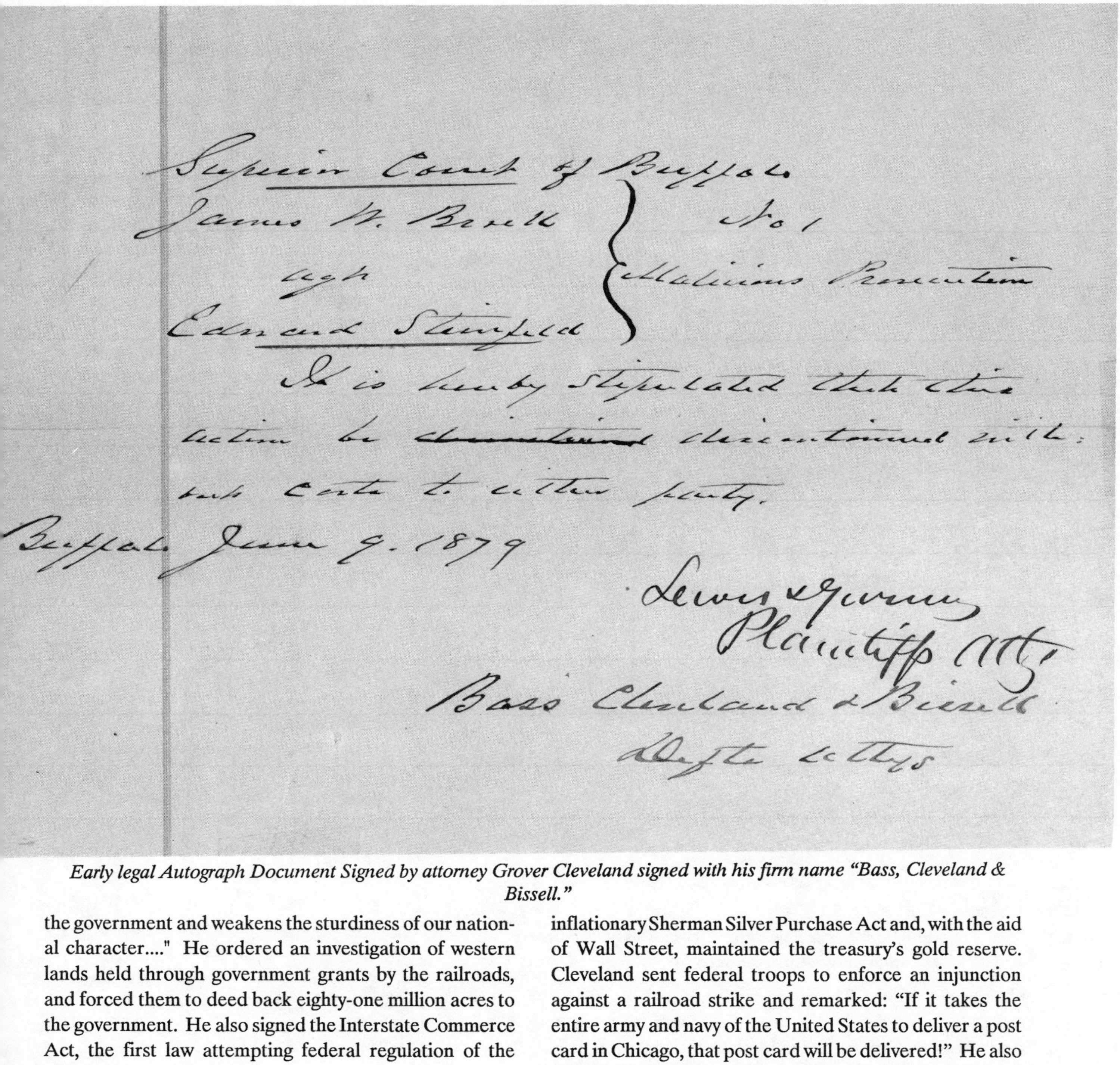

[Handwritten legal document reproduced at top of page:]

Superior Court of Buffalo

James N. Bevell

ugh

Edward Steinfeld

No. 1

Malicious Prosecution

It is hereby stipulated that this action be ~~discontinued~~ discontinued with out costs to either party.

Buffalo June 9. 1879

Lewis & Ginns
Plaintiffs Att[y]

Bass Cleveland & Bissell
Defts attys

Early legal Autograph Document Signed by attorney Grover Cleveland signed with his firm name "Bass, Cleveland & Bissell."

the government and weakens the sturdiness of our national character...." He ordered an investigation of western lands held through government grants by the railroads, and forced them to deed back eighty-one million acres to the government. He also signed the Interstate Commerce Act, the first law attempting federal regulation of the railroads.

Cleveland was defeated for reelection in 1892 by Benjamin Harrison, even though he won a large majority of popular votes. He won reelection in 1892, however, only to be immediately faced with a severe economic depression. Dealing directly with the treasury crisis rather than with business failures, he obtained the repeal of the mildly inflationary Sherman Silver Purchase Act and, with the aid of Wall Street, maintained the treasury's gold reserve. Cleveland sent federal troops to enforce an injunction against a railroad strike and remarked: "If it takes the entire army and navy of the United States to deliver a post card in Chicago, that post card will be delivered!" He also forced Great Britain to accept arbitration of a disputed boundary in Venezuela. Because his policies during the economic recession were unpopular, his party repudiated him in 1896 and instead nominated William Jennings Bryan.

In 1893 a cancerous growth was discovered in the roof of Cleveland's mouth, necessitating the removal of most

New York
May 8. 1889

H. R. Clarke Esq
My dear Sir:

Please accept my sincere thanks for the fine trout you kindly sent me. They were certainly beauties and the evidence their receipt afforded of your friendliness was much gratifying.

Yours very truly
Grover Cleveland

Autograph Letter Signed on Cleveland's typical octavo size stationery, written between his presidential terms.

his children were playmates of Woodrow Wilson's daughters and they acted in amateur plays together, but Cleveland held Professor Wilson in a "minimum of high regard."

With the exception of the last few years when poor health forced him to employ a secretary, Cleveland personally wrote all of his letters during all periods of his life, including the presidency when he fired the White House secretary in an economy move and even personally answered the White House telephone! Cleveland's Ls.S. are much scarcer than his A.Ls.S. Cleveland never had the franking privilege. He is relatively common in presidential documents and early legal documents dating from his legal career, and he is the most common and least expensive of the nineteenth century presidents in both signed Executive Mansion cards and signed photographs which were invariably cabinet-size. Only a few examples are known to exist of Cleveland's early signature "S.G. Cleveland," incorporating the initial of his first name, Stephen. They would command a high price should any appear on the market.

In terms of content Cleveland was one of the better letter writers among the presidents. He wrote a number of candid and interesting letters, many of which contained humorous commentary on the issues or prominent personages of the day. Most of Cleveland's letters, even routine ones, were longer than one page, and if Cleveland considered them important they frequently ran to many pages.

of his upper left jaw. The serious and major operation was a closely guarded secret because Cleveland feared that concerns about his health might make the bad economic situation even worse. The surgery was a success and Cleveland was fitted with an artificial jaw of vulcanized rubber.

After Cleveland left the White House he lived in retirement in Princeton, New Jersey. Two of his five children, his two sons, were born after he left office. At Princeton

Cleveland's handwriting is extremely difficult to read and he holds, with Van Buren and Kennedy, the dubious honor of having the worst penmanship of the presidents. Cleveland's writing is tiny, with many ill-defined individual letters, which were often represented merely by a single stroke, or not at all. He left open his small case "d's," "p's," "a's" and "o's" making his handwriting a nightmare to read. One is almost tempted to resort to the Rosetta stone for assistance in translating his hieroglyphics.

23. BENJAMIN HARRISON

August 20, 1833 - March 13, 1901

Twenty-Third President
March 4, 1889 - March 4, 1893

Republican

Highlights in office:
Pan-American conference;
Sherman Antitrust Act;
Sherman Silver Purchase Act.

Benjamin Harrison was from a very prominent American family. His great grandfather, Benjamin Harrison, was a signer of the Declaration of Independence, and his grandfather, William Henry Harrison, on whose farm he was born, was the ninth president. His father, John Scott Harrison, who served in Congress, holds the distinction of being the only man to be the son of one president and the father of another.

Harrison was a graduate of Miami University in Ohio and practiced law in Indianapolis. He was known as a brilliant lawyer and had a lucrative law practice, was active in Republican politics, and was elected reporter of the state supreme court. He was commissioned a second lieutenant at the beginning of the Civil War, during which it was charged that he used political influence to rise to the rank of general despite a lackluster battlefield record. Harrison was twice defeated in bids for the governorship of Indiana, but won election to the U.S. Senate.

When James G. Blaine withdrew from contention for the Republican presidential nomination in 1888, the party began to look for a moderate, scandal-free Republican from a "swing" state, someone with political experience, name recognition, and service in the Civil War. Benjamin Harrison filled the bill in all respects and was nominated on the eighth ballot.

Harrison married the daughter of one his college professors when he was only twenty. He and his wife, Caroline, were deeply religious and devout members of the Presbyterian Church. For many years Harrison taught a men's Bible class and served as Sunday school superin-

tendent. Caroline Harrison died following a long illness during her husband's last year in the White House. Three years later the sixty-two year old Harrison married his wife's niece, a young thirty-seven year old widow named Mary Scott Lord Dimmick, who had lived with the family for several years and who had served as official White House hostess during her aunt's illness. Harrison's two children were so disturbed by the match that they boycotted the wedding. A year later a daughter, Elizabeth, was born who was younger than Harrison's grandchildren, thus creating a genealogical nightmare in family relationships.

Outside the family circle, Harrison was personally cold and humorless. As one acquaintance stated: "Harrison can make a speech to ten thousand men and every one of them will go away his friend. Let him meet the same ten thousand men in private, and every one will go away his enemy." Harrison's only self-indulgence was his love for fine cigars.

The first electric lights were installed in the White House while Harrison was president, but the Harrisons were so fearful of the new device they refused to touch the switches and would let the lights burn all night if there were no servant to turn them off.

Harrison promulgated a vigorous foreign policy during his single term. The first Pan American Congress met in Washington in 1889, establishing an information center which later became the Pan American Union. Harrison also submitted a treaty to the Senate to annex Hawaii but the treaty was later withdrawn by Cleveland. Congress

J. W. Weidemeyer, Esq.
63 Barker St,
New York City. N.Y.

My dear Sir:—

I have your letter of the 13th inst, in which you say, "Genl. Wilsons letter"— referring, I suppose, to yours of the 11th inst—"was concerning an article on President Harrison and also, to his best portrait, and that a likeness of Mrs Harrison would also be desirable". In your letter of the 11th inst, no reference was made to President Harrison: You said: "Genl. Wilson desires me to inquire if you would have the kindness to ~~inquire~~ refer him to some particularly competent person that would furnish a biographical sketch for our Encyclopedia," &c. You add; "A faithful likeness and autographic signature would also be desirable. I could only understand your letter to refer to some sketch of myself as the letter

Manuscript Letter Signed by Senator Benjamin Harrison mentioning his grandfather, President William Henry Harrison, and his grandmother, First Lady Anna Harrison. (reduced 82%)

was addressed to me and no other person was named. If the sketch desired is one of my Grandfather, President Harrison I will try to find someone to prepare it and would be glad to undertake the work myself but for the fact, that my engagements will not allow me to do so within the time you limit.

Very truly yours,

Benj Harrison

Your brother, Your Affectionate Brother

Benj Harrison

Close of an Autograph Letter Signed of Benjamin Harrison illustrating his illegible handwriting.

passed its first peace-time billion dollar appropriation during Harrison's administration.

The Sherman Antitrust Act was signed by Harrison, but it was the tariff issue which was to prove Harrison's most troublesome domestic problem—how to deal with the surplus in the treasury created by high tariff rates! Although Harrison was renominated by his party in 1892, he was defeated by Cleveland. His last years as a respected elder statesman were spent in contentment with his young wife and child and as an orator, author, and successful lawyer.

Harrison wrote a heavy, bold hand with a broad-nibbed pen. The angularity of his individual letters, which increased over time, combined with his heavy pen strokes, make his writing quite difficult to read. Harrison employed secretaries during most periods of his career,

making his A.Ls.S. somewhat scarce, particularly of presidential date. In content, his letters were quite dry and generally written in lawyerly phraseology. Letters of interesting or historic content are rare.

Harrison always signed his name in full. His early signatures were signed "Benja. Harrison" with the "a" connected to the "H" of Harrison. Sometime after 1881 and before 1886 he dropped the "a" in "Benja." and thereafter simply signed "Benj. Harrison," always connecting his first and last names.

Harrison's Ls.S. were both manuscript and typed, and he favored octavo personalized stationery, although his official letters written as senator were primarily on quarto stationery. Harrison's post-presidential letters were normally typed on personalized, oblong, octavo stationery imprinted "Benjamin Harrison, 874 North Delaware

Manuscript Letter Signed by Senator Benjamin Harrison with the early form of his signature: Benj ᵃ Harrison. He later dropped the small "a" from "Benjamin."

Street, Indianapolis, Indiana." Harrison is obtainable in presidential Ds.S. and in signed Executive Mansion cards and engravings, although he is not nearly so common as he once was. He is scarce and expensive in signed photographs.

25. WILLIAM McKINLEY

January 29, 1843 - September 14, 1901

Twenty Fifth President
March 4, 1897 - September 14, 1901

Republican

Highlights in office:
Hawaii annexed;
Spanish-American War.

Born in Ohio of poor parents, William McKinley was a sickly, bookish child who was reared by a staunch Methodist mother who wanted him to be a minister. He began his career as a postal clerk and later worked as a school teacher. When the Civil War began he volunteered as a private when he was only nineteen years old, and served in the Twenty-third Ohio Volunteer Infantry under the command of Rutherford B. Hayes, who later described McKinley as "one of the bravest and finest officers of the army." McKinley served with great valor and rose to the rank of major. After the war he returned to Ohio and studied law. He was elected prosecuting attorney of Stark County and served six terms in the U.S. House of Representatives and two terms as governor of Ohio.

McKinley had a very tragic personal life. After only four years of marriage his wife, Ida, suffered a mental and physical collapse following the deaths of their two infant daughters and her mother. She never recovered and spent the rest of her life as a tormented epileptic on the border of sanity. McKinley remained totally devoted to her and often neglected presidential business to lie across her bed and soothe her. He violated protocol at official White House functions and state dinners to sit beside his wife in case she had an epileptic seizure, in which case he would calmly put a napkin or handkerchief over her face until the seizure had passed and he would continue his conversation as if nothing had happened. Even at the moment of his own assassination his thoughts were of his wife's delicate health: "My wife . . ." he gasped to a trusted aide, ". . . be careful how you tell her, oh, be careful."

In personality, McKinley has often been often compared to Lincoln. He was gentle and kind, possessed tremendous charm and charisma, and was quite concerned about the welfare of others. It was these traits of character which brought him to the attention of Mark Hanna, a wealthy Republican from Cleveland who became his staunch and loyal mentor and promoted his political career tirelessly and selflessly. Hanna once said: "I love McKinley. He is the best man I ever knew." Hanna engineered McKinley's two gubernatorial campaigns as well as his presidential nomination and election.

In 1896, McKinley won the presidential nomination on the first ballot and faced the Democratic nominee William Jennings Bryan. Despite a strong campaign by Bryan, business interests united behind McKinley and helped win him the election.

In the friendly atmosphere of the McKinley administration, industrial corporations developed at an unprecedented pace, but it was foreign policy which dominated McKinley's administration. McKinley was no warmonger, but popular opinion compelled him to request that war be declared against Spain, a recommendation which Congress was most happy to approve. In the ensuing one hundred day war the U.S. destroyed the Spanish fleet in Cuba, seized Manila in the Philippines, and occupied Puerto Rico. After the war, acquiescing to imperialistic sentiments in the country, McKinley annexed other Spanish possessions: the Philippines, Guam, and Puerto Rico.

In 1900 McKinley again faced Bryan in the presidential election and again handily defeated him. While Bryan

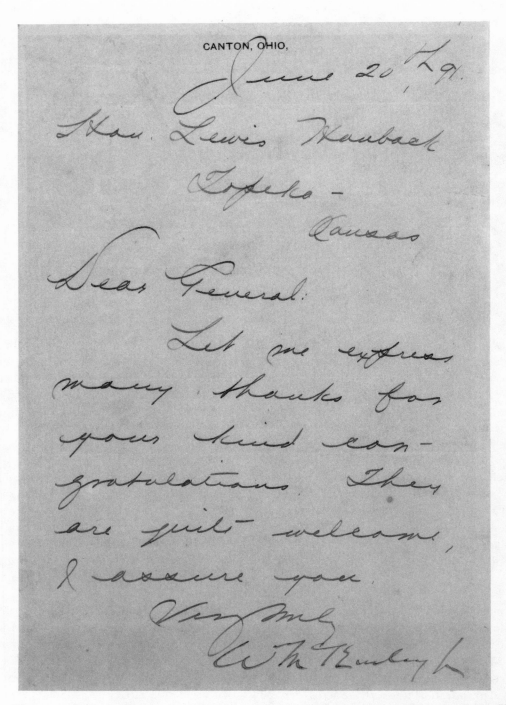

CANTON, OHIO,

Manuscript Letter Signed written by Congressman William McKinley to fellow congressman Lewis Hanback acknowledging congratulations on his gubernatorial nomination, signed "W McKinley Jr."

spoke against imperialism, McKinley quietly stood for "the full dinner pail." His second term, so auspiciously started, ended tragically in a receiving line at the Pan American Exposition in Buffalo, when a deranged anarchist named Leon Czolgosz shot him twice. As Mckinley collapsed, bystanders grabbed Czolgosz and started pummeling him. McKinley murmured: "Don't let them hurt him." He died eight days later.

McKinley was not an interesting letter writer, seeming to shirk from putting his intimate views or feelings on

EXECUTIVE MANSION,
WASHINGTON.

Executive Mansion card signed by William McKinley.

paper. He is scarce in A.Ls.S. of all dates, particularly as president. However, during the Spanish-American War he wrote hundreds of telegrams, mostly in pencil, many with significant content. His presidential documents are readily obtainable. He is obtainable, too, in signed Executive Mansion cards and signed photographs, usually cabinet-size, although they are not common and are relatively expensive. Until shortly before becoming president, McKinley usually signed his name "W. McKinley, Jr."

using his first initial only. On documents and some letters, seemingly by whim, however, he signed himself in full.

McKinley's handwriting is difficult to read, and his holographs are often characterized by ink blots, smeared letters, and crossed-out words. His script is also characterized by open "a's" and "o's," uncrossed small case "t's," and many ill-formed letters, which make his script very difficult to read. He favored a medium-to-heavy pen nib.

home during my visit to Albany, if it would not conflict with the arrangements of the committee. I would suggest that you see the committee in order that there may be no misunderstanding or conflict.

With kindest regards,

Very truly yours,

Mr. John A. Sleicher,
        The Mail & Express,
            New York City.

Letter Signed by William McKinley as governor of Ohio.

26. THEODORE ROOSEVELT

October 17, 1858 - January 6, 1919

Twenty-Sixth President
September 14, 1901 - March 4, 1909

Republican

Highlights in office:
Trust busting; Pure Food and
Drug Act; Departments of
Commerce and Labor established.

At age forty-two Theodore Roosevelt was the the youngest man ever to become president.* He was America's first "modern" president, the first to travel by motorcar and by airplane. A one-man orchestra, his contemporaries said: "He wanted to put an end to all evil in the world between sunrise and sunset"; "He killed mosquitoes as if they were lions"; "A mixture of St. Paul and St. Vitus." Roosevelt had great vitality and charisma, and was a brilliant conversationalist as well as an author of acclaim in his own right.

Roosevelt was from a wealthy and socially prominent New York family. A sickly child who suffered from asthma, he turned to gymnastics and boxing to strengthen his "constitution." By the time he reached Harvard he had become a wiry extrovert. He was a most unlikely politician because his social class was disdainful of both politics and politicians; the more plebian voters, in turn, were likely to be suspicious of the "dude" with the squeaky voice. However, he confounded both classes by winning a seat at age twenty-three in the New York Assembly. The deaths on the same day of his first wife, Alice Lee, in childbirth, and of his mother, from typhoid, temporarily ended his political career. He went west, to the Dakotas, and ranched for two years while his deep emotional scars healed. However, he never again mentioned his first wife, even to their only child, Alice.

Roosevelt, a Phi Beta Kappa graduate of Harvard, studied law at Columbia. He gained a reputation as an outspoken reformer, but was defeated in his bid to become mayor of New York City. At one time he was a professional writer of historical and autobiographical volumes. He was appointed to the Civil Service Commission and later became New York City police commissioner before becoming assistant secretary of the navy. At the outbreak of the Spanish-American War he resigned to organize the "Rough Riders," a volunteer regiment, and became the hero of the Battle of San Juan.

After the Spanish-American war, political boss Tom Platt needed a hero to draw attention away from the political scandals in New York state, and accepted Roosevelt as the Republican gubernatorial candidate in 1898. Within two years, the same political boss was anxious to get rid of the new reform governor and arranged to "kick Roosevelt upstairs" as the Republican vice-presidential nominee. A year later, following McKinley's assassination, conservatives were appalled to find, as Mark Hanna stated, "that damned cowboy" in the White House. Roosevelt was extremely popular, however, and was easily renominated by his party in 1904. He won 57 percent of the popular vote and carried every state outside the South.

As president, Roosevelt emerged as a "trust buster" under the terms of the new Sherman Antitrust Act.

He led the United States into a more active role in world

---

* John F. Kennedy, at age forty-three, was the youngest man *elected* president.

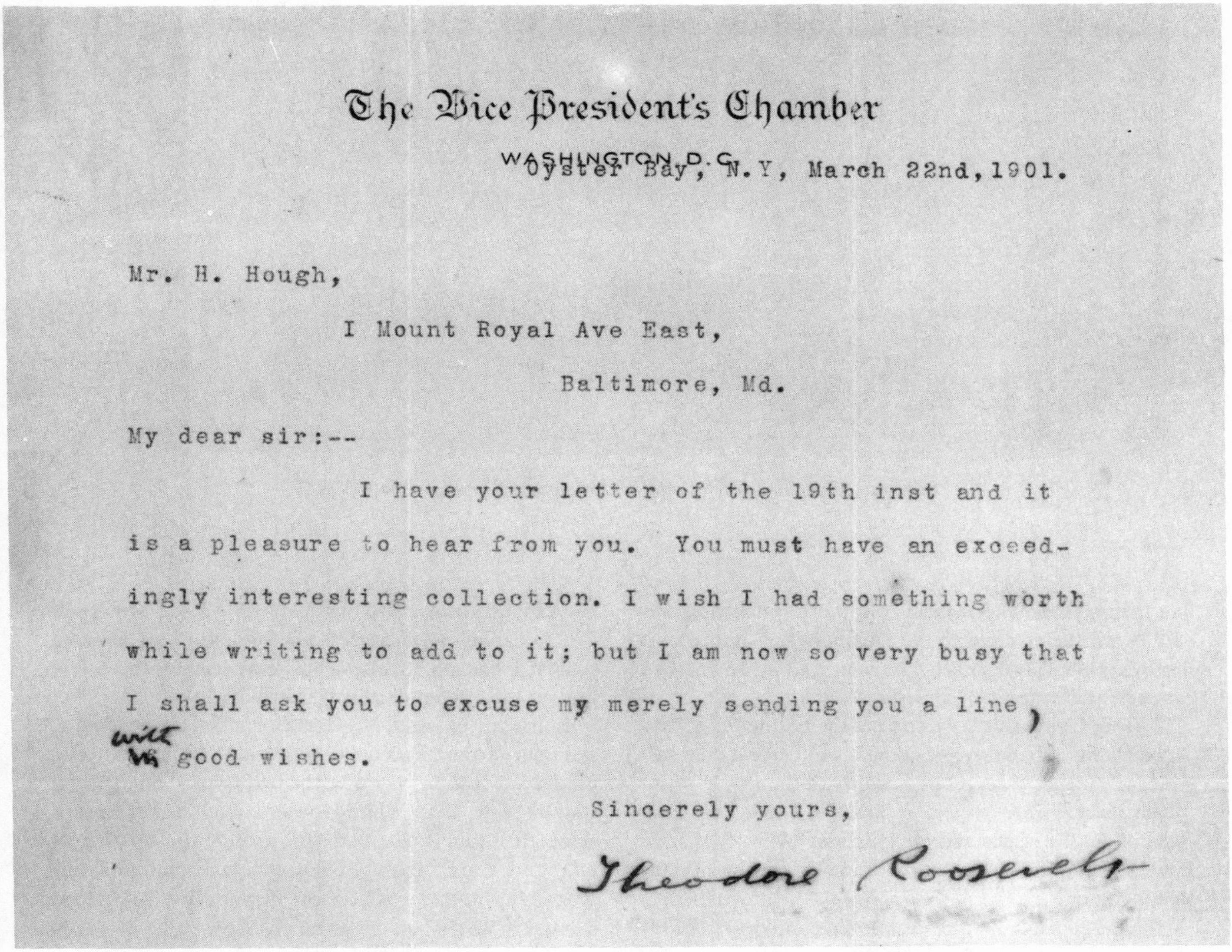

The Vice President's Chamber

WASHINGTON, D.C.
Oyster Bay, N.Y, March 22nd, 1901.

Mr. H. Hough,

I Mount Royal Ave East,

Baltimore, Md.

My dear sir:--

I have your letter of the 19th inst and it
is a pleasure to hear from you. You must have an exceed-
ingly interesting collection. I wish I had something worth
while writing to add to it; but I am now so very busy that
I shall ask you to excuse my merely sending you a line,
with
good wishes.

Sincerely yours,

Theodore Roosevelt

Letter signed by Theodore Roosevelt as vice president. He served as vice president slightly less than six months.

politics and popularized the proverb "Speak softly but carry a big stick" which became known as the "Roosevelt corollary."

Aware of the pressing strategic need for a short-cut between the Atlantic and Pacific, Roosevelt master-minded the construction of the Panama Canal. His corol-lary to the Monroe Doctrine prevented the establishment of foreign bases in the Caribbean and appropriated to the U.S. the sole right of intervention in Latin America.

Roosevelt won the Nobel Prize for mediating the Russo-Japanese War and reached a "Gentlemen's Agree-ment" on immigration with Japan. He also sent the "Great White Fleet" on a goodwill tour of the world.

Some of Roosevelt's most significant achievements were in the field of conservation. He added enormously to the national forests in the west and reserved vast lands for public use. He also promoted large irriga-tion projects.

Leaving the presidency in 1909, Roosevelt went on an extended African safari but, upon his return, again turned to politics. After breaking ties with President Taft, formerly his closest friend, Roosevelt ran for president on

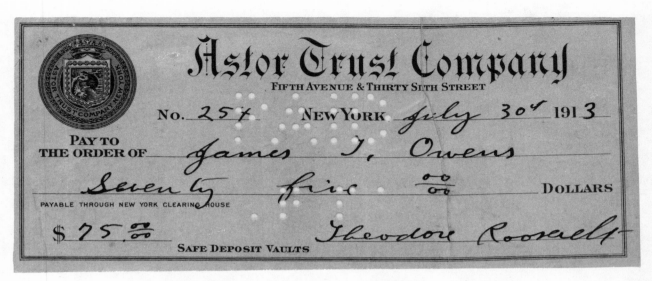

Personal bank check completed and signed by Theodore Roosevelt.

the Progressive ticket, which split the Republican party and threw the election to the Democrats. Although his last years were anticlimactic, he remained active but died when he was only sixty years old.

Theodore Roosevelt was one of the best letter writers of all twentieth century presidents. He carried on a vast correspondence with a large and varied number of individuals on a wide range of topics. He articulately commented on the issues and personalities of the day, often quite unflatteringly. Taft and Wilson were victims of many of his barbs.

Roosevelt's handwriting was legible and devoid of ornamentation, and he favored a heavy-nibbed pen. His script changed little during his adult life. He usually signed his name in full but, on occasion apparently dictated by whim and no doubt by considerations of time, he also frequently signed himself "T. Roosevelt."

To his children he wrote many charmingly illustrated letters, which are now quite scarce and desirable.

He is abundant in Ls.S. and, although somewhat scarce and expensive, he is also obtainable in A.Ls.S. Roosevelt is obtainable, too, in signed photographs, ranging from postcard size up to mammoth, two feet by three feet portraits which he selectively distributed.

Roosevelt changed the name on official presidential stationery from "Executive Mansion," which had been used since Lincoln instituted the first printed presidential stationery, to "The White House," which has been used since that time. He had the presidential stationery changed soon after becoming president, and any Roosevelt letter written on "Executive Mansion" stationery would be a great rarity. Roosevelt is also obtainable in quite-desirable A.Qs.S., often concerning courage and character.

During Roosevelt's tenure as governor of New York, he employed a stamped signature, and letters written during his last few post-presidential years were sometimes secretarially signed.

Roosevelt also authored several books, and signed copies are highly prized by collectors.

Typical signature of Roosevelt signed with
his initial "T. Roosevelt"

27. WILLIAM HOWARD TAFT

September 15, 1857 - March 8, 1930

Twenty-Seventh President
March 4, 1909 - March 4, 1913

Republican

Highlights in office:
16th Amendment; Payne-Aldrich
Tariff Act; "Dollar Diplomacy."

William Howard Taft was from a distinguished family, the son of a former U.S. attorney general and secretary of war under President Grant. He graduated second in his Yale law school class and served as prosecuting attorney in Cincinnati, then became superior court judge, U.S. solicitor general, federal district judge (at age thirty-four), governor general of the Philippines and secretary of war under Theodore Roosevelt. After his presidential term he became a law professor at Yale before being appointed chief justice of the U.S. supreme court by President Harding.

Taft was perhaps unique among presidents in his considering the presidency to be the nadir of his life: "I don't remember that I was ever president." His appointment as chief justice was to him the zenith of his life. Justice Louis Brandeis remarked "It's very difficult for me to under-

stand how a man who is so good as chief justice could have been so bad as president."

Against his better judgment, Taft's ambitious and imperious wife, Helen (Nellie) Herron, pressured him to seek the presidency. Ironically, Mrs. Taft was unable to enjoy her years as first lady because she suffered a severe stroke in 1909. During her slow recovery the president lovingly taught her to speak again.

Taft's presidency occurred during a period of intense struggle and tension between progressive and conservative forces, culminating in the famous break between Taft and his mentor, former president Theodore Roosevelt, which resulted in his losing his reelection bid. In the angry Progressive attacks against him, credit was given to neither his administration's initiation of eighty antitrust suits, nor to the submission to the states of constitutional

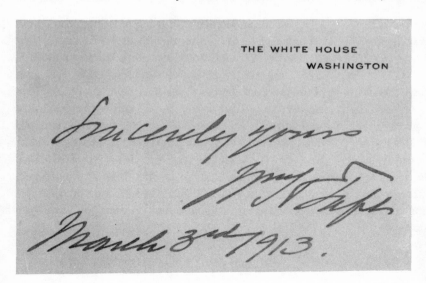

White House card signed by William Howard Taft on his last full day as president.

Autograph Document Signed in the third person by Taft as president, being his list of invitees for the Vice President's Dinner, listed according to rank.

amendments for a federal income tax and for the direct election of United States senators. A postal savings system was established, and the Interstate Commerce Commission was directed to set railroad rates.

Taft summed up his feelings when he said "Politics, when I am in it, makes me sick."

Taft's autographs are among the most common of all the presidents. His material is obtainable in most forms, although he is rare in presidential A.Ls.S.and White House cards, and his S.P.'s, while obtainable, are somewhat scarce. Taft wrote large numbers of routine-content letters, but he was also quite capable of writing witty and interesting letters. His good-content letters are rare and desirable.

Taft wrote an attractive, flowing hand with the letters carefully connected within the words. His simple, bold signature is one of the most attractive of all the presidents.

Taft is also obtainable in presidential Ds.S. as well as in documents from his brief tenure as collector of the internal revenue in Cincinnati. Ds.S. from both periods are quite attractive and desirable. He was known to his friends as "Bill," and his letters to them are signed either "Bill" or "Bill Taft," a rare and desirable form of his signature. Throughout his life his usual and customary signature was "Wm. H. Taft." A full signature of Taft's would be a great rarity, and such an example is unknown to the authors.

Supreme Court of the United States
Washington, D.C.

Mr. Orenstein

Mrs. Taft tells me
you wish my auto-
graph - Well here
it is - With best
wishes

Wm H Taft

Jany 15th 1929

Autograph Letter Signed by William Howard Taft as Chief Justice.

28. THOMAS WOODROW WILSON

December 28, 1856 - February 3, 1924

Twenty-Eighth President
March 4, 1913 - March 4, 1921

Democrat

Highlights in office:
Federal Trade Commission created;
World War I; Versailles Peace Conference.

Thomas Woodrow Wilson (he dropped the "Thomas" in favor of his more dignified middle name) was the son of a messianic Presbyterian minister and grew up in "genteel poverty." Although he was not the sanctimonious Calvinist portrayed by his critics, he did in fact subscribe to an ardent belief in predestination. Wilson was a scholar and the only president to have an earned a Ph.D. (from Johns Hopkins). He was also a graduate of the University of Virginia Law School, but practiced law less than a year. He held teaching positions at Bryn Mawr, Wesleyan, and Princeton, where he was named president at age forty-six and became noted for his educational reforms. Mentioned as a possible presidential candidate as early as 1906, he was elected governor of New Jersey in 1910, and two years later won the Democratic presidential nomination.

Like other great men, he was both strengthened and weakened by his idiosyncrasies. When he had his own way he was dazzlingly impressive; however, when crossed he was irritable, self-righteous and obstinate, traits much in evidence during the latter stages of his reign at Princeton and during his second presidential term, both of which ended sourly. Wilson and his arch-enemy, Theodore Roosevelt, had much in common: both were idealists and reformers, both had stronger wills and more self-confidence than most men, and both yearned for public adulation.

In 1914 Wilson faced a mammoth problem when Europe went to war. Justifiably skeptical of European motives and horrified by the blood bath on the western front, he campaigned for reelection on the basis of maintaining American neutrality, using the slogan "He Kept Us Out of War." In this he was completely sincere; however, within a few months America found itself heavily embroiled in the war. The feeling that he had sent thousands of young Americans to their deaths made Wilson pursue peace with the ardor of a zealot. He believed the war would be tragically pointless unless it led to a lasting peace and made "the world safe for democracy."

Wilson enunciated American war aims in his "Fourteen Points"—his critics said God could state His law in Ten Commandments but Wilson had to have Fourteen! The League of Nations, his cenotaph for the war dead, was rejected by the Senate because Wilson was too stubborn to compromise and made the tactical error of not inviting any Republican senators to accompany him to the Versailles Peace Conference. An amended version of the treaty could have been ratified had Wilson been willing to compromise, but for him it was all or nothing. During the ratification controversy, Wilson made a national speaking tour to mobilize public sentiment for the treaty. Exhausted from the tour, he suffered a paralytic stroke from which he almost died. During his last year in office he was too incapacitated to tend to executive business, and there is much truth to the accusation that his second wife, Edith, was the de facto president.

Although Wilson was more inflexible than almost any other president, he was also more imaginatively bold. The great irony is that, by having loftier aspirations than many other presidents, he may have achieved less. Nonetheless,

SCHEDULE FOR ACADEMIC SPECIAL STUDENTS.

1st Term 190*1*–190*2*.

Name *A. H. McLane*   No. *26*

DIRECTIONS TO INSTRUCTOR.

The instructors designated in the opposite column will sign this slip, and specify by name or number the course or courses to which the bearer is admitted, and also the hours at which the class, or the division thereof to which the bearer is assigned, will meet. The signature will imply that the student's name has been entered by the instructor upon the class roll and seating-list.

DIRECTIONS TO STUDENT.

Obtain from all the instructors designated above, their signatures in the column opposite. In case any signature cannot be promptly obtained, or in case any two courses taken are given at the same hours, consult the Secretary of the Special Student Committee immediately. **Obtain all signatures promptly, and mail this schedule fully signed to the Secretary of the Special Student Committee at once.**

BY ORDER OF THE FACULTY COMMITTEE
ON ACADEMIC SPECIAL STUDENTS.

Document Signed, being an academic schedule signed twice by Professor Woodrow Wilson.

Wilson's vision, whatever its defects, of a world made safe for democracy, was more inspired than the cautious conservatism of his opponents.

Wilson enjoyed the company of clever women. Although he was accused of philandering with a widow named Mrs. Peck (which gave rise to his political opponents' labeling him "Peck's Bad Boy") prior to being elected to the presidency, his devotion to his first wife, Ellen Axson Wilson, was passionate and obsessive. They had three daughters. When she died in the White House in 1914, he sat beside her body for two days and refused to allow it to be moved. He came close to a total nervous breakdown and, in order to restore his mental balance,

friends engineered a meeting between him and a beautiful Washington widow, Edith Bolling Galt.

Wilson's courtship of Mrs. Galt received national attention. In 1915 a typographical error in the *Washington Post* made the president the object of lewd laughter. In describing an evening at the theatre spent by the president and his fiancee, a society reporter wrote that, instead of watching the performance, "the President spent most of his time entertaining Mrs. Galt." Unfortunately, a typographical error caused "entertaining" to be printed as "entering" in the newspaper's earliest edition. They were married in December, 1915, only sixteen months after the death of his first wife, despite fears that his early remar-

Pencil Autograph Letter signed by Wilson as president to his daughter, being a telegram which was written after his first wife's death in August 1914 and before his remarriage in December, 1915. Dr. Grayson was Wilson's White House physician.

White House card signed by Woodrow Wilson. Wilson always signed White House cards at the top so that nothing could be written above his signature.

riage might damage his reelection chances.

Wilson was tall and thin, with sparse, steel-grey hair and vivid blue eyes. He wore rimless glasses, had a square heavy jaw, a strong tenor voice, and thought of himself as unattractive.

Several of Wilson's quotes are illuminating but are little remembered today. To a group of black leaders he said in 1913: "Segregation is not humiliating but a benefit, and ought to be so regarded by you gentlemen." In 1919 he said: "Why has Jesus Christ so far not succeeded in inducing the world to follow his teachings? . . . I am proposing a practical scheme to carry out His aims," and "I believe in Divine Providence. If I did not I would go crazy."

Woodrow Wilson was the first president to personally type on a typewriter, composing almost all his pre-presidential correspondence and, after becoming president, drafting important documents on it. For this reason Wilson is rare in A.Ls.S. of all dates, but particularly those of presidential date; however, his graceful and legible penmanship is one of the most attractive of all presidents. His script varied little throughout his adult life until after his stroke in September, 1919. Anything signed by Wilson after he suffered his paralytic stroke is scarce, particularly of presidential date. The stroke noticeably affected the appearance of his signature, which never regained its handsome and graceful appearance. It became cramped and frequently had blobs of ink or smeared individual letters.

After approximately 1880 when he dropped his first name "Thomas," his signature was always signed "Woodrow Wilson." Anything signed with the earlier signature "Thomas W. Wilson" would be quite rare and desirable, but few such examples are known to exist.

Although Wilson discontinued the practice of personally signing military commissions, he is nonetheless readily obtainable in this form and other types of presidential Ds.S. Another quite interesting and charming form of his Ds.S. are signed student report cards from his academic career.

Wilson wrote terse, grammatical, formal but polite letters, which were seldom interesting. Nonetheless, there is great demand for his material.

Wilson's signed White House cards are moderately scarce and display one of his idiosyncracies: he invariably wrote his signature at the extreme top of the card to prevent anyone's writing anything above it as if he had written or approved it himself.

29. WARREN G. HARDING

November 2, 1865 - August 2, 1923

Twenty-Ninth President
March 4, 1921 - August 2, 1923

Republican

Highlights in office:
Washington Disarmament Conference;
supported U.S. participation in the Permanent
Court of International Justice; pardoned
Eugene Debs; persuaded the steel industry
to reduce from twelve to eight hour days.

Many historians rate Harding as the worst of all the presidents. Historical consensus is that he was congenial, gregarious and genuinely good-natured, but quite mediocre and immoral. "I am not fit for this office and never should l have been here," he said. He was tenaciously loyal to his friends but, sadly, the converse was not true. His father, Dr. George Tryon Harding, a country physician, once told him "It's a good thing you weren't a girl, Warren, you'd be in the family way all the time. You can't say no."

In all fairness, Harding has probably been excessively condemned. Despite his legendary heavy drinking and all-night poker sessions, at which the liquor flowed freely in the White House despite Prohibition, he was extremely hard-working. His sexual escapades were not of great consequence. Although Harding's views could be characterized as right-wing, he released socialist leader Eugene V. Debs from the penitentiary where he had been sent by the Wilson administration. In truth, Harding was the president the country desired and deserved, and had been elected by the greatest landslide in history to that time.

Harding was born in the village of Corsica, later Blooming Grove, Ohio. In his early career he was a school teacher, insurance salesman, and small town newspaper publisher. Later he served as an Ohio state senator, lieutenant governor and U.S. senator. Perhaps his greatest asset was that he "looked like a president," attractive, well-built, six feet in height, with blue eyes, white hair,

and swarthy complexion. There were persistent rumors in his hometown, however, that the Harding family was "tainted" by Negro blood. When questioned on this point during the presidential campaign by a friendly reporter, he replied "How do I know if one of my ancestors jumped the fence?"

At age twenty-five he married a divorcée, Florence Kling DeWolfe, who was five years his senior and who had a son by her prior marriage. She was the daughter of the town's richest banker. A cold, rather unattractive woman, she was dubbed "The Duchess" by Harding and his friends. Although their relationship was turbulent, and they were not close for most of their marriage, Mrs. Harding helped mastermind her husband's career. Her political judgment was normally more accurate than that of her husband.

Harding carried on a passionate fifteen year affair with the wife of one of his friends. Later, as U.S. senator and president, he carried on a torrid, clandestine affair with a beautiful young blond named Nan Britton who was in her twenties. She bore him an illegitimate daughter, his only child. Britton later claimed the child was conceived in a White House closet.

Despite his apparently easygoing personality, Harding suffered nervous breakdowns in times of stress. His first serious breakdown at age twenty-two necessitated his spending several weeks in a sanitarium. He suffered a total of five such episodes over the next twelve years.

LEGAL NOTICE.

Sarah E. Koons, residing at Lebanon Illinois, will take notice that on August 1, 1896, H. L. Simons filed his petition against her in the court of common pleas of Marion County, Ohio, Case 887, asking judgment against her for $11 18, with interest from July 28, 1896, and costs; that on said date an attachment was issued in said case out of said court; that she is required to answer herein on or before October 17, 1896.
H. L. SIMONS.
L. E. MYERS, his attorney.
Marion, Ohio, August 1, 1896. 11-16

Proof of Publication.

W. J. Harding , of lawful age, being sworn, says that a printed notice, a copy of which is hereunto attached, was published for *six* consecutive weeks in THE MARION STAR, a newspaper published and in general circulation in said Marion County, immediately previous to the *19th* day of *September* A. D., 1896, and that at the time he was *pub* of said paper.

W. J. Harding

Publication, - - $ *6.00*

Proof - - - - $ *.20*

Total - - - $ *6.20*

Sworn to and subscribed beforn me, this *20* day of *Sept* A. D., 1896

M. Waddel Clerk
By .... Dep

Partially printed Autograph Document Signed, signed twice, by publisher Warren G. Harding. (Reduced 82%)

Envelope postmarked from Washington D.C. and addressed by Senator Warren G. Harding to his long time mistress Carrie Phillips. One can only speculate as to the contents!

85

Harding always retained great personal popularity with the public. His cabinet consisted of both very able and very corrupt men. In what is now known as the Teapot Dome Scandal, his secretary of the interior, Albert B. Fall, was convicted and sent to prison for fraudulent transfers of government oil reserves. When Fall's corruption first came to Harding's attention he said: "It's not my enemies who worry me. It's my friends, my goddamned friends, who make me walk the floor at night." He seems not to have suspected the extent of the corruption until it was too late. Although a number of Harding's cronies were corrupt, he himself was honest.

After several weeks of not feeling well, he died on August 2, 1923, in San Francisco while on a tour of the west, the sixth president to die in office. His sudden death during a presidential good will tour led to speculation that he had been poisoned by his wife in order to avoid disgrace and probable impeachment as the corruption of his administration became known. Mrs. Harding refused to allow an autopsy on her husband's body, and spent days secluded in the White House burning her husband's papers.

Harding wrote a neat, generally legible hand, although his penmanship was not particularly attractive. His script is characterized by often failing to cross lower case "t's" even at the beginning of a sentence. Some words were connected, and he always connected his signature. He usually signed his signature as "W.G. Harding" before the presidency, and "Warren G. Harding" after becoming president.

During his senatorial career between approximately 1918 and 1921, Harding employed a secretary, George B. Christian, to sign his name by proxy, and also used a rubber stamp. After becoming president, Harding personally signed all documents and letters.

Harding's A.Ls.S. are rare for all dates, particularly presidential. He is readily obtainable both in Ls.S. from his pre-presidential period, and in Ds.S.—legal notices or "Proofs of Publication," many of which he signed twice—dating from his publishing career. His White House letters are rare, and his S.P.'s and White House cards are not common. In terms of numbers, Harding material is scarce, but because there is little demand it remains relatively obtainable at moderate prices. Good-content Harding letters are quite rare. He tended to ramble and use colloquialisms in his letters, which were at times ungrammatical, particularly his A.Ls.S. Still, his letters exude his innate good will and friendliness and have a certain charm.

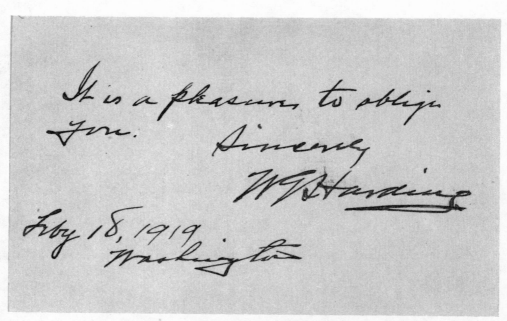

Autograph Noted Signed of Senator Warren G. Harding.

30. JOHN CALVIN COOLIDGE

July 4, 1872 - January 5, 1933

Thirtieth President
August 3, 1923 - March 4, 1929

Republican

Highlights in office:
Cut federal budget;
U.S. foreign service created;
Kellogg-Briand Peace Pact ratified.

John Calvin Coolidge was born at Plymouth, Vermont, on July 4, 1872, the son of a village storekeeper and minor politician. He received word that he was president on August 3, 1923, at 2:30 a.m. while visiting his father, a notary public, who administered the presidential oath of office by lantern light.

Alfred E. Smith, a Democrat and admirer of Coolidge, said Coolidge was "distinguished for character more than achievement. His great task was to restore the dignity and prestige of the presidency when it had reached the lowest ebb in our history."

Coolidge was an Amherst graduate and a lawyer. He was elected to the Northampton Common Council, then became city solicitor, state representative, mayor, state senator, and lieutenant governor. He was elected governor of Massachusetts in 1918 and won national attention when he broke the strike by the Boston police unionizers. He stated "There is no right to strike against the public safety by anybody, anywhere, anytime."

Coolidge's conservative laissez-faire political philosophy was "don't rock the boat." H.L. Mencken stated that "Coolidge's chief feat was to sleep more than any other president . . . the itch to run things did not afflict him; he was content to let things run themselves." The most significant foreign policy achievement of his administration, the Kellogg-Briand pact, was primarily the work of subordinates, and he made no mention of foreign affairs in his autobiography.

Coolidge was frugal both fiscally and with words. His legendary taciturnity became his trade mark. His frugality

with words stemmed to some degree from shyness, but he was also quite witty. In paying tribute to his wife, Grace Goodhue Coolidge, who was a teacher at a school for the deaf when he married her, he remarked that "having taught the deaf to hear, Miss Goodhue might perhaps cause the mute to speak." Once at a presidential dinner party, a young lady who was sitting next to him confided that she had placed a bet that she could get at least three words of conversation from him. Without looking at her he quietly replied "You lose." Alice Roosevelt Longworth said Coolidge "looked like he was weaned on a pickle."

In retrospect, it should be noted that Coolidge was not so dull as the contemporary wits portrayed him. Within his limits, he was a logical, capable, thorough and honest individual who was well-respected by his associates. However, Coolidge was gradually worn down by the strain of office. The tragic death of his son Calvin from blood poisoning devastated him. He seemed to sense that the United States was economically unstable, and he probably realized he was not equipped to deal with major problems. As a result, Coolidge issued another laconic statement while vacationing in the Black Hills of South Dakota: "I do not choose to run for president in 1928."

When the great depression struck, Coolidge was in retirement, but before his death in January, 1933, he told a friend, " . . . I feel I no longer fit in with these times." When Coolidge's death was announced, however, a wit had the last word: "How could they tell?"

Coolidge is common or at least obtainable in all forms of material, although expensive in A.Ls.S., particularly of

CALVIN COOLIDGE
GOVERNOR

THE COMMONWEALTH OF MASSACHUSETTS
EXECUTIVE DEPARTMENT
STATE HOUSE. BOSTON.

15th April, 1920.

Brigadier General Newton E. Turgeon,
Buffalo, New York.

My dear General Turgeon:

Thank you most
heartily for the beautiful photograph
you have sent me. I was very pleased
indeed to hear from you in this way.

Very truly yours,

O

E

Letter Signed by Calvin Coolidge as governor of Massachusetts.

presidential date. Most of Coolidge's A.Ls.S. are from pre- and post-presidential periods.

Coolidge's script was legible and characterized by its large size, usually completely filling the page. He dropped the use of his first name, John, about 1895, and thereafter signed himself as "Calvin Coolidge." Anything signed with his first name is extremely desirable, but very few such examples are known to exist.

Coolidge employed secretaries to sign his name at various times prior to becoming president, including his term as lieutenant governor and governor of Mas-

sachusetts. However, he personally signed all presidential and post-presidential material.

In content, Coolidge ranks as one of the poorest and most uninteresting presidential letter writers. No other president's letters cause such widespread drowsiness as those of "Silent Cal." His letters often concern such stultifying topics as repairing the plumbing or inquiring into the butcher's bill. There may be no such thing as an interesting Coolidge letter—certainly none has ever been seen by the authors.

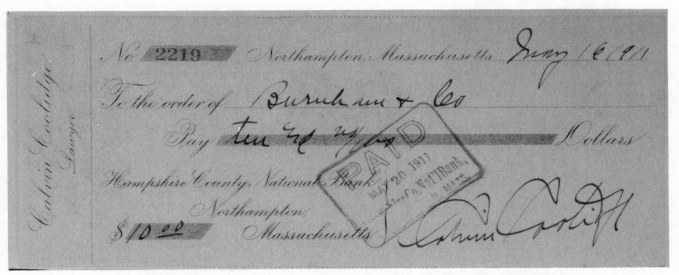

Personal bank check completed and signed by Calvin Coolidge. (Reduced 82%)

Signature of Calvin Coolidge.

31. HERBERT HOOVER

August 10, 1874 - October 20, 1964

Thirty-First President
March 4, 1929 - March 4, 1933

Republican

Highlights in office:
Great Depression; Veterans Administration
and Recovery Finance Corporation created;
20th Amendment.

Herbert Clark Hoover, the son of an Iowa Quaker black-smith, was orphaned at the age of eight and reared in Oregon by his grandparents. He entered Stanford University when it opened in 1891 and was graduated with a degree in mining engineering. He met his wife, Lou Henry, the daughter of a local banker, at Stanford, and they shared a life-long interest in minerals and mining. They were married in 1899, when he was twenty-four, by a Catholic priest, a good friend, shortly before they sailed to China.

In China, Hoover worked for a private corporation and became one of China's leading engineers. In June, 1900, during the Boxer Rebellion, the Hoovers were trapped at Tientsin for almost a month under heavy fire. Hoover directed the building of barricades while his wife worked in the hospitals, and he risked his life to rescue Chinese children. Both Hoover and his wife spoke fluent Chinese and, after he became president, frequently spoke to each other in Chinese to prevent the staff or others from knowing what they were discussing.

Hoover made a large fortune as a mining engineer, a profession which took him all over the world. He was the most traveled of all our presidents.

His two sons were born in London where he lived for some years before World War I. His presidential eligibility was later challenged on the erroneous basis that, as a British rate payer, he had voted in a foreign election.

One week before Hoover's fortieth birthday, and while he was living in London, Germany declared war on France. The American consul-general asked his help in getting stranded tourists home, and during the next six weeks Hoover's committee helped 120,000 Americans return to the United States. Hoover next tackled the far more difficult job of feeding Belgium, which had been overrun by the German army.

After the United States entered the war, President Wilson appointed Hoover as U.S. food administrator. He succeeded in cutting the consumption of foods and avoided rationing at home, and at the same time kept the Allies fed. After the war he was a member of the Supreme Economic Council and head of the American Relief Administration which fed starving millions in central Europe and Soviet Russia.

Hoover attended the peace conference in Paris, where an English observer commented that he was the only man to emerge with an enhanced reputation. Franklin D. Roosevelt, who became acquainted with him in wartime Washington remarked: "He is certainly a wonder, and I wish we could make him president of the United States".

Hoover served brilliantly as secretary of commerce and "assistant secretary of everything else" under Presidents Harding and Coolidge, and in 1928 he became the Republican presidential nominee. In his first try for public office he overwhelmingly defeated Al Smith. His election was thought to ensure prosperity, and Hoover stated at the time: "We in America today are nearer to the final triumph over poverty than ever before in the history of any land." Within a few months after this statement, however, the nation suffered the stock market crash of October, 1929, and entered the worst economic depres-

THE WHITE HOUSE
WASHINGTON

White House card signed by Herbert Hoover.

sion in the nation's history. After the crash Hoover announced that he would keep the federal budget balanced, as well as cut taxes and expand public works spending, but the economic condition of the entire world continued to worsen.

Given Hoover's personal economic philosophy of rugged individualism, by which he had achieved success and from which he never waivered, there was little he could do about the depression. The most he could countenance, by means of the Reconstruction Finance Corporation, was a program to lend money to "worthy businessmen," for Hoover did not believe in the "dole" for the unemployed on the basis that it would sap their initiative in looking for work. He also distrusted Europe and believed the depression resulted from foreign economic errors. Instead of seeking international agreement on monetary and trade policies, he sanctioned economic nationalism and the raising of trade barriers which only worsened Europe's economic plight. Hoover also resisted giving diplomatic recognition to Soviet Russia, and he supported Prohibition, which he referred to as "an experiment noble in motive."

Hoover also had no words of solace for the "bonus marchers" who descended on Washington in 1932, and his name became linked to every evil feature of the depression. The tarpaper shacks of the unemployed were "Hoovervilles"; empty pockets turned inside out were "Hoover flags"; old newspapers wrapped around the body for warmth were "Hoover blankets"; broken down automobiles pulled by mules were "Hoover wagons." A joke current at the time had Hoover asking a congressman if he could borrow a nickel to phone a friend. The congressman told Hoover "Why don't you take a dime and call them all!"

Overwhelmingly defeated for reelection by Franklin D. Roosevelt, Hoover left office under a dark cloud. Over thirty years of life were left to him, however, and before he died he had become the well-respected elder statesman of the Republican party. Under Presidents Truman and Eisenhower, he served on commissions to streamline and economize the structure of the federal government.

Herbert Hoover's public offices required him to write and sign large numbers of letters. Post-presidentially he personally responded to almost every request, and he lived to be ninety years old. Hoover, therefore, in terms of numbers, is probably the most common of all presidents in nearly all forms of material. Hoover himself once said that after leaving office all he did was "write letters, take pills and dedicate libraries."

As a correspondent Hoover was dull. He wrote very brief, formal letters which rarely had interesting content. Good-content Hoover letters of any period are rare and desirable. Until about 1915 he signed his name "H.C. Hoover"; afterwards he always signed "Herbert Hoover." Examples of the early form of his signature are both rare and expensive.

In addition to having the most available autographs, Hoover also wrote more books than any other president,

91

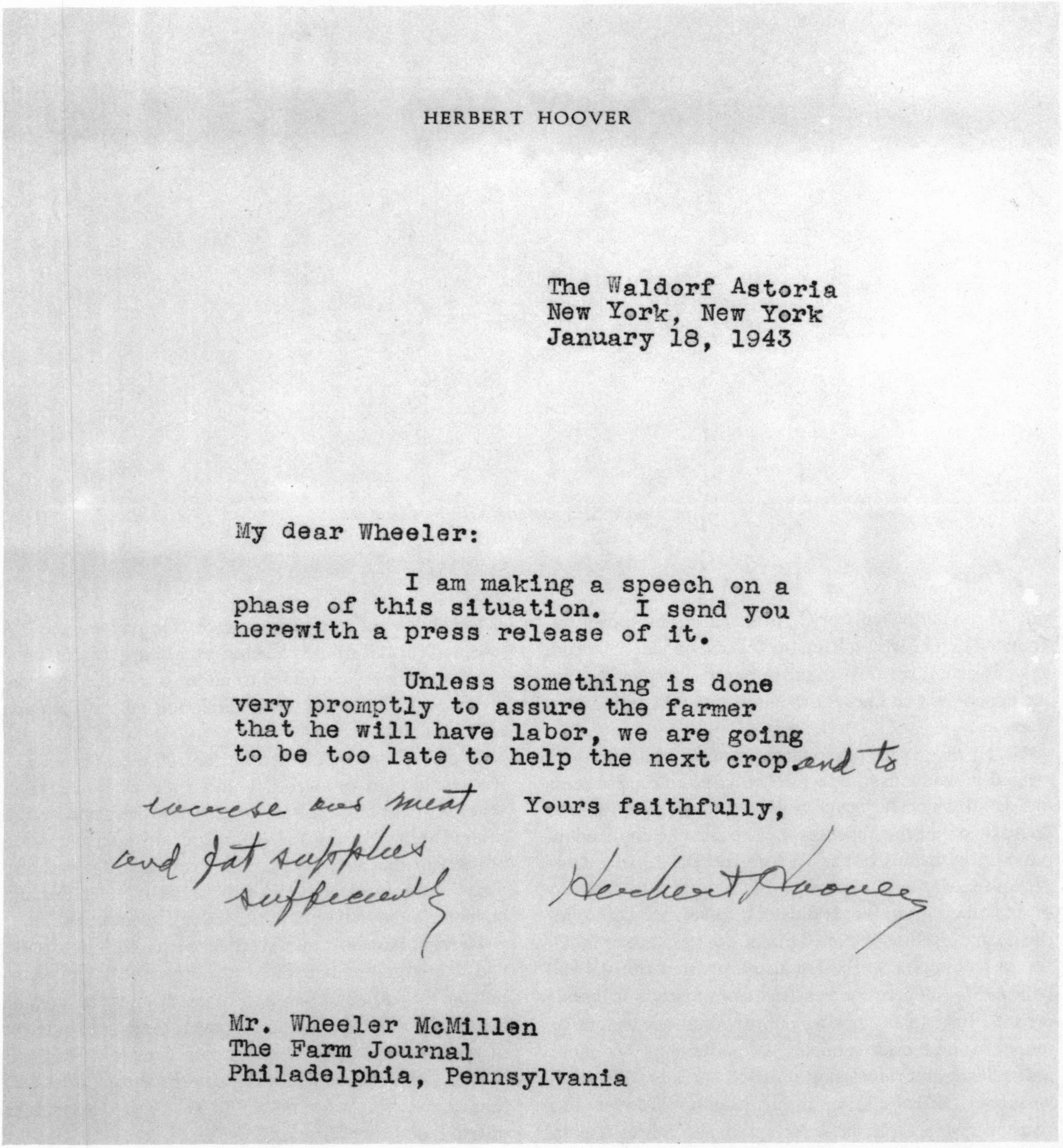

HERBERT HOOVER

The Waldorf Astoria
New York, New York
January 18, 1943

My dear Wheeler:

I am making a speech on a
phase of this situation. I send you
herewith a press release of it.

Unless something is done
very promptly to assure the farmer
that he will have labor, we are going
to be too late to help the next crop *and to*

increase our meat   Yours faithfully,
and fat supplies
sufficiently   *Herbert Hoover*

Mr. Wheeler McMillen
The Farm Journal
Philadelphia, Pennsylvania

*Post presidential letter of Hoover containing a rare holographic addition. Hoover's handwritten letters are virtually
unobtainable.*

although Nixon and Carter may ultimately exceed his record. Signed copies of most of Hoover's books can be obtained at moderate prices. An exception is the early metallurgical work which Hoover and his wife translated in 1912, Agricola's *De Re Metallica*, first published in 1556. These rare volumes also contain Hoover's scarce early signature "H.C. Hoover."

In A.Ls.S. of all dates, Hoover is one of the scarcest of

HERBERT HOOVER

The Waldorf-Astoria Towers
New York, New York   10022
March 22, 1964

My dear President Moses:

I have not forgotten.

And if I am not able to be present
at the inaugural ceremony on April twenty-
second I shall send a message, as you
suggest.

Yours faithfully,

Herbert Hoover

The Honorable Robert Moses
President
New York World's Fair 1964-1965
World's Fair, New York   11380

One of Herbert Hoover's last letters. He was bedfast most of 1964 and died in October, 1964. He signed virtually nothing during his last year.

all presidents. He once wrote that he had probably not written over a dozen handwritten letters in his entire life. Only a handful of presidential A.Ls.S. are known to exist, most of which were written at the request of influential autograph collectors. Hoover's script, while legible, is sometimes difficult to decipher, particularly in handwrit-ing during his old age. He had the peculiar characteristic of looping many of his small case letters, such as his "r's" and "w's." A very peculiar Hoover characteristic was writing words which began with small case "t's," such as "the" and "though," with tiny and barely definable "t's" incorporated into, and almost obscured by, the second

Personal bookplate of Herbert Hoover. Notice the mining theme of the drawing which reflects his training as a mining engineer.

letters of the words, which were also written far above the base line and sometimes represented only by a loop. Another peculiarity of Hoover's extremely rare A.Ls.S. was his often writing the date diagonally upward at the top of the letters. Still another peculiarity was his adding extra strokes to some letters, *e.g.,* his "m's" and "n's."

Almost the only obtainable examples of Hoover's rare holographs are inscriptions on photographs and in books, and infrequently as postscripts on letters. Strangely, the scripts of Hoover and his wife bear great similarity, particularly at first glance. Hoover is also scarce in Ds.S. of all periods. Most of his presidential documents contained facsimile signatures.

Although obtainable, his presidential letters and signed White House cards are not common.

As Hoover obtained the franking privilege late in life, his handwritten franking signatures are quite rare, and few examples are known to exist.

With kind regards,

Yours faithfully,

H.H.

. Wheeler McMillen
m Journal

Uncommon form of Herbert Hoover's signature.

32. FRANKLIN D. ROOSEVELT

January 30, 1882 - April 12, 1945

Thirty-Second President
March 4, 1933 - April 12, 1945

Democrat

Highlights in office:
21st Amendment; National Industries
Recovery Act; Worker Progressive Admin-
istration; Social Security Act; World War II.

Franklin Delano Roosevelt was one of the most hand-some, charming and affable men ever to be president. Winston Churchill once said "meeting him is like opening a bottle of champagne," and Woodrow Wilson described the six feet two inch broad-shouldered "FDR" as the "handsomest young giant I have ever seen." With his patrician and aristocratic background, he was also one of our most "blue-blooded" presidents. His maternal genealogy was traceable to William the Conqueror, and he had at least twelve Mayflower ancestors. He was re-lated to Mrs. James Monroe through the Aspinwall family, through the Delano family he was a fourth cousin once removed to President Grant, and through his maternal grandmother's family he was a seventh cousin once removed to his wartime colleague Sir Winston Churchill. Educated by private tutors, he had toured Europe eight times by the time he was sixteen.

Roosevelt attended Groton and Harvard, where he was a mediocre student who maintained a "gentleman's C" average. As might be expected, however, he was quite a social success and enjoyed a great deal of reflected glory since his fifth cousin, Theodore Roosevelt, was then presi-dent. He was elected editor of the Harvard *Crimson* for which he wrote articles urging the football team to victory. After graduation from Harvard he attended Columbia Law School but, totally bored by the study of law, flunked several courses and dropped out before he was graduated. He nevertheless passed the New York bar examination and became associated with a fashionable New York City law firm.

When he was twenty-eight, the Democratic leaders in his home district of Hyde Park, which had been carried by only one Democrat since 1856, became interested in the personable and handsome young lawyer with the famous name. Roosevelt also filled another qualification of the party leaders—he was able to pay his own expenses. To the surprise of all and the horror of some, Roosevelt ran a flamboyant door-to-door campaign in a red touring car and achieved an upset victory for a seat in the state senate.

In Albany he identified himself with the "genteel reform" element. He was an early supporter of Woodrow Wilson's presidential bid, and when Wilson was elected he appointed FDR as assistant secretary of the navy, a position previously held by his cousin Theodore. Roosevelt proved to be a capable administrator. He had long advocated increased naval power and, with the onset of World War I, he gained stature as a prophet. In 1920 the thirty-eight year old Roosevelt was selected as his party's vice-presidential nominee, just as his famous cousin Theodore had been in 1900. The Democrats hoped that FDR's famous last name would attract Progressive Republicans to the Democratic ticket, but he and his running mate, James M. Cox, suffered a crushing defeat in the Harding-Coolidge landslide. Roosevelt emerged as an effective campaigner, however, and after the election his political prospects were enhanced.

But tragedy at age thirty-nine seemed to put an end to Roosevelt's political career. While vacationing at his family's summer home at Campobello Island, in New Brunswick, Canada, he contracted a severe case of

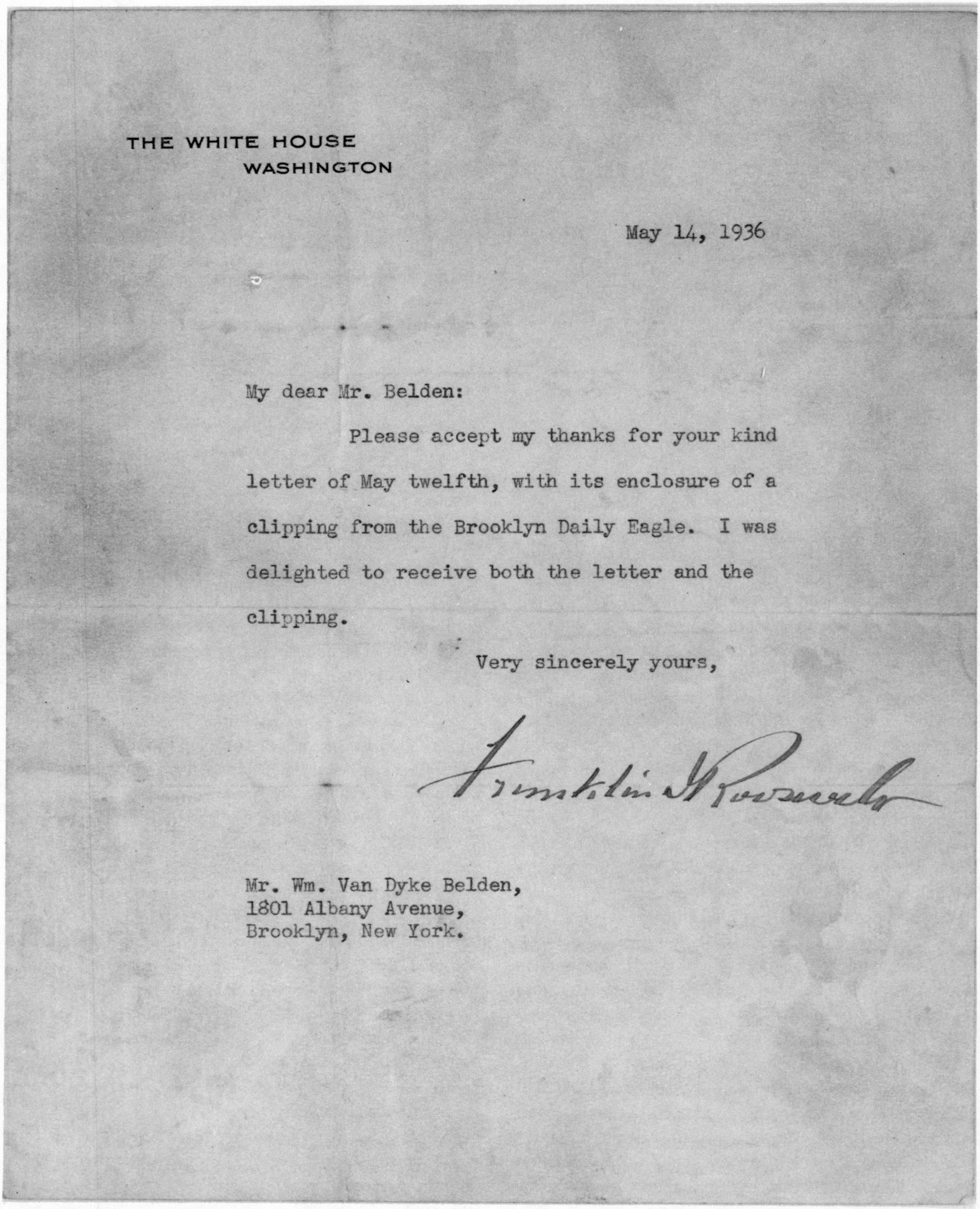

THE WHITE HOUSE
WASHINGTON

May 14, 1936

My dear Mr. Belden:

Please accept my thanks for your kind
letter of May twelfth, with its enclosure of a
clipping from the Brooklyn Daily Eagle. I was
delighted to receive both the letter and the
clipping.

Very sincerely yours,

Franklin D Roosevelt

Mr. Wm. Van Dyke Belden,
1801 Albany Avenue,
Brooklyn, New York.

Presidential Letter Signed by Franklin D. Roosevelt written on pale green stationery, which he first initiated, and which is still used today.

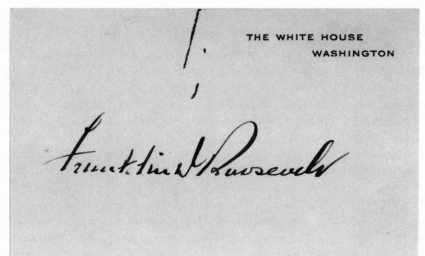

THE WHITE HOUSE
WASHINGTON

White House card signed by Franklin D. Roosevelt.

poliomyelitis. Unfortunately, it took the physicians over a week to correctly diagnose his condition, and by that time he was totally and permanently paralyzed from the waist down. Hopelessly crippled, Roosevelt never regained the use of his legs.

He set out to prove to his family and the world that he need not live the life of an invalid, working tirelessly at exercises and traveling to Warm Springs, Georgia, for water therapy. In time he learned to walk a few steps on crutches with the help of braces and weights on his legs, an important triumph, psychologically and otherwise, because it allowed him to resume his political career—he could now walk from a hidden wheelchair to the speaker's platform.

The influence of Louis Howe, a chain-smoking gnome of a man, cannot be underestimated in terms of FDR's career. Howe, rekindling both FDR's will to fight and his interest in politics, engineered Roosevelt's reemergence at the 1924 Democratic National Convention where he gave his now immortal "Happy Warrior" nominating speech for Al Smith, a speech which electrified the delegates to whom his paralysis seemed to increase his appeal. In a very real sense polio became his "log cabin."

In 1928 when Al Smith was nominated for president, Roosevelt was nominated for governor of New York and won by a narrow margin even though Smith lost the state to Hoover by over 100,000 votes. As governor, he used his office to win relief for the hungry and unemployed of his state, and in 1930 won reelection by the biggest margin in New York history to that time.

Roosevelt's emergence as a leading contender for the 1932 Democratic presidential nomination was largely engineered by Louis Howe and James A. Farley. The delegates to the convention knew, given Hoover's great

unpopularity, that they were nominating the next president. Although FDR had earlier won several impressive primary victories, he had lost Massachusetts to Al Smith and had lost the crucial California primary to John Nance "Cactus Jack" Garner of Texas. A deal was struck for Garner to receive the second spot on the ticket, and FDR was nominated on the fourth ballot. Told by Senator William Gibbs McAdoo that "Now all you have to do is stay alive until the election," Roosevelt carried forty-two of the forty-eight states and won in the electoral college 472 to 59.

Roosevelt's administration faced the worst depression in our history. He was no economic expert and had been reared to believe that budget balancing and economy were the only remedies for depressed times. Keynesian deficit financing was a mystery to him. Despite the accusations of his enemies, he had no intention of revolutionizing our social and economic order. Ironically, he probably had less inherent compassion for the plight of the poor than did his aristrocratic wife.

Under Roosevelt, Washington in the 1930's was a maze of overlapping bureaus and agencies whose activities were poorly coordinated. Roosevelt made some bad errors of judgment, one of the worst of which was his court-packing scheme of 1937-38, by which he attempted to increase the composition of the supreme court from nine to twelve members so he could appoint three additional justices favorable to his policies.

Because FDR was temperamentally unable to rebuke or fire incompetent or insubordinate associates, he occasionally appeared to be devious or dishonest, jocularly evading unpleasant topics. Nevertheless, his weaknesses were outweighed by his great strengths.

Roosevelt did not succeed in totally wiping out unemployment, and it took the boom years of World War II to restore prosperity to the country. What Roosevelt did accomplish, however, was restoration of the nation's self-confidence and courage. When he became president in 1933, Hitler was coming to power in Germany and many feared a similar, ultra-right-wing fate awaited this country. Roosevelt admirably lived up to his inaugural assurance that "the only thing we have to fear is fear itself," projecting his paternalistic confidence in a series of perfectly timed radio broadcasts known as the "fireside chats." He also developed a consummate skill in dealing with the press, and no other president has had such a good relationship with the Fourth Estate.

Roosevelt was reelected in 1936 in a landslide victory, but had to deal with the approach of World War II, for which he was not equipped by previous training. He was interested in naval questions but not versed in diplomacy or strategy. His basic assets remained confidence and readiness to act. For FDR the unforgivable sin was to do nothing—errors could be corrected but a vacuum was disastrous. He perhaps welcomed the Japanese attack on Pearl Harbor; according to Admiral Husband E. Kimmel, the Pearl Harbor commander, there is evidence to indicate that Roosevelt knew in advance of the Japanese attack but failed, possibly deliberately, to notify the commander because he wanted to involve the United States in the war against the Axis powers before it was too late to defeat them. War silenced the critics who had opposed his unprecedented election to a third term.

Great controversy surrounds Roosevelt's role as a wartime leader. In 1944, with the war clearly in its last phase, he was honored by the nation with an unprecedented fourth term. The charges that Roosevelt knew his health was failing, and that he was no match in summitry for Churchill and Stalin, have the advantage of hindsight. The truth may be that he did not know precisely what he was aiming for but, being an American, he believed his nation had a moral obligation to shape the peace. A confidant optimist, he believed everything would come out right in the end.

Since Roosevelt's death, there have been interesting revelations about his personal life which in retrospect help to understand the man. Although Roosevelt was considered to be devastatingly handsome, he showed no interest in women until his junior year at Harvard when he fell in love with his fifth cousin once removed, Anna Eleanor Roosevelt. Eleanor, the orphaned niece of Theodore Roosevelt, was painfully shy and insecure and had an unhappy Dickensian childhood. What attracted the dashing FDR to her remains a mystery. After his death, Eleanor destroyed all of his love letters to her, so it is doubtful that their early relationship will ever be understood. He may have been attracted to her brilliant mind or to her social consciousness (she spent her free time doing volunteer work at a Manhattan settlement house). It is also possible that FDR was impressed and swayed by Eleanor's close connection to her famous uncle, Theodore Roosevelt, who gave her away at their wedding in 1905. Their marriage floundered almost from the beginning. The first problem was interference from Franklin's strong-willed and domineering mother. Franklin was her only child and she had even moved to Boston to be near him while he was at Harvard. After his marriage, she moved in with the newlyweds. She made all the decisions and dominated the still-shy Eleanor.

There were even deeper tensions. Family papers which were first revealed in 1971 indicate that Eleanor always considered sex an ordeal and that Franklin had a very high libido. He usually had his way until 1916 when, after the birth of her sixth child, Eleanor terminated their sexual relationship. During their remaining twenty-nine years of marriage, they never slept together again, maintaining different bedrooms and even different wings in the White House. Not surprisingly, FDR turned elsewhere for companionship. His first and most serious affair was with Eleanor's beautiful social secretary Lucy Mercer. Eleanor found a batch of their love letters and offered to give FDR a divorce, but Franklin's domineering mother intervened and threatened to cut off his allowance if he did not terminate his affair and remain married. Nevertheless, FDR never lost interest in Lucy Mercer and remained discretely in touch with her. (She was with him in Warm Springs when he collapsed, but left before he died and before the arrival of Eleanor and the press.)

Medical reports indicate that polio did not impair FDR's sexual prowess, and rumors continued to link him with other women. Wartime gossip centered around the beautiful young Princess Martha of Norway. In 1973 Roosevelt's son Elliott published a book in which he wrote that FDR's long-time secretary, "Missy" LeHand, was his father's mistress for twenty years. Elliott also asserted that his mother not only knew but approved of their relationship and even allowed FDR and Missy to occupy adjoining bedrooms. Eleanor's seeming open-mindedness may possibly be explained by the recently published love letters between herself and a newspaper woman named Lorena Hickock. Eleanor apparently maintained a series of lesbian relationships for the rest of her life after the cessation of her intimate relationship with her husband. She built a separate cottage on the Hyde Park estate which she shared with two other women who were lesbians, according to Elliott, and she even had their three initials embroidered on their cottage linen. Eleanor's acid-tongued first cousin, Alice Roosevelt Longworth, called Eleanor's mannish lady friends "female impersonators."

Despite their totally separate personal lives for most of their marriage, the Roosevelts formed one of the most effective husband-and-wife political teams ever to occupy the White House.

Like most twentieth century presidents, Franklin D. Roosevelt is scarce in holographic material, particularly A.Ls.S., although not as scarce in this format as either of the Johnsons, Hoover, Eisenhower, Kennedy, or our living former presidents. Most of his A.Ls.S. are of pre-presidential date from approximately 1920 to 1932, or from the period of time between his position as assistant secretary of the navy and his election as governor of New York. It was during this period of time that he was recuperating from polio and had more free time than he ever would again. His presidential-date A.Ls.S. are extremely rare and expensive. Most of his presidential-date holographic material is in the form of brief notes and is usually signed with initials. In fact, many of his letters and notes to intimates, holographic and otherwise, are signed only with his famous initials "FDR."

Roosevelt wrote an interesting semi-cursive script which at first glance appears almost to be printed, as many or all of the individual letters within the words are disconnected. This trait is evident even in his signature. While Roosevelt's penmanship is attractive, it is also somewhat difficult to read. As a student and young man he signed him name with his initials "F.D. Roosevelt," a form in vogue at the time. Roosevelt continued signing his name in this fashion after he became assistant secretary of the navy; however, he eventually dropped this form in favor of the signature he employed the rest of his life, "Franklin D. Roosevelt."

While the basic appearance of Roosevelt's signature remained similar throughout his adult life, it grew in size and, like many other presidents, reached its zenith during his presidency. However, toward the end of his life as his health deteriorated, his signature once again diminished in size, became quite crabbed and tremulous, and bore little resemblance to his earlier, bolder presidential signatures. Roosevelt's full signatures "Franklin Delano Roosevelt" are extremely rare and were written primarily

on legal documents. Few such examples have appeared on the market. The example illustrated in this book is the only one the authors have ever seen.

As a letter writer, FDR does not rate high marks. Most of his letters are routine and boring; he seemed to reserve his famous lines and quotes for speeches. His presidential T.Ls.S. are among the most common of all presidents, for the obvious reason that he served as president longer that anyone else ever has or will. As in the case of many other presidents, good-content FDR letters of all periods are extremely rare.

White House cards of FDR are also plentiful, as well as attractive official cards signed as governor of New York.

Although rare in terms of numbers, highly desirable items are books from Roosevelt's private library, most of which are miniatures and which are generally signed "Franklin D. Roosevelt, Hyde Park." A portion of his personal library was willed to his children, several of whom sold their precious bequest. The bulk of FDR's personal library remains intact in his presidential library and will never appear on the market.

Another interesting type of FDR items are stamps or covers from his famous stamp collection, which was also bequeathed to his children and which they also sold. These philatelic items all bear the authenticating legend and stamp of the auction house which handled the sale: "From the Franklin D. Roosevelt Collection, Authenticated by H.R. Harmer, Inc., N.Y."

Another interesting but little-known fact about FDR is that he was one of only two of our presidents who were autograph collectors, the other being John F. Kennedy.

Signed photographs of FDR are not common but are obtainable. Large, folio size signed engravings of his likeness, quite attractive and desirable, were given in appreciation to large benefactors of polio research in connection with the National Foundation of Infantile Paralysis.

Prior to becoming president and also during the period of time between 1920 and 1932, Roosevelt employed at least nine secretarial or proxy signers. Most of the proxy signatures are easily discernable, but three or four of his secretaries were quite skillful, and letters from this period should be closely scrutinized. Also, a rubber-stamp signature was sometimes used during his terms as governor of New York. Roosevelt is thought to have personally signed everything bearing his signature after he became president; however, there is some suspicion that a forerunner of the autopen may have been used in the Roosevelt White House. To the knowledge of the authors there is

Typical signature of Franklin D. Roosevelt.

Extremely rare full signature of Franklin Delano Roosevelt.

no concrete proof of any such use.

One idiosyncrasy of FDR's was his preference for jet-black India ink, particularly on documents, which made some of his authentic signatures appear to be facsimiles, but close scrutiny of these signatures will reveal individual strokes and shading within the letters which is not present in facsimile signatures. To make matters more difficult, some of Roosevelt's presidential documents, particularly postmaster commissions, do bear facsimile signatures. For these reasons, Roosevelt's presidential documents, which are not common but occasionally available, should be closely examined.

The demand for Roosevelt material is strong, but his routine material is plentiful and still moderately priced. As with most presidents, however, his fine-content letters, particularly A.Ls.S., are both rare and expensive.

33. HARRY S. TRUMAN

May 8, 1884 - December 26, 1972

Thirty-Third President
April 12, 1945 - January 20, 1953

Democrat

Highlights in office:
U.N. Charter ratified; first atomic
bombs; Taft-Hartly Act; Korean War;
Berlin Air Lift; 22d Amendment.

Harry S. Truman was the only twentieth century president who did not attend college but, nevertheless, was one of our most widely read presidents and a first-rate historian. He was the son of John Truman, a farmer and mule trader. Because of poor eyesight, which necessitated his wearing glasses from an early age, Truman was never able to engage in sports and games. He became somewhat of a "mama's boy" who spent his spare time reading and playing the piano and, by age fourteen, had read every book in the Independence, Missouri, library.

Truman was not able to attend college because of family financial reverses. After being graduated from high school at age seventeen, he began a long series of menial jobs, including timekeeper for a railroad gang, bookkeeper in a bank in which his boarding-house roommate Edgar, Dwight D. Eisenhower's brother, also worked, and mail room clerk for the Kansas City *Star*. Most of Truman's earnings were devoted to helping his parents build up a new family farm.

At age thirty-three Truman was still living at home when he volunteered to fight in World War I. He was popular among his army comrades, who soon elected him captain of his unit. He proved to be a highly competent and courageous commander who kept his troops in line with colorful language. After the war, in partnership with an army comrade he opened a haberdashery which was a financial failure, and Truman spent the next fifteen years paying off the debts even after he became a United States senator.

At this juncture Truman turned to politics. During the war he had become friendly with Mike Pendergast, nephew of the Missouri political boss "Big Tom" Pendergast whose political machine was glad to sponsor the young war hero. With its support, in 1922 Truman was elected judge of the Jackson County Court, an administrative position in which he saved the taxpayers thousands of dollars by his efficiency and honesty, unknown qualities in the Pendergast machine. "Big Tom" was hesitant about promoting his incorruptible lieutenant but, in 1934 when three other chosen candidates declined to enter the race for the U.S. Senate, Pendergast reluctantly turned to Truman. Truman won both the primary and general elections by a narrow margin. At first known derisively in Washington as "The Senator from Pendergast," by hard work and integrity Truman earned the affection and respect of other members of the Senate "club" but stayed out of the limelight.

In 1940, with the Pendergast machine in ruins, he faced an uphill reelection fight against a tough primary challenge by a popular former governor. To make matters worse, President Roosevelt favored his opponent and urged Truman to drop out of the race and accept an appointment to the Interstate Commerce Commission. Truman refused, telling Roosevelt he was going to run if the only vote he got was his own. He waged a tireless underdog campaign and won reelection by a narrow margin. Struck by the waste and inefficiency of the army bases he visited during his campaign, he returned to Washington with a new sense of mission and was appointed chairman of a committee to investigate government waste. Known

Christmas 1946

Handsome 1946 Christmas greeting signed by both President and Mrs. Harry S. Truman.

as the "Truman Committee," during World War II this committee saved taxpayers about $15 billion.

In 1944 Roosevelt chose Truman as his fourth-term running mate to replace Henry A. Wallace. During his few weeks as vice president, Truman scarcely saw Roosevelt, and was not briefed on the development of the atomic bomb or the developing difficulties with the Soviet Union. On April 12, 1945, while presiding over the senate, he wrote a note to his mother and sister: "I am trying to write you while a windy Senator is making a speech on a subject with which he is in no way familiar." Then he strolled over to Speaker Rayburn's celebrated "Board of Education" to "strike a blow for liberty" by enjoying some bourbon and branch water but, instead of a drink, Rayburn handed him a message to go immediately to the White House. Upon arrival he was informed by Mrs. Roosevelt that the president was dead.

As president, Truman made some of the most difficult and crucial decisions in history. Shortly after VE Day the war against Japan reached its final stage, but the Japanese stubbornly refused to surrender. Truman ordered atomic bombs dropped on Hiroshima and Nagasaki, cities devoted to munitions production, and the Japanese quickly surrendered, ending World War II. Truman, who had ordered the bombs dropped only after being told they would save American lives and hasten the war's end, maintained to the end of his life that he had done the right thing and had no regrets about his decision.

In June, 1945, Truman observed the signing of the charter of the United Nations, established with the hope it would preserve world peace. Soon thereafter he presented Congress with a twenty-one point program which included an expansion of Social Security, a full-time unemployment program, a permanent Fair Employment Practices Act, public housing and slum clearance. His programs became known as the "Fair Deal."

In 1947, as the Soviet Union was pressuring Turkey and threatening to overthrow Greece, Truman asked Congress to aid the two countries and promulgated the program that bears his name—the Truman Doctrine. He also stimulated remarkable economic recovery in Europe by the Marshall Plan, which he named for his secretary of state.

When the Russians blockaded Berlin, Truman engineered the massive airlift to supply Berliners until the Russians backed down. In the meantime he negotiated a military alliance, to protect western nations, which was established in 1949 and which became known as the North Atlantic Treaty Organization.

In 1950 the Communist government of North Korea attacked South Korea. There was never a suggestion by Truman that either the United States or the United Nations should back away from the confrontation. A long and frustrating struggle ensued, but Truman managed to keep the war a limited one rather than risking a major confrontation with China or the Soviet Union. During the height of the Korean War Truman faced still another crisis, the insubordination of the popular General Douglas MacArthur, which resulted in Truman's firing MacArthur. Truman later wrote: "I fired MacArthur because he wouldn't respect the authority of the President. I didn't fire him because he was dumb son-of-a-bitch, because he was, but that's not against the law for generals. If it was, half to three quarters of them would be in jail."

Truman will perhaps be best remembered for his stunning upset victory in 1948 over Republican Thomas E. Dewey, one of the biggest upset victories in history. For almost everyone except Truman, the campaign appeared to be a foregone conclusion, a landslide victory for Republican Thomas E. Dewey, since southern Democrats had broken away to back their "Dixiecrat" candidate Strom Thurmond and since the left wing of the party had been weakened by Henry Wallace's Progressive movement.

Truman ran an old-fashioned "whistle stop" campaign, making innumerable speeches to small town audiences from the back of his train, from which he introduced Mrs. Truman as "The Boss" and his daughter, Margaret, as "The Bosses' Boss." Although the first election-night returns looked grim, Truman defeated Dewey by over two million votes.

Truman's personal life was simple and impeccable. After a twenty-nine year courtship he married his childhood sweetheart, Elizabeth Virginia (Bess) Wallace. At the time of their marriage he was thirty-five and Bess was thirty-four. They met in Sunday school when he was six and she was five. He later wrote that she was "a beautiful little girl with golden curls. I was smitten with her at once and still am." Bess was the opposite of Truman in almost every respect: he was bespectacled and bookish, she was athletic and tom-boyish. She had won a local shot-put championship and was locally renowned as the only girl in Independence who could whistle through her teeth. She was from one of the town's leading families and her relatives always looked down on Truman—even after be became president. Truman's mother-in-law, the aristocratic and overbearing Madge Wallace, in particular

OPA Form R-535
(Rev. 4-26-43)

Form Approved
Budget Bureau No. 08-R087

UNITED STATES OF AMERICA
OFFICE OF PRICE ADMINISTRATION

APPLICATION FOR SUPPLEMENTAL
AND OCCUPATIONAL MILEAGE RATION

NAME OF REGISTERED OWNER—(PRINT):
Bess W. Truman

VEHICLE LICENSE NO.:
369

ADDRESS—(NUMBER AND STREET):
219 No. Delaware

STATE OF REGISTRATION:
Mo.

CITY AND STATE:
Independence, Mo.

YEAR MODEL—MAKE:
1940-Chrysler

NAME OF APPLICANT—(PRINT)—(IF SAME AS ABOVE, WRITE "SAME"):
Hon. Harry S. Truman

ADDRESS—(NUMBER AND STREET):
U. S. Senate

CITY AND STATE:
Wash. D.C.

INSTRUCTIONS

This form is to be used by persons needing supplemental and occupational mileage rations for—

business, gainful employment, regular and recognized courses of study, or

other work regularly performed that contributes to the war effort or public welfare.

Do Not use this form for—

taxis, jitneys, ambulances, hearses, or other commercial vehicles.

RECORD OF BOARD ACTION
(NOT TO BE FILLED IN BY APPLICANT)

DATE: **9/21/43**

BOARD NO.: **92**

COUNTY AND STATE: **Jc. C.**

BOOKS APPROVED FOR BULK TRANSFER:
☐ YES ☐ NO

(CHECK ONE)
☐ REJECTED ☑ APPROVED

IF APPROVED—LIST MILEAGE ALLOWED:

SIGNATURE OF BOARD MEMBER:

LIST BELOW ALL OTHER PASSENGER CARS AND MOTOR-
CYCLES OWNED OR OPERATED BY YOU
(which are available for your occupational use)

NOTE
All applications for supplemental rations for these vehicles must be filed together.

COUPON BOOKS B, C, AND D			
CLASS OF BOOK	SERIAL NO.	EARLIEST RENEWAL DATE	COUPONS IN BOOK
C	223192	10/30/43	64
C	223193	"	9

SIGNATURE OF ISSUING OFFICER: issued to Stevens
Carger 9/21/43

NAME OF REGISTERED OWNER:

ADDRESS—(NUMBER AND STREET):

CITY AND STATE: 　　　　TYPE OF RATION NOW HELD:

NAME OF REGISTERED OWNER:

ADDRESS—(NUMBER AND STREET):

CITY AND STATE: 　　　　TYPE OF RATION NOW HELD:

4. Principal occupation of principal user of vehicle.
(Examples: Bookkeeper, doctor, machinist, etc.)

U. S. Senator

Employed by—(Name): **U. S. Gov't**

(Employer's address): **U. S. Senate**

Industry, business, or profession in which employed.
(Examples: Shipbuilding, wholesale grocery, etc.)

1. Has any other application been made for a supplemental ration for this same period for the vehicle for which this application is made? If "Yes," state when, where, and action taken.
　YES ☐　NO ☐

→ **Official Trip to Missouri and return**
-2500 Miles - 9/22/43 10/30/43

5. Specific uses of this vehicle by the principal user in the above occupation. (Examples: Driving between home and work, repair calls, sales trips, etc.)

2. Are you employed in the area served by the Board with which you will file this application?
　YES ☐　NO ☐

Is the vehicle usually kept in the area served by the Board with which you will file?
　YES ☐　NO ☐

If neither of above is "Yes," give reason for applying to this Board:

6. Is vehicle now in use?
　YES ☐　NO ☐

7. List below types and serial numbers of mileage ration books outstanding for use with this vehicle.

3. Is the gasoline used by this vehicle taken from bulk storage facilities of either the owner or applicant?
　YES ☐　NO ☐

16—34387-1

Interesting partly printed Autograph Document Signed of Senator Truman for "supplemental mileage ration" for an official trip to Missouri in connection with his famous "Truman Committee" W.W. II investigating committee. The document contains a rare printed signature of Truman. Embarrassingly, Truman had to list his wife as owner of his home. (Truman never owned a home of his own.)

Signature of Senator Truman on verso of the mileage ration senatorial document.

disliked her son-in-law. She lived with the Trumans in the White House and let it be known publicly she thought Dewey would defeat him and that she thought Eisenhower was more qualified than Truman to be president.

Truman never owned a home of his own. After his marriage he moved into the Gates mansion where Bess was living with her mother and grandmother, and there he and Bess lived for the rest of their lives.

Truman's greatest fears were indecision, uncertainty, and weakness. Historians agree that the worst characteristics of his presidency stemmed from his need to make instant decisions on complex matters, and from his even more unfortunate tendency to shoot from the hip. For example, in 1960 the Associated Press reported that in one of his speeches he said extemporaneously "that anyone who votes for Nixon ought to go to Hell" and that Nixon "never told the truth in his life." Later Truman denied having made the first statement but added "they can't challenge the second."

His penchant for colorful language was legendary. He once offended a friend of his wife's at a Washington horticulture show by repeatedly referring to the "good manure" that must have been used to grow the lovely blossoms. "Bess, couldn't you get the president to say fertilizer?" complained the woman. "Heavens no," replied the first lady, "It took me twenty-five years to get him to say manure."

In the middle of a speech someone yelled "Give 'em Hell, Harry," and Truman responded: "Well, I never gave anybody hell—I just told the truth on these fellows and they thought it was hell."

Truman's presidency can perhaps best be summed up by a statement he made in 1964 in old age: "There is an epitaph in Boot Hill Cemetery in Arizona which reads: 'Here lies Jack Williams. He done his damndest.' What more can a person do? I did my damndest, and that's all there is to it." However, perhaps Dean Acheson best summed up the opinion of many others about Truman when he wrote: "I have read over and over again that he was an 'ordinary' man—I consider him one of the most extraordinary human beings who ever lived."

Truman was in public office for much of his adult life and lived to be eighty-eight years old. He wrote large numbers of letters throughout his career and, after leaving the White House, tried to accommodate all requests for autographs as long as his health permitted. In terms of numbers, his material is plentiful. However, in recent years, Truman has become quite a folk hero, increasing the demand for his material, particularly with good content.

After leaving office Truman graciously autographed many interesting souvenir items such as copies of legislation, photographs showing him holding the famous "Dewey Defeats Truman" issue of the Chicago *Tribune* aloft, and philatelic items.

Although Truman personally signed almost everything throughout his career, he did employ proxy signers during his senatorial term; however, fortuitously, they bear little resemblance to his authentic signature.

Throughout his life Truman signed his full name "Harry S. Truman." The "S" in his name is not an abbreviation but, rather, his complete middle name. His parents could not agree whether the "S" should stand for his paternal or maternal grandfathers whose names were, respectively, Anderson Shippe Truman and Solomon Young, and so the noncommittal initial was diplomatically chosen as a compromise.

Truman's signature changed markedly in appearance during his adult life both in size and appearance, the most notable distinction being that his middle initial was written more cursively and distinctly in both his early and in his old-age signatures. Many of his old-age signatures bear a disconnected cursive middle initial and are often much smaller and more crabbed than his earlier signatures.

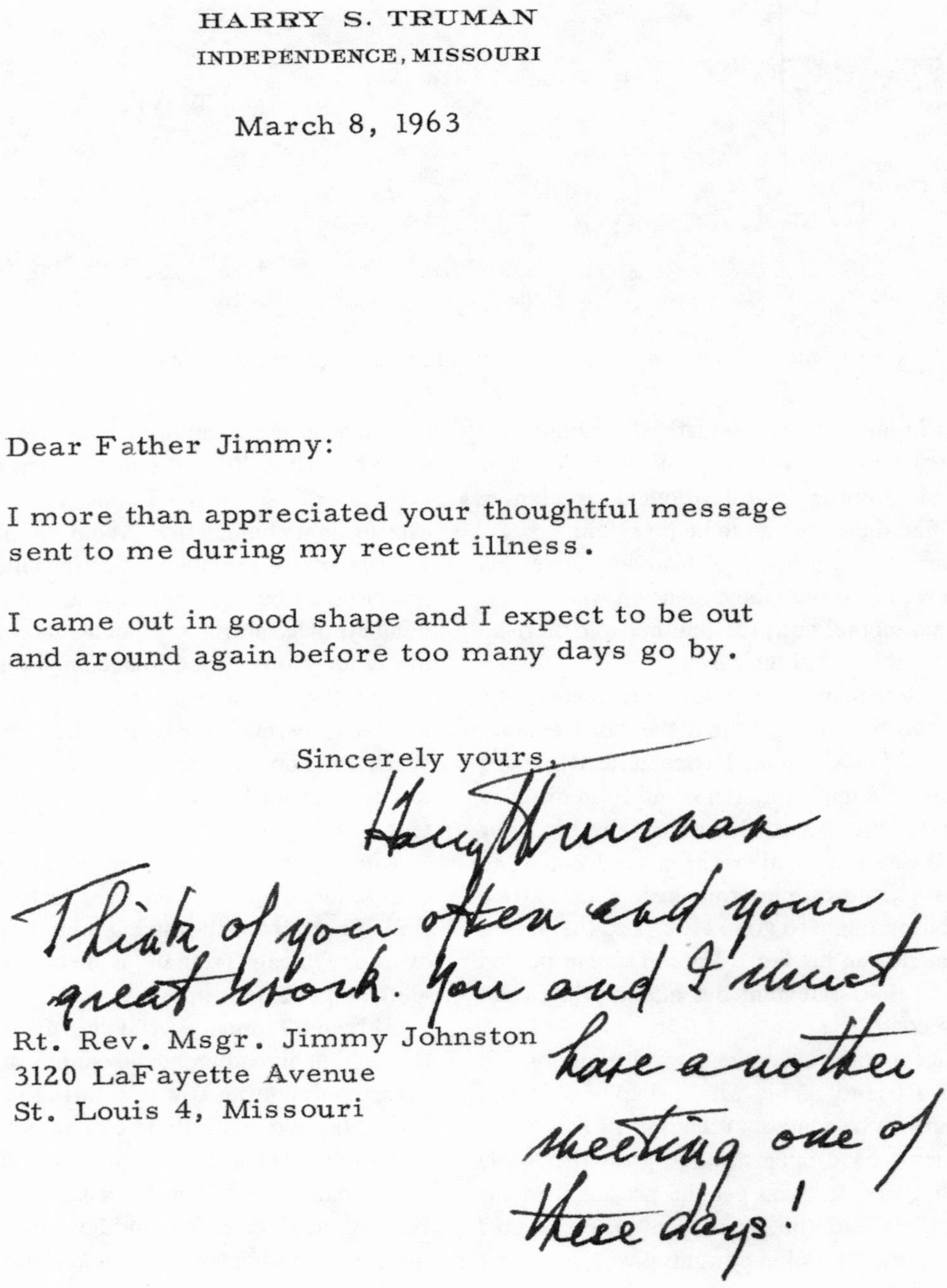

HARRY S. TRUMAN
INDEPENDENCE, MISSOURI

March 8, 1963

Dear Father Jimmy:

I more than appreciated your thoughtful message
sent to me during my recent illness.

I came out in good shape and I expect to be out
and around again before too many days go by.

Sincerely yours,

Harry Truman

*Think of you often and your
great work. You and I must
have another
meeting one of
these days!*

Rt. Rev. Msgr. Jimmy Johnston
3120 LaFayette Avenue
St. Louis 4, Missouri

Health-content, post presidential Truman letter with scarce holographic postscript.

Truman, who was one of our few left handed presidents, wrote a bold, attractive and legible hand which changed little throughout his adult life. Like most twentieth century presidents, his A.Ls.S. are scarce and expensive for all periods, particularly of presidential date.

Unlike most of the other twentieth century presidents,

Truman wrote a good letter. He was not afraid to state his mind—forcefully—often in the form of highly desirable holographic postscripts, and he peppered his correspondence with his earthy and forceful opinions. Usually a master of brevity, he nevertheless wrote newsy commentaries on the issues of the day in gossipy letters to his to his wife, daughter, mother, and sister during his White House tenure. These letters have today become primary sources for historians.

After leaving office, Truman developed the curious habit of dating almost everything he signed, although during his presidency he had dated few things he autographed. Undated Truman items, such as books and photographs, are probably of presidential date, particularly if they bear his bold vintage presidential signature which reached its zenith during his presidency.

Although Truman had the franking privilege both as senator and former president, his hand-signed franks are extremely rare.

Pre-presidential bank checks, both as county judge as well as from his personal account, have appeared on the market but are considered rare and quite desirable, especially the personal checks.

At various periods after leaving office, Truman employed facsimile copies of holographic letters or notes to acknowledge letters of congratulations, get-well wishes, etc. All these letters and notes are without salutations and were mailed in typed envelopes.

Signature of Truman at age eighty-two on philatelic cover.

34. DWIGHT D. EISENHOWER

October 14, 1890 - March 28, 1969

Thirty-fourth President
January 20, 1953 - January 20, 1961

Republican

Highlights in office:
Korean War ended; tariffs reduced;
minimum wage increased; social security
benefits broadened; Alaska and Hawaii
admitted to the Union; Saint Lawrence
Seaway built; Air Force Academy established.

Dwight David Eisenhower was one of the most popular men ever to hold the presidential office. As the preeminent hero of World War II he was the most celebrated man in America, and both parties wanted him for their candidate. He declined the Republican presidential nomination in 1948 but accepted it in 1952, winning an overwhelming victory of 442 electoral votes to 89 over Democrat Adlai Stevenson. In 1956, Stevenson was again the Democratic presidential nominee, but Eisenhower defeated him even more soundly with 457 electoral votes to 73 and almost 58 percent of the popular vote.

Eisenhower was born in Denison, Texas, the third of seven sons. Before his first birthday his family moved to Abilene, Kansas, where he was reared. At birth he was named David Dwight Eisenhower, but later reversed his Christian names. Eisenhower was an excellent high school athlete and received an appointment to West Point, where he played halfback on the football team and badly injured his knee while tackling the famous Jim Thorpe. He was graduated sixty-fifth in his class of 165.

In his early army career Eisenhower excelled in staff assignments and served under Generals John J. Pershing, Douglas MacArthur, and Walter Krueger. After Pearl Harbor, General Marshall called him to Washington for a war-plans assignment, testing him out in North Africa, Sicily and Italy.

By the end of 1943, there was an urgent need for a supreme allied commander to supervise the forthcoming invasion of northern Europe. Since the Americans were providing most of the men and materials, the appointment was their prerogative. Roosevelt conferred with Marshall, who could have secured the coveted honor for himself but who dispassionately renounced the appointment in favor of Eisenhower. Eisenhower ably fulfilled the position, one which demanded great tact in dealing with other branches of the service as well as commanders of other countries, including temperamental and prima donna commanders such as Patton and Montgomery. The political consequences of Eisenhower's position as supreme commander were inevitable.

As president, Eisenhower was criticized for keeping too clean a desk and delegating too much authority to his formidable assistant, Sherman Adams, and his even more formidable secretary of state, John Foster Dulles. He was also criticized for not standing up to McCarthyism and for hiding behind the supreme court in civil rights controversies. Eisenhower badly mishandled the U-2 incident when the Russians shot down a U.S. spy plane, initially denying the plane's activities and then admitting them publicly. Eisenhower's critics charged, with some truth, that he lacked the executive boldness to make a great president.

In domestic policy Eisenhower pursued a middle course, continuing most of the New Deal and Fair Deal programs and emphasizing a balanced budget. When public school desegregation began, he sent troops to Little

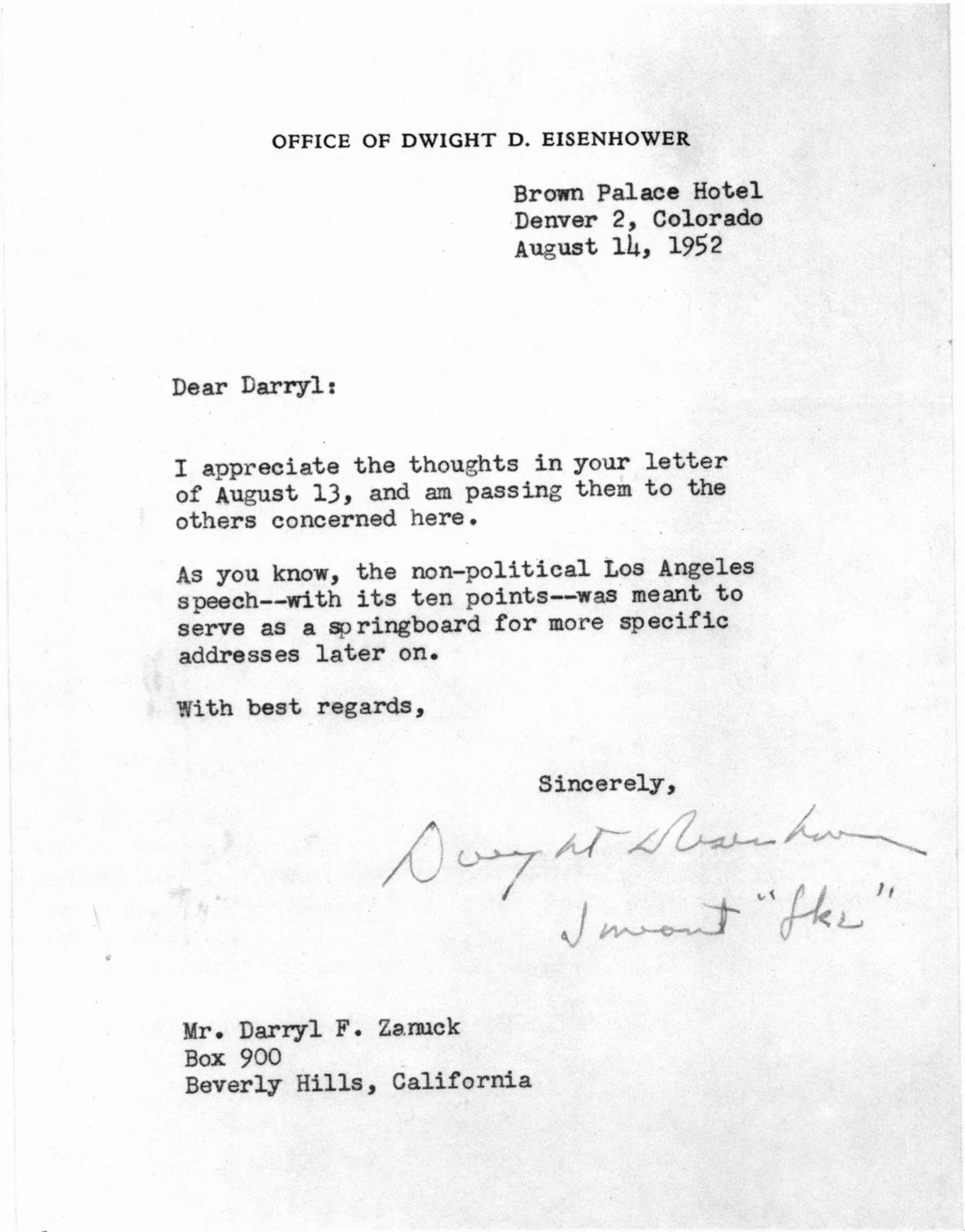

Brown Palace Hotel
Denver 2, Colorado
August 14, 1952

Dear Darryl:

I appreciate the thoughts in your letter
of August 13, and am passing them to the
others concerned here.

As you know, the non-political Los Angeles
speech--with its ten points--was meant to
serve as a springboard for more specific
addresses later on.

With best regards,

Sincerely,

Dwight D. Eisenhower
I meant "Ike"

Mr. Darryl F. Zanuck
Box 900
Beverly Hills, California

Intriguing content Eisenhower letter to movie producer Darryl Zanuck signed with a rare double signature.

Rock, Arkansas, to assure compliance with federal court orders. He also ordered complete desegregation of the armed forces, stating "there must be no second-class citizens in this country."

Eisenhower concentrated on maintaining world peace and watched with pleasure the development of the "atoms for peace" program, the loan of American uranium to have-not nations for peaceful purposes.

Before leaving office in 1961 he gave a speech urging the maintenance of adequate military strength but warn-

Very rare type of Eisenhower presidential cards, with gilt edges and raised, embossed gold Presidential seal. One is signed by both President and Mrs. Eisenhower.

THE WHITE HOUSE
WASHINGTON

Authentically signed Eisenhower White House card.

ing the country against the inherent dangers of "the military-industrial complex." He concluded the speech with a prayer for peace "in the goodness of time."

Eisenhower's desire to please was so strong that he was probably not firm enough on occasion. Unlike Truman, he was not a political fighter. He also had no passion for far-reaching social changes, and his administration was accurately labeled a "businessman's administration." It was said that his cabinet was comprised of "eight millionaires and a plumber" (the latter being his secretary of labor). Eisenhower's great passion and burning issue was peace. He made good on his word to end the Korean conflict, and during his eight years in office America did not take part in any other armed interventions.

Eisenhower's personal life and marriage were never as perfect and happy as they appeared to be on the surface. At West Point Ike was known as somewhat of a "woman hater," but nevertheless at age twenty-five he married the vivacious, small town belle Mamie Doud. During the next twenty years the Eisenhowers lived in thirty different homes as Ike climbed up the military ladder. The death in 1921 of their first child, Doud Dwight, "Icky," at the age of three devastated both parents. Ike never fully recovered, and their marriage was never again quite the same. During World War II there were persistent rumors that General Eisenhower was having an affair with his pretty WAC chauffeur and aide, Kay Summersby. Nonetheless, he and Mrs. Eisenhower weathered the storm and remained together.

Ike's chief relaxations were golfing, painting, and cooking. As president he practiced putting on the White House lawn, and had the squirrels trapped and taken away when they stole his golf balls. Eisenhower never took himself too seriously and once said: "I can think of

110

nothing more boring for the American public than to have to sit in their living rooms for a whole half-hour looking at my face on their television screens."

After the presidency Eisenhower retired to his Gettysburg farm. Although his health steadily declined, he had several productive and pleasant years. He died at Walter Reed Hospital in Washington following his seventh heart attack.

Eisenhower wrote a bold, plain hand and favored a broad-nibbed pen. Until approximately 1940 at the onset of World War II, he normally signed himself "D.D. Eisenhower." To intimates he usually signed himself "D.E." or, less frequently "D.D.E." Items signed with all three of his initials are quite rare. Even more rarely he would sign himself "Ike E." Possibly the rarest and certainly one of the most desirable forms of his signature incorporated his famous nickname, "Ike Eisenhower."

Eisenhower is one of the rarest of all presidents in A.Ls.S. for all periods, particularly of presidential date. In fact, in over thirty years the authors do not recall having seen a presidential-date Eisenhower A.L.S., nor are we personally aware of any although some must exist.

Eisenhower rarely wrote good-content or interesting letters, but they were usually friendly, charming, and exuded Eisenhower's innate good will. He is moderately scarce in presidential T.Ls.S., and quite rare in presidential Ds.S. Rare, too, are signed Eisenhower White House cards. He introduced White House cards signed with facsimile signatures which bore a printed legend on the verso, indicating that the signature and inscription were facsimiles. Signed photographs of Eisenhower of all periods are moderately scarce and in good demand, particularly those in uniform of World War II date.

Generally speaking, as with Washington and Grant, Eisenhower's war-date material, especially as supreme commander, is in greater demand than his presidential-date material. However, much of his war-date material was secretarially signed, particularly routine correspondence, fan mail, autographs, and even photographs. In

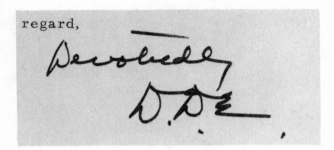

Signature from a 1948 letter signed as "Ike Eisenhower," the rarest form of his signature.

Signature from a 1968 letter signed by Eisenhower with his scarce full initials.

her posthumously published autobiography, Kay Summersby stated that she and other members of Eisenhower's staff and entourage spent the evenings answering and signing his fan mail. Later, both as president of Columbia University and as NATO commander, Eisenhower employed an autopen. As a presidential candidate in 1952 he employed at least two secretaries to sign for him, and after leaving the White House he again resumed the practice of allowing a secretary to sign for him. However, his post-presidential secretarial signatures are normally devoid of his middle initial "D," and the "E" of Eisenhower is much more legibly written than in his authentic signatures.

As a former president, Eisenhower was granted the franking privilege, but his hand-signed franks are extremely rare.

35. JOHN F. KENNEDY

May 29, 1917 - November 22, 1963

Thirty-Fifth President
January 20, 1961 - November 22, 1963

Democrat

Highlights in office:
Bay of Pigs invasion; progress in
civil rights; intervention in Viet Nam;
Cuban missile crisis.

At age forty-three, John Fitzgerald Kennedy was the youngest man ever elected president. At age forty-six he was also the youngest to die. He served scarcely a thousand days as president.

Kennedy was the first, and thus far the only, Roman-Catholic president besides being one of the most brilliant, witty, handsome, charming and wealthy men ever to occupy the oval office. He was a war hero, a Pulitzer Prize-winning author, and may have led the most unconventional personal life of any president. His very great virtues were coupled with very great faults. His inaugural address is probably the most famous of all presidential inaugural addresses and contains a number of now-immortal phrases: "Ask not what your country can do for you — ask what you can do for your country"; "Let us never negotiate out of fear, but let us never fear to negotiate"; "If a free society cannot help the many who are poor, it cannot save the few who are rich."

Of him, the famous author John Steinbeck wrote: "What a joy that literacy is no longer prima facie evidence of treason, that syntax is no longer subversive at the White House." A critical southern senator said of him: "He seems to combine the best qualities of Elvis Presley and Franklin D. Roosevelt."

Of Irish descent, "Jack" Kennedy was born in Brookline, Massachusetts, on May 29, 1917, thus becoming the first president to be born in this century. The second-oldest child and son of a large family, he was a weak and sickly child who was plagued by a myriad of childhood diseases. His brother Robert once said "when we were

growing up together, we used to laugh about the great risk a mosquito took in biting Jack — with some of his blood the mosquito was almost sure to die." As in the case of Theodore Roosevelt, Kennedy overcompensated for his childhood weaknesses by an almost desperate emphasis on physical fitness and competition. Kennedy's domineering father, the financier Joseph P. Kennedy, encouraged this tendency by teaching his sons that second-best was not acceptable. Even after becoming president, Kennedy called his father at least once a day.

The other dominant figure in Kennedy's life always remained his older brother, Joe, Jr., who was killed during World War II. Kennedy once said: "Joe was the star of our family. He did everything better than the rest of us." There was a constant and often violent struggle between the siblings while they were growing up. After Joe was killed, Jack was left to compete with a ghost. No matter what his accomplishments, neither he nor his father ever thought he could fill Joe's shoes.

Kennedy was an average student and maintained a "C" average. In college he preferred to devote most of his time to athletics until he seriously injured his back playing football. He dropped out of school the second semester of his junior year to travel through Europe, where his father's position as the U.S. ambassador to Great Britain admitted the young Kennedy to high-level diplomatic and political circles throughout Europe.

When he returned to Harvard, he used his experiences as the basis for his senior thesis, a study of England's complacency on the eve of World War II, for which he was awarded a magna cum laude from the Harvard political science department. His thesis, later rewritten and retitled *Why England Slept*, became a bestseller, resulting in a desire to pursue a writing career.

He studied briefly at the Stanford School of Business after being graduated from Harvard, but as America moved closer to war he dropped out of school to accept a naval commission in October, 1941. The most memorable event of Kennedy's war career was when his boat, PT-109, was rammed and sunk by a Japanese destroyer. His back was seriously reinjured, but he managed to swim to safety as well as to save a wounded comrade by taking the man's life preserver in his teeth. Kennedy was awarded the Navy Medal and the Purple Heart. He was recuperating in a naval hospital from malaria and his back injuries, from which he lived in constant pain for the rest of his life, when he learned that his elder brother Joe had been killed while flying a dangerous mission. Although Kennedy still hoped for a writing career, his family demanded he take up the political career that had been planned for Joe. Years later Kennedy's father said: "I told him Joe was dead and it was his responsibility to run for Congress. He didn't want to. But I told him he had to."

The Kennedy family selected a congressional district in which his maternal grandfather, John "Honey Fitz" Fitzgerald, still had great popularity as a former mayor of Boston. Kennedy's well-organized and well-financed congressional campaign emphasized his record as a war hero and he won an easy victory, entering Congress in 1947 at age twenty-nine. He was twice reelected to Congress by large margins.

When Kennedy was thirty-six, he married the twenty-three year old, socially prominent Jacqueline Bouvier in a society wedding which received national publicity. Kennedy met Jacqueline at a dinner party and later recalled that "I reached across the asparagus and asked her for a date." Over the course of their marriage Mrs. Kennedy was pregnant five times, but suffered two miscarriages and lost her last child when he was two days old. The Kennedys were never publicly affectionate, but Kennedy was obviously proud of his brilliant and beautiful wife and he doted on their children.

Much has been written about Kennedy's personal life. Suffice it to say that he was a womanizer both before and during his marriage and presidency. He was not unique among presidents in this respect.

In 1952, Kennedy felt strong enough politically to challenge his state's incumbent Republican senator, the patrician Henry Cabot Lodge. Kennedy's senatorial cam-

paign was the most expensive and professional campaign in Massachusetts history up to that time. After the Kennedys made a timely $500,000 "business loan" to the financially ailing Boston *Post*, the influential, usually Republican newspaper strongly endorsed Democrat John F. Kennedy for the senate. Although Eisenhower decisively carried the state, Kennedy beat Lodge by an impressive 70,000 votes. At the age of thirty-five, John F. Kennedy entered the United States Senate.

By 1954, Kennedy's painful back condition had deteriorated to the point that he had to walk on crutches. He was forced to undergo two, then-risky, spinal-fusion operations, the first of which was not successful and as a result of which Kennedy almost died. During his lengthy recuperation at his father's Palm Beach home, he wrote another book, *Profiles in Courage*, about U.S. senators who had defied public opinion in order to "do right." A bestselling sensation, it won the Pulitzer Prize for Kennedy.

Kennedy was regarded as "soft" on the issue of McCarthy, even though he was recuperating from back surgery when the Senate voted on censure, because he refused to issue a public statement clarifying his position. A critic later jibed that Kennedy should "show less profile and more courage."

In 1956 Kennedy narrowly missed winning the Democratic vice-presidential nomination. His exposure at the convention won him national recognition, however, and in 1960 he gained the first-ballot nomination for president, with Lyndon B. Johnson as his vice-presidential running mate.

The Kennedy-Johnson ticket beat the Nixon-Lodge team by one of the slimmest margins in presidential election history, with 34,227,096 votes for the Democrats and 34,108,546 for the Republicans, a margin of less than three-tenths of one percent. Most of the states voted against Kennedy, as did majorities of whites, college graduates, high-income people, Protestants, women, senior citizens, businessmen, professionals and farmers. With the help of Lyndon Johnson's support in the "Solid South," however, and some highly questionable and disputed votes from Chicago's political boss and king maker, Mayor Richard Daley, Kennedy won by 303 to 219 electoral votes.

As president, Kennedy set out to honor his pledge to get America moving again, and his economic programs launched the country on its longest sustained expansion since World War II. Before his death he had formulated plans for a war on poverty and had called for vigorous new

United States Senate

WASHINGTON, D. C.

May 13, 1957

J.L. _____ S. D. E. C. _____
                 J.J.P. _____

REC'D MAY 14 1957

REMARKS _____

Mr. Jim Lindsey, Chairman
State Democratic Executive Committee of Texas
1010 Lavaca Street
Austin, Texas

Dear Jim:

Thank you for your letter of May 6 and for keeping me informed of the situation in your state.

I was most disturbed by the clipping you sent me and your observations on it. I have no wish to become involved in any factional difficulties concerning the Democratic Party in Texas or any other state; nor have I ever encouraged any individuals to use my name in a way that might indicate I was involved. The only time I had previously met Woody Bean was when Lyndon Johnson introduced him to me as our host in El Paso last fall; and consequently when he dropped by my office, and offered to bring the National Committeewoman from Texas by, I of course raised no objection. I knew nothing else about his relationship, or that of Mrs. Randolph, with Lyndon and other party leaders. I told both of them that it has always been my assumption, and still is, that Lyndon would lead the Texas delegation in 1960 and its votes would be pledged to him, if he so desires. As for myself, I have no plans beyond my reelection to the Senate in 1958, and never indicated to the contrary to Woody Bean or anyone else.

As you can see, the story in the Austin newspaper was inaccurate and misleading in many respects. It was certainly never checked with this office for accuracy or authorization by either the writer or his source.

I wish you would come to Washington and drop in! In any event, I hope to see you in the not too distant future.

With every good wish.

Sincerely yours,

John F. Kennedy

JFK:gl

Historically significant and ironic letter, in light of subsequent events, from Senator John F. Kennedy to the Chairman of the Texas Democratic Party denying he had meddled in Texas Party politics and mentioning Lyndon B. Johnson and Johnson's arch political enemies. Kennedy ends by saying he has "no plans beyond my reelection to the Senate in 1958."

civil-rights legislation. With the Alliance for Progress and the Peace Corps, he brought American aid and idealism to developing countries. He also expanded the country's space efforts.

Soon after Kennedy's inauguration he permitted a band of Cuban exiles, already armed and trained, to invade Cuba in an unsuccessful attempt to overthrow Castro. In short order the Soviet Union renewed its campaign against West Berlin, to which Kennedy responded by reinforcing both U.S. troop strength in Berlin and the nation's overall military strength. The Soviet Union responded by building the Berlin Wall, and initiated plans to install offensive nuclear missiles in Cuba. When air reconnaissance revealed the Russian missiles sites in October, 1962, Kennedy imposed a naval blockade on the Cuban-bound missiles. As the world trembled on the brink of nuclear war the Russians, apparently convinced, by this strong American response, of the futility of nuclear blackmail, backed down and agreed to remove the missiles.

Kennedy had relied on bad advice from the joint chiefs of staff, which had hatched the invasion scheme prior to 1961, and from his other military advisers. He frankly admitted his blunder and, according to the polls, Kennedy's highest rating as president came immediately following the Bay of Pigs fiasco. The American people rallied to support their president, and 82 percent expressed approval of his handling of the situation. No one was more shocked at this pleasant and unexpected turn of events than Kennedy himself. He said: "My God, it's as bad as Eisenhower. The worse I do the more popular I get." He also stated: "All my life I've known better than to depend on the experts. . . . How could I have been so stupid, to let them go ahead?"

After the missile crisis, Kennedy contended that both sides had a vital interest in stopping the spread of nuclear weapons and slowing the arms race. His determined efforts toward this goal led to a nuclear test ban treaty in 1963.

Kennedy was widely criticized for appointing his brother as attorney general. The president deflected the criticism with his sparkling wit by replying that his brother was a young lawyer and needed legal experience.

When the president visited Texas in November, 1963, accompanied by his wife, he had been warned that there might be hostility. Even in his own bailiwick Vice President Johnson had earlier experienced a hostile reception, as had U.N. Ambassador Adlai Stevenson who was struck and spat upon in Dallas shortly before Kennedy's visit.

However, the president remained cheerfully philosophical and, ironically, while in Fort Worth the morning of his assassination, remarked that anyone with a rifle with a telescopic scope positioned on a tall building could kill him if they wanted to. A few hours later while Kennedy was riding in a motorcade in downtown Dallas with Texas Governor and Mrs. John B. Connally, he was shot in the head, neck, and back by a sniper. He died soon thereafter at Parkland Hospital in Dallas. Immediately after Kennedy's assassination, reports were circulated that Kennedy had traveled to Texas to heal a breach between Governor Connally and Senator Ralph Yarborough. Since Senator Yarborough had not even been consulted about the trip, his friends widely believed that the charges were made to make Yarborough the scapegoat of the assassination and to draw attention away from the planners of the trip.

John F. Kennedy's mercurial and illegible signature and penmanship are the scourge of historians and autograph collectors. Without question Kennedy had the most illegible handwriting and signature of all presidents. Even as a child and adolescent, his handwriting was very poor and barely legible, and it worsened with time. He wrote very rapidly in an apparent attempt to keep up with his lightning-quick thinking processes. To make matters more difficult, the appearance of his signature varied greatly and, on one occasion, he was known to have signed himself in quick succession "John Kennedy," "John F. Kennedy," and "Jack Kennedy" — and all three signatures looked vastly different.

Kennedy's mood seemed to dictate how he signed his name. If there is a single hallmark of authenticity of Kennedy material it is that no two authentic signatures look alike. Complicating an already nightmarish situation regarding Kennedy's material is his employment throughout his public career of both secretaries and robot autopens to sign his name, even in books and on photographs. Like Lyndon Johnson's autographic material, all autographic material of John F. Kennedy's should be regarded as not being genuine unless proven otherwise. Even the experts frequently disagree as to what is or is not genuine. A rash of forged Kennedy material, some of it expertly done, has appeared on the market, so even "personally witnessed" examples must be closely scrutinized. Normally, holographic postscripts written by presidents on letters can be accepted as genuine, and they also authenticate the signature on the letter, but in Kennedy's case clever forgers have forged even postscripts, particularly on purported drafts of presidential letters, including forged additions and postscripts on some genuine drafts. A collector should bear in mind that a president would not normally sign drafts of letters or speeches, and all such items should be regarded with great caution. Caveat emptor is the rule for the material of John F. Kennedy, as well as for his successor, Lyndon B. Johnson, whose authentic material may be even rarer than that of Kennedy's.

John F. Kennedy is therefore scarce in all forms of authentic material for all dates, and extremely so for presidential-date items. Only a few unquestionably genuine signatures of Kennedy have come on the market. His A.Ls.S. are extremely rare and normally date from his World War II service. Few presidential A.Ls.S. are known to exist or to have ever come on the market. To the knowledge of the authors, no unquestionably genuine

Kennedy White House cards are known to exist. The authors are aware of only two genuinely signed octavo-size pieces of Air Force One stationery.

Unlike Johnson, who enjoyed signing photographs of himself, Kennedy apparently did not, and he is particularly rare in this format for all periods. His secretaries inscribed and signed almost all of his photographs for him, using the same stereotypical phrases. They also signed copies of his books, although more of his autographed books seem to be genuine than his signed photographs.

Kennedy wrote a fair number of good-content letters, many of which evidenced his excellent but erudite sense of humor. He had a flair for writing, and some of his letters have almost a literary turn of phrase. Most of Kennedy's letters were rather brief and to the point.

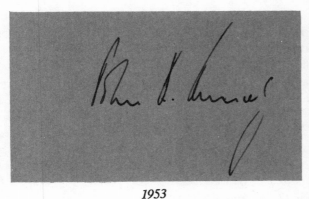

1953

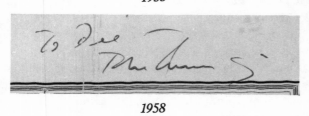

1958

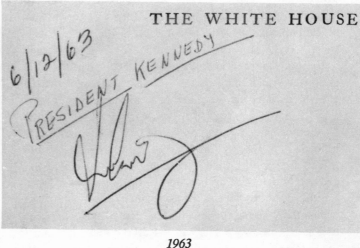

1963

Scarce authentic in-person signatures of John F. Kennedy.

36. LYNDON B. JOHNSON

August 27, 1908 - January 22, 1973

Thirty-Sixth President
November 22, 1963 - January 20, 1969

Democrat

Highlights in office:
Escalation of Viet Nam War; voting rights legislation; federal aid to education; Medicare; Department of Housing and Urban Development; Model Cities Program; Office of Economic Opportunity; Job Corps; "War on Poverty."

Lyndon B. Johnson's vision for the country and the world was for a "Great Society." A legislative genius and a veteran of twenty-five years on Capitol Hill, in his first years in the White House he obtained passage of one of the most extensive legislative programs in our history. Emphasizing cooperation between the executive and legislative branches, he used the veto sparingly and had none of his thirty vetoes overridden. Adlai Stevenson described him as "a master of the art of the possible in politics" who possessed "extraordinary managerial skill." In foreign affairs, Johnson carried on both the rapidly growing struggle to restrain encroachment in Viet Nam and the maintenance of collective security.

The "Johnson treatment" was legendary, for he had the unerring ability to size-up his victim and select the proper treatment from his bag of persuasive tricks, even including a measure of physical assault. As one victim of his persuasive treatment recalled: "Lyndon got me by the lapels and put his face on top of mine and he talked and talked and talked and talked. I figured it was either getting drowned or joining." If gentler methods were called for, Johnson might grab his victim's knee with a massive hand or slowly massage his shoulder in order to bring him around.

Johnson came from the barren hill country of central Texas, where his parents' families combined farming and politics, and he felt the pinch of rural poverty as he grew up. He worked his way through Southwest Texas State

Teachers College, progressing from janitor to a position as assistant to the president, and began his career as a school teacher, learning compassion for the poverty of others when he taught students of Mexican descent in South Texas. He then worked several years as secretary to Texas Congressman Richard Kleberg, and served as state director of the National Youth Administration. In 1937 he campaigned successfully for the House of Representatives on a New Deal platform. Tremendously aided by his talented wife, Claudia Alta "Lady Bird" Johnson, he beat seven other candidates.

Johnson was the first member of Congress to enlist in the military service after Pearl Harbor. He served in the navy until President Roosevelt ordered the return to Washington of all members of Congress who were serving in the armed forces.

After six terms in the House, Johnson was elected to the Senate in 1948, by a margin of only eighty-seven votes, in one of the closest and most controversial elections in Texas history. There were widespread charges of voting fraud, and Johnson's narrow victory gave rise to his nickname "Landslide Lyndon." In later years Johnson himself could joke about this close election. He liked to tell the story of a small Mexican-American boy who was found sitting on the curb of a South Texas town and crying. A neighbor asked the boy what was wrong and the child answered that his father hadn't come to visit him. "Why, son," the neighbor declared, "You know your daddy has been dead for six years." "I know," said the boy, "but he came back last Tuesday to vote for Lyndon Johnson and didn't even stop to see me."

In 1953 Johnson became the youngest minority leader in the Senate's history, and the following year when the Democrats won control he became the youngest majority leader. As a consummate powerbroker with great legislative skills, he obtained passage of a number of key Eisenhower legislative programs, which he favored.

In 1960 Johnson sought the Democratic presidential nomination, but had to be satisfied with the second spot under Kennedy. The Kennedy-Johnson ticket narrowly beat the Republican Nixon-Lodge ticket. Johnson became president on November 22, 1963, when Kennedy was assassinated in Dallas, and took the president's oath aboard Air Force One with the slain president's blood-soaked widow looking on.

As president, Johnson obtained passage of President Kennedy's stalled legislative programs, including a tax cut and a new civil rights bill, then urged Congress to enact the massive legislation for his "Great Society," which included poverty, Medicare, and education legislation among its many programs.

In 1964 Johnson was elected president in his own right with 61 percent of the electorate, the greatest popular margin in American history.

The Johnson administration sponsored spectacular space explorations, including three astronauts who successfully orbited the moon. Johnson had championed the space program from its beginning.

There were two overriding crises in the Johnson administration: racial unrest and Viet Nam. Although President Johnson had secured passage of the broadest civil-rights legislation in U.S. history, there was no early or easy solution to the racial problem. In Viet Nam the fighting continued, despite Johnson's efforts to end communist aggression and achieve a settlement, and controversy over the war became acute. In March, 1968, Johnson limited the bombing of North Viet Nam in order to initiate peace negotiations, then shocked the world by withdrawing as a candidate for reelection so he could devote all his energies to the quest for peace which, sadly, eluded him. When he left office the peace talks were under way, but he did not live to see them succeed. Johnson had prophesied "When [The Great Society] dies, I, too, will die." He suffered his fatal heart attack the day after President Nixon announced plans which would essentially kill the Great Society.

Lady Bird Johnson's contribution to her husband's suc-

cess cannot be underestimated. It is doubtful he could have achieved the presidency without her able help and support. As Sam Rayburn aptly observed, "Marrying her was the smartest thing Lyndon ever did." In the years following their marriage Mrs. Johnson ran the household with little help from her hard-working husband, and also managed to overcome her natural shyness in order to help Johnson politically.

Early on, the Johnsons had to live frugally in order to make ends meet on his congressional salary. After eight years, Lady Bird received a $64,000 inheritance from her father and invested it in a ramshackle Austin radio station. Using her remarkable business skills, Mrs. Johnson parlayed her investment into a multi-million dollar communications empire. During the White House years Mrs. Johnson proved herself to be one of the most influential first ladies in history. She helped Johnson campaign for reelection on "The Lady Bird Special" campaign train, and also helped win approval for her beautification bill known as "The Lady Bird Bill," a significant piece of highway beautification legislation which eliminated thousands of unsightly bill boards and junk piles along the highways of America.

Without question, Lyndon Johnson was one of our most brilliant and hard-working presidents. Whether or not one agrees with his politics, no president ever tried harder than Lyndon Johnson. His energy and stamina were phenomenal. He always drove himself—and others—to the limit. Mrs. Johnson once observed that "Lyndon acts as if there is never going to be a tomorrow." As president, Johnson began every day with a bedroom conference at 6:30 a.m., then worked straight through until 2:00 p.m. when he had lunch, relaxed, sometimes with a swim, and took a quick nap. By 4:00 p.m. he was ready to go again. "It's like starting a new day" Johnson observed, and he would then proceed to work straight through to one or two in the morning. This Johnsonian "double day" amazed the press and exhausted and frustrated his over-worked aides. His assistant Jack Valenti opined that Johnson had "extra glands" that gave him energy that ordinary men did not possess: "He goes to bed late, rises early, and the words I have never heard him say are 'I'm tired'."

Johnson had trouble relaxing. He tried but disliked golf and bowling—he was not happy unless he made a hole-in-one or a strike. He finally settled on swimming for exercise and relaxation, but he turned every lap into a political conference and had floating telephones installed so he could work in the water.

It was assumed until quite recently that, in light of his

February 27, 1968

Dear

I return in a few hours to Washington. With me I will
carry part of your heartache and, I am thankful to say,
some of the great courage you have shown in face of
tragedy.

The loss of two good and brave sons on the battlefield
of freedom is the cruellest affliction. I wanted you to
know that Mrs. Johnson and I have offered prayers for
you here at the Ranch. We feel very close to you --
not only as nearness is measured by miles, but in
that special kinship we find in admiring the teachings
by which you raised your sons.

Your lessons have not been lost. They live in the
gallant example of Eddie and Dale. Boys they were;
but by their convictions they have taught countless
Americans to stand like men when freedom is threatened and peace imperiled by aggression.

In achieving that, they have also given the inspiration
of your instruction to the world, promising all men a
better chance to "stand tall and walk straight."

God bless you for that selfless gift. I pray that you
will find comfort in His mercy now. This nation
will always offer you the strength of its deep gratitude
and pride.

Sincerely,

Authentically signed Viet Nam content Typed Letter Signed of President Lyndon B. Johnson.

thirty-seven year political career, the autographed material of Lyndon B. Johnson would be among the most common of all of the presidents, but it now appears that Johnson may be the rarest of all presidents in all forms of material from all periods. Johnson employed secretaries, and later autopens, throughout his career, and seems to have signed virtually nothing personally. Unfortunately, those items which are currently considered to be authentically signed are suspect because not all of his secretarial, and particularly autopen, patterns are yet known. Although not common, Johnson is probably more easily obtainable in authentically signed books and photographs than letters. He enjoyed signing photographs and books by or about himself. The majority of his authentically signed letters seem to be signed either "Lyndon" or "L.B.J." His post-presidential memoirs, *The Vantage Point*, are probably the best source of unquestionably authentic full signatures. Lengthy inscriptions in books and postscripts on letters are virtually the only source of his very rare holographs and are perhaps the closest one can come to Johnson's A.Ls.S.

Without question, Johnson is the rarest of all presidents in A.Ls.S. from all periods; only a handful are known to exist. With the exception of a cache of early love letters to Mrs. Johnson, which will remain sealed until after her death, there are only two A.Ls.S. in the Lyndon B. Johnson Library — one written to his grandmother while he was at college, and the other to his mother during his school teaching days. There are only two standard file drawers of Johnson's holographic material in the entire L.B.J. Library, and even this small number contains papers on which he wrote only a check mark, "O.K.", or his single initial "L."

Lyndon B. Johnson wrote a neat, usually legible hand, normally with every letter meticulously formed and connected to the other letters within the words. His penmanship changed little throughout his adult life, although it did diminish somewhat in size.

Johnson was noted for warm and folksy personal letters. As might be expected, he used his correspondence quite effectively as a political tool. He had a firm, unbreakable rule for his staff members: they could not quit work or go home until every letter received that day was answered — even if it were only to tell his constituents that he was working on their problems. He might write as many as a half-dozen letters to the same constituent,

advising him of the status of his request or problem. The recipients always received the intended — and accurate — impression that Johnson was tending to business and diligently working on their matters. No president has used correspondence more effectively than did Lyndon B. Johnson. Ironically, almost all of Johnson's "warm and folksy" correspondence was secretarially or autopen-signed.

Johnson was capable of writing eloquent, charming, and well-thought out letters but, like most modern presidents, he is not noted for good-content letters. Most of his letters deal with boring and routine political matters. Many of Johnson's early letters were to grassroots or precinct-level political leaders or postmasters with whom he kept in close touch.

Although there are exceptions, more fully discussed in the monograph on the handwriting and signature of Lyndon B. Johnson in the appendix, the cardinal sign of authenticity of Johnson's signatures is the presence of a period, after his middle initial, which he normally placed far below and to the left of the lower loop of the "J" in "Johnson." Unfortunately, on occasion he also wrote signatures without the period, sometimes did not connect his middle initial "B" to "Johnson," and his later secretaries started adding the telltale period, further complicating matters. His chief amanuensis, Bruce Thomas, using the same stereotype phrases such as "With best wishes," could more closely imitate Johnson's handwriting than he could his signature.

To the knowledge of the authors, all of Johnson's post-presidential material is authentic. With the exception of his book plates and signed copies of his memoirs, he signed virtually all his post-presidential material with his initials "L.B.J.," probably an energy-conserving device as his health rapidly deteriorated after he left office. He lived only four years after leaving the White House.

In summary, all the material of Lyndon B. Johnson should be regarded with great caution and should probably not be regarded as genuine until proven and until additional in-depth study is done on his material.

The appendix entitled "The Surprising Modern Presidential 'Button Gwinett'" is the first and thus far only study of Lyndon B. Johnson's autographic material. It provides a more complete study and discussion of the handwriting and signature of Johnson.

37. RICHARD NIXON

January 9, 1913 -

Thirty-Seventh President
January 20, 1969 - August 9, 1974

Republican

Highlights in office:
U.S. withdrawal from Viet Nam War;
visit to Red China;
Watergate scandal; resignation from office.

It will be many years before a fair and dispassionate verdict can be reached about Richard Milhous Nixon, the second president to face impeachment and the first to resign from office. Even Nixon critics, however, must agree that Nixon made the most of his assets, certainly in a political sense. He did not have the social connections of Franklin D. Roosevelt nor the wealth of Kennedy; he did not have the family political tradition of Robert A. Taft nor the popularity of Eisenhower; he was not a war hero nor was he handsome, athletic, photogenic, charming or even affable, and he was not a particularly good orator. He was defeated for president in 1961 and for governor of California in 1962, but he refused to give up and fade away. Resilient and resourceful enough to secure a lucrative position in a New York law firm, he used it to rebuild his political base and was rewarded for his tenacity in 1968 with the Republican presidential nomination.

Nixon was born in California in 1913, the second oldest of five sons. Two of his brothers died from tuberculosis while they were adolescents, and Nixon seemed to feel strangely responsible for, and guilty about, their deaths. Nixon's mother wrote: "I think that Richard may have felt a kind of guilt." After the tragic early deaths of his two brothers, Nixon seemed to feel the need to prove that he deserved to live.

He had a brilliant record both at Whittier College and at Duke University Law School where he graduated third in his class. As a student Nixon was never popular with the other students. In law school, he was nicknamed "Iron Butt" because of his long hours in the library. Other students called him "Gloomy-Gus." After graduating from law school, he was turned down for several jobs with New York law firms. He was even turned down by the FBI for a position. (Interestingly, FBI Director J. Edgar Hoover was one of his personal heroes.) He eventually landed a job with a small law firm in California, and in his first case as a trial lawyer in 1937, ten days after being admitted to the California bar, he represented a Los Angeles woman attempting to recover a bad debt. During the trial, Nixon was accused of unethical behavior by the trial judge and threatened with disbarment. He was also sued by his client for mishandling her case, but Nixon's partner subsequently settled with the client by giving her $4,000.

Although Nixon was exempt from military service in World War II because of his Quaker religious beliefs, he nevertheless enlisted and served as a naval lieutenant commander in the Pacific, where he divided his time between building airstrips and playing poker. By the end of the war his poker winnings totaled over $10,000.

In 1946, after leaving the service, Nixon responded to a newspaper advertisement placed by one hundred wealthy California Republicans seeking a congressional candidate. After some hesitation they agreed to sponsor Nixon. As one of them put it: "He was the best of a bad lot." Nixon made his first campaign appearances dressed in a naval uniform. He unmercifully attacked his Democratic opponent, Jerry Voorhis, as being soft on communism and "a lip-service American who is fronting for un-American elements, unwittingly or otherwise."

Post presidential Nixon inscription on a photograph.

Three days before the election Nixon charged that Voorhis had consistently voted the "Moscow—PAC—Henry Wallace" line in Congress. Voorhis was in fact a dedicated anti-Communist as well as a member of the House Un-American Activities Committee. Nixon's vicious and false rhetoric made mincemeat of the mild but truthful Voorhis, and on election day Nixon soundly defeated him.

After Nixon took his seat in Congress he introduced a piece of "anti-subversive" legislation known as the Mundt-Nixon bill, which was so repressive that even Nixon's fellow Republicans opposed it. Thomas E. Dewey condemned it as an attempt "to beat down ideas with clubs." Still, Nixon emerged from his first term in Congress as a leading red-baiter.

In 1950 Nixon ran for the Senate against Congresswoman Helen Gahagan Douglas, a liberal and a former actress. Nixon immediately dubbed her the "Pink Lady" and circulated libelous campaign literature about her on pink paper. It was during this race that a newspaper dubbed Nixon "Tricky-Dick." Nixon won the senatorial election by over 70,000 votes, easily crushing Douglas, and became the Senate's youngest member at age thirty-eight. As a senator he worked closely with Senator Joseph McCarthy. In one memorable statement which did not endear him to Harry Truman, Nixon said: "Ninety-six percent of the 6,926 Communists, fellow-travelers, sex perverts, people with criminal records, dope addicts, drunks and other security risks removed under the Eisenhower security program were hired by the Truman administration."

At the 1952 Republican convention many delegates still had their doubts about Nixon, but did not have the time or energy to act on them. As one delegate recalled: "We took Dick Nixon not because he was right wing or left wing—but because he was from California and we were tired." Shortly after Nixon's nomination, he was attacked for his secret "slush-fund." Eisenhower refused to commit himself one way or the other, forcing Nixon to make his now-classic "Checkers" speech in a last-ditch effort to save himself. During the speech Nixon tearfully defended himself, and the public responded favorably. Eisenhower was personally disgusted with Nixon's performance but was forced to keep him on the ticket. After the speech Hollywood producer Darryl Zanuck called Nixon and congratulated him on "the most tremendous performance I've ever seen."

Eisenhower always kept Nixon at arm's length, and wanted to drop Nixon from the ticket in 1956. In a tense oval office meeting, Nixon refused Eisenhower's offer of any post in his cabinet, except secretary of state, if he would voluntarily step down. With Nixon's strong support from conservative elements, Ike could not have dropped him without a fight, which he chose to avoid. However, even though Eisenhower again reluctantly accepted Nixon as a running mate, he continued to snub him both politically and socially. (When Lyndon Johnson was president, he took Nixon on a tour of the White House and showed him parts of the building he had never seen.) In 1960 Eisenhower was asked at a press conference: "What major decisions of your administration has the vice president participated in?" Eisenhower's instantaneous flip response was: "If you give me a week, I might think of one."

In 1960 Nixon was nominated for president by acclama-

tion. He lost the election to John F. Kennedy by a narrow margin, but continued campaigning for Republican candidates. In his ill-advised California gubernatorial campaign in 1962 he was haunted by the "Hughes Loan," a secret loan of $200,000 from billionaire Howard Hughes to Nixon's brother Donald. At a public ceremony in Chinatown Nixon totally lost his composure when he opened a fortune cookie which contained the message: "What about the Hughes Loan?" The cookie had been placed there by political prankster Dick Tuck.

Nixon was humiliatingly defeated by Pat Brown by 350,000 votes but stubbornly refused to concede defeat. When his press aide Herb Klein told him the next morning that reporters were still waiting for a statement he replied "screw them," and then sent Klein down to make a statement in his place. While Klein was in front of television cameras from all the major networks, Nixon, disheveled and unshaven, interrupted him and gave a rambling and disjointed tirade which ended with "you won't have Nixon to kick around anymore." His speech was described by one of the reporters as a "nervous breakdown in public." His jerky, convulsive gestures and nervous giggles gave the impression that he was a man who had been pushed to the very brink of sanity. Nevertheless, by 1964, Nixon was back on the campaign trail and in 1968 was again his party's nominee, defeating Democrat Hubert H. Humphrey and third-party candidate George C. Wallace.

Reconciliation was the primary goal of Nixon's presidency. The nation was dangerously divided, with racial violence in the cities and continuing demonstrations throughout the country against our involvement in Viet Nam. In his first term Nixon proposed tax reforms in such areas as welfare, tax laws, and the structure of the government itself. His accomplishments in office included revenue-sharing, the end of the draft, new anti-crime legislation, and a broad environmental program. As he had pledged, he appointed philosophically conservative supreme court justices. One of the most memorable and dramatic events in the history of mankind occurred during his presidency when, in 1969, American astronauts landed on the moon. Although Nixon succeeded in ending American fighting in Viet Nam and in improving relations with China and the U.S.S.R., the Watergate affair brought even deeper divisions to the country and ultimately brought down his presidency.

Although Nixon had defeated Democrat George McGovern in 1972 by one of the widest margins in American political history, within a few months his administration was embroiled over the Watergate scandal, stemming from a break-in, and the ensuing cover-up, at the offices of the Democratic National Committee during the 1972 campaign. The break-in was traced to officials of the "Committee To Reelect The President." A number of administration officials resigned, and some were later convicted of various offenses stemming from the cover-up. Nixon denied any personal knowledge or involvement in the Watergate imbroglio, but the courts forced him to produce tape recordings of oval office conversations which proved that he had in fact tried to thwart the investigation. Simultaneously, a series of unrelated scandals in Maryland forced Vice President Spiro T. Agnew to resign in 1973. Nixon's nominee for vice president to replace Agnew was House Minority Leader Gerald R. Ford, who was overwhelmingly approved by Congress.

Faced with certain impeachment, Nixon announced on August 8, 1974, that he would resign the next day.

From the beginning Nixon, seemingly most comfortable in the role of a pious martyr, echoing his saintly mother, seemed to sense that he would ultimately fail. Lyndon Johnson recognized this trait in Nixon, and once said about him: "He's like a Spanish race horse who runs faster than anyone for the first nine lengths, and then turns around and runs backward. You'll see, he'll do something wrong in the end. He always does."

Nixon seemed to set himself up for defeat. In 1952, after his nomination for vice president, he had made himself politically vulnerable by continuing to accept contributions to his political "slush fund." In 1960, when he was running well ahead of Kennedy in the polls, he had again invited disaster by agreeing to debate the handsome and articulate Kennedy in televised debates. During one of the debates Nixon demanded that Kennedy apologize for the salty language used by former President Truman in a ringing anti-Nixon campaign speech. Nixon then said to the audience: "I can only say that I am very proud that President Eisenhower restored dignity and decency, and frankly, good language to the conduct of the presidency. And I can only hope—should I win this election—that I would approach President Eisenhower in maintaining the dignity of the office." Kennedy's reaction was hearty off-camera laughter. Shortly after the debate was over, Nixon retired to his dressing room and exploded in front of reporters: "the f---g b---d—he wasn't supposed to use notes." After his defeat one of his aides confessed: "Dick didn't lose this election. Dick blew this election."

Nixon had also come dangerously close to "blowing it" in 1968, despite the most expensive campaign in U.S. history to that time, when he polled two and one-half million fewer votes than he had in his losing 1960 presidential bid. His overall percentage of the popular vote, 43.4 percent, was lower than any winning candidate since 1912, and he won only because of the presence of third-party "American Independent" candidate George C. Wallace, whose law and order candidacy drew off almost ten million votes, 13.5 percent of the total. Wallace received enough of the normally Democratic, blue-collar votes in key industrial states to swing them to Nixon, who won 301 electoral votes to Humphrey's 191 even though the difference in the popular vote was less than one percent. Nixon had won in 1968 in spite of himself. In 1972, even though he won one of the greatest landslides in history, he had sown the seeds of his own undoing by the inept and stupid Watergate cover-up.

One interesting characteristic of Nixon is that all his life he has had a difficult time coordinating his body. Although he played college football for four years, he warmed the bench because he had "two left feet." One teammate recalled that anytime Nixon was put in a game "we knew a five-yard penalty was coming up" because in his eagerness Nixon would invariably rush ahead before the play started. In later years Nixon's habit of clumsily banging into car doors led to a serious knee injury that slowed down his campaigning in 1960, and as president his coordination problems surprised and shocked observers. He was patently incapable of getting the tops off either pill bottles or ceremonial pens and would often resort to trying

Signed Nixon calling cards.

to bite and gnaw them off. On one occasion, after unsuccessfully attempting to bite off the top of a pill bottle, he finally resorted to stomping on it. At one press conference he raised his hands with the classic gesture for those in the room to stand, but told them "would you please be seated." On still another and even more embarrassing occasion, while delivering a major speech he pointed to the audience and said "I," then pointed to himself and said "you." Nixon was often so physically tense that if anyone happened to touch him on the arm he would jump as if he had been struck by a heavy blow.

As he was growing up Nixon expressed little interest in women or their company. One former classmate recalled: "Oh, he used to dislike us girls so! He would make horrible faces at us. As a debater, his main theme in grammar school and his first years in high school, was why he hated girls." Nixon's mother later recalled: "Richard was not much of a mixer in college." The only girl who managed to arouse Nixon's interest prior to his marriage was Ola Florence Welch, whom he dated for several years. On their dates Nixon preferred to discuss such topics as how history would have been changed if the Persians had conquered the Greeks, and Ola ultimately dropped him. In 1938, after Nixon was out of law school, he met his future wife in an amateur theatrical group which he attended specifically to meet Pat. After a rehearsal he called her aside and asked her to marry him. She later said: "I thought he was nuts." For the next two years Nixon doggedly pursued Pat, one of the most popular young women in Whittier, who continued to date all the town's eligible young bachelors. She later said that Nixon "would drive me to meet other beaux, and then wait around to take me home." After two years Pat capitulated and agreed to marry him. Although she has always been supportive of his career, Pat wanted him to withdraw from politics and twice extracted his written promise to do so. He broke both promises.

Intentionally or otherwise, Nixon has publicly humiliated his wife on a number of occasions. In 1969, at one of his inaugural balls, he broke tradition by failing to introduce the new first lady. At the next ball he introduced his daughters and son-in-law, and only then remembered to introduce his wife. Later, as he was about to get into his limousine to go to still another ball, he had to be reminded by an aide that he had left Mrs. Nixon standing alone inside.

As one might expect, Nixon's personality has caused strong reactions from others over the years: "He is the kind of politician who would cut down a redwood tree, then mount the stump and make a speech for conservation" (Adlai E. Stevenson); "I think basically he is shy, and like a lot of shy people he appears not to be warm" (Rose Mary Woods); "Nixon is a shifty-eyed goddam liar and people know it. He's one of the few in the history of his country to run for high office talking out of both sides of his mouth at the same time and lying out of both sides. . . I don't think the son-of-a-bitch knows the difference between telling the truth and lying" (Harry S. Truman); "He has no taste" (John F. Kennedy); "Dick's a team man" (Gerald R. Ford); "I just knew in my heart it was not right for Dick Nixon to ever be president of this country" (Lyndon B. Johnson); "That man is not fit to be president" (Henry Kissinger); "He has never cared about money in his whole life . . . . In that innocent mind of his, he left his tax work for others to do because he was working on world problems." (Bebe Rebozo).

Strangely enough, Nixon's favorite form of relaxation seems to be sitting in a room with his best friend, Florida banker Bebe Rebozo, in total silence for hours on end. The same pattern is apparently followed aboard Rebozo's luxury yacht.

Nixon's genuine signatures, like the man, are the subject of controversy. His post-presidential office staff steadfastly maintains that everything bearing Nixon's signature is genuine, but a noted autograph dealer and handwriting expert doubts the authenticity of Nixon's post-presidential San Clemente period signatures because of their small size and similarity. Whether or not this is the case, the authors have seen numerous items from Nixon's retirement period, including his San Clemente period, particularly book plates and photographs, which had holographic inscriptions in Nixon's distinctive script and which are unquestionably genuine. Many of them are dated in his own hand. However, it appears that, post-presidentially, Nixon signs autographs episodically, and the size of his signature and writing seems to vary according to his mood. The authors own a signed engraving of Nixon which he dated "12-25-79," and sense that the lonely former president did not have a joyous Christmas if he spent the holiday signing autographs.

Nixon's scarce holographs are legible and attractive. One distinctive feature of Nixon's handwriting is his habit of crossing some of his lower case "t's" with a bar like a horizontal fish hook, and his small case "f's" have a backward lower loop which often gives them the appearance of a figure eight.

Early on, Nixon wrote some of his signatures as "R. Nixon," particularly during his war career period, but now typically signs himself either "Richard Nixon" or "R.N." Most of his authentic presidential letters are signed with his initials "R.N." although to intimates he signs as "Dick" or "Dick Nixon." Rarely does he sign his name in full or with his middle initial, and such full signatures are both rare and desirable. Even congressional bills which Nixon approved as president were signed simply "Richard Nixon." Nixon's signature is one of the most bold and legible of the presidential series, except during his presidency when his signature deteriorated startlingly, particularly during the Watergate period. By the time of his resignation Nixon's authentic signature, as evidenced on approved congressional bills, had deteriorated to a weird series of overlapping lines which would be totally unidentifiable standing alone. One interesting characteristic of these illegible presidential signatures is that the initial stroke for the "N" in Nixon sometimes stretches back and completely across his first name. Another is that the signatures vary drastically in appearance, almost as much as did Kennedy's signatures, and they look nothing like his pre- and post-presidential signatures. They do not, in fact, look like they were penned by the same person.

Throughout Nixon's public career, as well as during the period of time between his vice presidency and presidency (1961-69), he always employed secretaries and autopens to sign his correspondence and other items. As with all presidents since Kennedy, virtually everything bearing Nixon's presidential signature was autopen or secretarially signed. The autopen and secretarial signatures were legibly written, which in and of itself should give cause for suspicion. Although Nixon's signature on his letter of resignation is legible, it was obviously written with great care and deliberation and is definitely a deviation from his other, normally totally illegible, presidential signatures.

There are at least a dozen known Nixon presidential autopen patterns, as well as a number of different secretarial signatures, many of which were probably signed by his veteran secretary Rose Mary Woods, who is perhaps best remembered for her claim that she accidentally erased eighteen minutes of an incriminating Watergate tape which she was transcribing. The torturous position she assumed to demonstrate how the erasure occurred would have done credit to Houdini. There are also several well-known vice-presidential autopen and secretarial patterns.

The various autopen patterns include all forms of Nixon's signature: "Richard Nixon," "Dick Nixon," "Dick," and "R.N." Coincidentally, although Mrs. Nixon also had one or more autopen patterns as first lady, much of her material is genuine, particularly items dating from early in the Nixon administration. Nixon's presidential aides purportedly made fun of Mrs. Nixon for personally signing her mail!

Nixon's A.Ls.S. are rare and costly, especially of presidential date, and those few which do surface usually date from Nixon's military or early congressional careers, although examples of his A.Ls.S. from all periods are known. However, Nixon's A.Ls.S., while extremely rare, are in no way as scarce as those of Kennedy and Johnson.

The content of Nixon's letters, like the man, has a stiff, formal, and somewhat awkward quality, especially his A.Ls.S.

Since leaving the presidency, Nixon's signature and handwriting have resumed their pre-presidential appearance and their legibility has greatly improved. One has but to compare them to authentic Nixon presidential signatures at the time of the Watergate crises and his resignation to realize how frighteningly near breakdown he actually was.

With the exception of post-presidential material, Nixon is to be considered rare in unquestionably genuine material of all periods. There has also been a recent increase in the demand for Nixon material, which gives every appearance of continuing to escalate.

Authentically signed Nixon White House cards are virtually unknown and unobtainable. Collectors should be wary of reproduction White House cards signed—and occasionally dated—after their presidential terms by Nixon, Ford and Carter. While these are attractive and desirable souvenir items, they are not authentic White House cards signed during their presidencies. Collectors should be particularly wary of authentic White House cards signed jointly by President and Mrs. Nixon; such cards were almost certainly post-presidentially signed by Nixon, and most of Mrs. Nixon's White House cards were autopen signed. The same also holds true of the other living former presidents whose signatures sometimes appear on White House cards with their wives.

Nixon has authored a number of books, most of which he wrote after leaving the White House, more than any other president except Hoover although Carter is running a close third and could easily outdistance both Nixon and Hoover. Nixon has graciously signed countless copies of his books on flyleaves, on bookplates, and in signed limited editions. To the knowledge of the authors, virtually all of Nixon's various books were authentically autographed by him with one notable exception: his first and perhaps best-known book, *Six Crises*, which he wrote shortly after losing the 1960 presidential election. A "signed edition" sold by the publisher was "signed" with an autopen signature on the first blank end paper. Authentically signed copies of *Six Crises* are rare, and the few authentic copies seen by the authors were post-presidentially signed by Nixon.

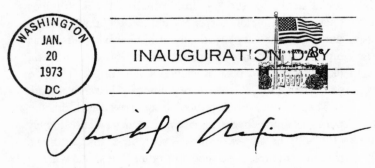

Philatelic cover signed by Nixon commemmorating his fateful second inauguration.

Cover of Inauguration Program signed by both "Dick" and Pat Nixon on his first day as Vice President.

RICHARD NIXON

January 13, 1981

Dear Mr. Minor,

    Christmas this year was a very
splendid day because Jennie, Christopher,
and Alex joined us around our Christmas
tree. What made the occasion even more
memorable was your thoughtfulness in
remembering us as you did.

    Pat joins me in sending our very
best wishes for a very happy New Year.

        Sincerely,

        Richard Nixon

Mr. Mike Minor
Assistant District Attorney
Courthouse
The State of Texas
Second Floor
Kaufman, Texas   75142

Post presidential Nixon Typed Letter Signed to the author.

38. GERALD R. FORD

July 14, 1913 -

Thirty-Eighth President
August 9, 1974 - January 20, 1977

Republican

Highlights in office:
Gave Nixon a full pardon;
Helsinki Accord; Red China
membership in United Nations.

Gerald R. Ford was the first vice president chosen under the provisions of the twenty-fifth amendment to the constitution. In the aftermath of the Watergate crisis which brought down Nixon's presidency, he succeeded the first president to resign. When Ford became president he said: "I assume the Presidency under extraordinary circumstances.... This is an hour of history that troubles our minds and hurts our hearts."

As president, Ford was confronted by almost insurmountable tasks: energy shortages, inflation, a depressed economy, and a volatile world situation. Perhaps his largest task, however, was restoring confidence in the presidency. In an effort to end the Watergate crisis, Ford granted former President Nixon a full pardon. He nominated former New York Governor Nelson A. Rockefeller as his vice president and selected his own cabinet.

Ford was born in Omaha, Nebraska, on July 14, 1913. His name at birth was Leslie Lynch King, Jr., the son of Dorothy Gardner King and Leslie King, a wool dealer. When the child was two years old his parents divorced and his mother took him with her to her parent's home in Grand Rapids, Michigan. Soon thereafter she married Gerald Rudolph Ford, a paint salesman who adopted the child and legally changed his name to Gerald Rudolph Ford, Jr. As he was growing up Ford was known as "Junior" or "Junie." He did not learn he was adopted until he was sixteen years old, and his younger half-brothers didn't learn the truth until even later. Ford saw his real father only twice, once when he was in high school and once when he was in law school. Both visits were short

and strained, and Ford chose not to have any additional contact with him.

Ford was a talented athlete and starred on the University of Michigan football team. He attended Yale Law School and served as assistant coach of the football team while obtaining his law degree.

In 1939, while he was coaching football and studying law at Yale, Ford's girl friend, Phyllis Brown, persuaded him to invest some money in a New York modeling agency. Later, Ford joined Phyllis and a *Look* magazine photographer on a trip to model winter clothes at a ski resort in Vermont. *Look* used twenty-one photographs of Ford and Phyllis in a feature article about a weekend in the life of "the beautiful people." Ford was the first president to be a male model. The second was Ronald Reagan.

Ford served in the navy during World War II and attained the rank of lieutenant commander. After the war he began a law practice in Grand Rapids and soon entered Republican party politics. Several weeks before he was elected to Congress he married an attractive divorcee named Elizabeth Bloomer, better known as "Betty." On the day of his wedding, Ford was reportedly so nervous that he wore one black shoe and one brown shoe to the ceremony.

The Fords have four children. Throughout most of their marriage he was away from home a great deal of the time, leaving Mrs. Ford with the full responsibility of rearing the children, causing her to remark humorously: "I wish I'd married a plumber. At least he'd be home by five o'clock."

GERALD R. FORD *Dec. 20, 1988*

Dear Michael:

Betty and I deeply appreciate your thoughtfulness at Christmastime. We are thoroughly enjoying the Australian Glazed apricots. Thanks so much.

We hope you and your family have a wonderful Holiday Season.

Warmest regards,

Jerry Ford

Post presidential Ford Autograph Letter Signed to the author signed "Jerry Ford," a form of signature he uses with friends.

Ford was a popular member of Congress throughout his twenty-five year congressional career and enjoyed a reputation for integrity and openness. He served as minority leader between 1965 and 1973.

During his first year in the presidential office, Ford battled inflation but had a difficult time getting his legislation through a heavily Democratic congress. He vetoed thirty-nine bills in his first fourteen months as president. One of his goals was to help the business community by giving it a tax cut and decreasing government regulation of business.

On the foreign policy front, Ford's major objective was preventing a new war in the Middle East while at the same time maintaining U.S. prestige after the collapse of Cambodia and South Viet Nam. Ford provided aid to both Israel and Egypt and convinced both countries to accept an interim truce. The Ford administration also continued the detente with the Soviet Union, and President Ford and Soviet leader Brezhnev agreed to new nuclear weapons limitations.

In 1976 Ford was the Republican presidential nominee but lost to Democrat Jimmy Carter. His pardon of Nixon had such an adverse effect in the highly charged post-Watergate atmosphere that it probably cost Ford the election. Since leaving office the Fords have lived in active retirement in Rancho Mirage, California.

Ford is one of our few left-handed presidents. He writes a plain, bold, legible and attractive hand. His handwriting and signature have changed very little during his adult life. On more formal documents he signs himself with the full "Gerald R. Ford," but to friends he signs "Jerry Ford" or simply "Jerry." He rarely signs with his initials.

Although Ford seems to have personally signed more of his congressional correspondence than other recent presidents, he nevertheless used a large number of secretaries and autopen patterns during all periods of his career, including his post-presidential period. He is particularly rare in authentic presidential material as he only served two and one-half years as president. He is rare in A.Ls.S. of all periods, and those few which have surfaced date from after the presidency.

In terms of content, Ford writes surprisingly candid letters with good content. He is not afraid to express his opinions and positions on the issues and personalities of the day, sometimes forcefully. This trait is somewhat surprising in light of Ford's "nice guy" image. His routine-content letters are unfailingly courteous and gracious, often with a well-turned phrase.

Ford is common in signed photographs from all periods except presidential. He has authored several books since leaving office, including his memoirs, *A Time to Heal*, many copies of which he graciously signed, normally with his handsome bookplate. There was a small, signed, limited edition of only 250 copies of these memoirs. Ford has done several signed, limited-edition books, primarily of speeches he has given. Perhaps the most striking and important souvenir item Ford has done is a handsome broadside measuring fifteen inches by twenty-two inches, containing the text of his remarks in the East Room of the White House upon becoming president, a color portrait, the presidential oath of office, and a raised, gold-embossed presidential seal. Since only 175 signed and numbered copies were done, the broadside is destined to escalate in value and perhaps will prove to be the most valuable of all Ford souvenir items, as well as the most attractive.

THE WHITE HOUSE
WASHINGTON

Uncommon form of Ford's signature on a reproduction of a White House card.

Signature of Gerald R. Ford signed without his middle initial.

Typical signature of Ford.

130

39. JAMES E. CARTER, JR.

October 1, 1924 -

Thirty-Ninth President
January 20, 1977 - January 20, 1981

Democrat

Highlights in office:
Emphasis on human rights; hostage crisis;
restored Panama Canal to Panamanians;
pardon of Viet Nam draft dodgers.

James Earl (Jimmy) Carter, Jr. is the first president to be elected from the deep South since Zachary Taylor's election in 1848, with the exception of the "accidental president" Lyndon B. Johnson.

Although Carter grew up in the rural south of the great depression without electricity, running water or indoor plumbing, his family was better off than most others in Plains, Georgia, and food was always plentiful. His father ran a successful supply business on the 3,200 acre farm to which the family had moved when Jimmy was four, and also sold insurance and ran a dry cleaning establishment. Over two hundred blacks worked for the Carters. Jimmy's father nicknamed him "Hot," short for "Hot Shot."

Carter was accepted by the U.S. Naval Academy and graduated in the top ten percent of his class in three years under the accelerated wartime curriculum. He subsequently served in the submarine branch, which included nuclear craft. His early ambition was to become the chief of naval operations but, upon the death of his father, he reluctantly returned to Plains to run the family peanut business.

In 1946 Jimmy made a happy marriage to a pretty Georgia girl, Rosalynn Smith. The Carters have three sons and a daughter.

Carter built the family businesses into a thriving operation and, in 1962, entered state politics, having begun public life earlier with the chairmanship of the Sumter County school board in 1955. Eight years later, after an unsuccessful initial effort, he was elected governor of Georgia. Among the new southern governors, he at-

tracted attention by emphasizing ecology, efficiency in government, and racial integration in all areas.

Carter's decision to run for president occurred during his gubernatorial term. One clear September morning in 1973 Governor Carter stopped by to visit his mother, who was resting in her bedroom. Carter pulled up a chair and propped up his feet on the foot of her bed. When his mother inquired as to his plans after leaving the governor's office, he replied: "I'm going to run for president." "President of what?" his mother asked, and Carter replied: "Mama, I'm going to run for president of the United States, and I'm going to win." Mrs. Carter then told him to get his feet off the bed.

Carter announced his candidacy for president in December, 1974, and began a strenuous two-year campaign that gained momentum as it went along. At the Democratic convention he was nominated on the first ballot and chose Senator Walter F. Mondale as his running mate. Carter campaigned hard against President Ford, debating him three times, and won by 297 electoral votes to 241 for Ford.

As president, Carter worked diligently to combat the issues of inflation and unemployment, and by the end of his administration he could proudly point to a decrease in the budget's deficit and an increase of nearly eight million jobs. However, inflation and interest rates remained at record highs, and the Carter administration's efforts to reduce them caused a brief but severe recession.

Carter scored a number of domestic achievements, particularly in the area of the energy shortage, by estab-

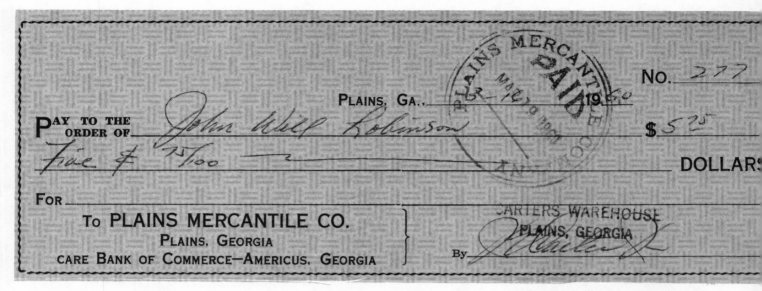

Early bank check completed and signed by Carter with his uncommon early signature: "J.E. Carter, Jr."

lishing a national energy policy and by decontrolling domestic petroleum prices to stimulate production. He promoted government efficiency through civil service reform and deregulated the trucking and airline industries. At the same time he sought to improve the environment, and he greatly expanded the national park system by including 103 million acres of Alaskan lands. He created the Department of Education in order to expand human and social services and he bolstered the sagging social security system.

His civil rights credentials were impeccable and he appointed record numbers of blacks, particularly black women, to federal positions. As early as 1965, as a deacon in the Plains Baptist Church, he had passionately but unsuccessfully argued that blacks be allowed to attend the church. The Reverend Martin Luther King, Sr. said of him: "I see a sincere man. Carter loves people, and that means all people. I know the man's heart and his intent."

Carter set his own style in foreign affairs by championing human rights, a policy coldly received by the Soviet Union and several other countries. He nevertheless made a significant contribution toward peace in the Middle East with his Camp David Accords between Israel and Egypt, and he was able to obtain ratification of the Panama Canal treaties. He also established full diplomatic relations with the People's Republic of China and completed the negotiation of the Salt II Nuclear Limitation Treaty with the Soviet Union.

There were, however, serious setbacks for Carter which evaporated his base of support. The major crisis was the seizure and taking as hostages of the entire staff of the U.S. embassy in Iran. The hostage crisis dominated the last fourteen months of Carter's administration and contributed heavily to his defeat in 1980. Even after his defeat, Carter continued the difficult hostage negotiations, which eventually resulted in Iran's releasing the fifty-two Americans still held captive when he left office.

Carter is a "born-again" Christian whose personal integrity is beyond reproach. His active retirement includes participating in the building of homes for the underprivileged. Although he left office an unpopular man, he is steadily gaining stature as a respected elder statesman. He was only fifty-six years old when he left office.

Jimmy Carter's penmanship is an attractive semi-cursive script in which many of the individual letters are disconnected, almost giving it the appearance of printing. Because his handwriting and signature are semi-cursive, or "semi-printed," they are perhaps the easiest to copy or forge of any president, which makes Carter material a nightmare for autograph collectors and dealers. Additionally, Carter signs many letters, even to strangers, with only his familiar first name "Jimmy." Unfortunately, his first name is the easiest part of his signature to duplicate secretarially as well as the most difficult part to authenticate, particularly when standing alone. To make matters even more difficult, Carter has had a number of secretaries who could skillfully imitate his signature, particularly Susan Clough, whose own handwriting is quite similar to Carter's.

At different times during his career Carter has varied his signature. During his military career and while running the family peanut operation he signed "J.E. Carter, Jr." Cancelled bank checks from this period are sometimes offered and are quite desirable both because personal presidential bank checks are scarce and because they contain this uncommon form of Carter's signature. During his political career he signed his name as "Jimmy Carter." On occasion, particularly post-presidentially as well as in-person, he has written his name "J. Carter," always connecting the "J" to the "C" of "Carter."

Although Carter, too, is rare in A.Ls.S., he and Reagan are not as rare as the other modern presidents in this form. Carter has a penchant for writing brief holographic A.Ls.S., technically memoranda, which are obtainable from most periods of his career, especially during the period when he first sought the presidency. An idiosyncracy of Carter's A.Ls.S. is his frequent use of the word "To" instead of the more usual salutation, as in "To Billy" rather than "Dear Billy." He frequently also deletes the complimentary closing before his signature, giving his letters the appearance of A.Ds.S.

In terms of content, Carter is a good letter writer, not afraid to state his position or opinion on major issues. His letters tend to be rather familiar and often intimate-sounding. Although he is quite capable of writing formal letters, informality seems to be his style.

Because of the relative ease with which Carter's plain, semi-cursive script and signature can be copied, and because of his extensive use of secretaries and autopens during his entire political and post-presidential career, all Carter material should be regarded with great caution.

JIMMY CARTER

September 11, 1981

To Charlie Brooks

Rosalynn and I enjoyed our visit to Yellowstone, and appreciate all that you did to make our trip a pleasure. We look forward to returning.

With best wishes,

Sincerely,

Jimmy Carter

Mr. Charlie Brooks
Star Route, Box 12
West Yellowstone, Montana 59758

The Grebe Lake trip was great, & we're so glad you're doing so well. Thanks again! Our love to Grace. — J

In-person post-presidential Carter signature, signed "J. Carter."

Post presidential Carter Typed Letter Signed with scarce holographic postscript signed with his first initial.

40. RONALD REAGAN

February 6, 1911 -

Fortieth President
January 20, 1981 - January 20, 1989

Republican

Highlights in office:
Economic reform;
air controllers' strike;
tax cut; rebuilding defenses.

Ronald Reagan was one of the most popular and charismatic of all our presidents and holds the rare and virtually unique honor among them of leaving office more popular than when elected. He also holds the distinction of being the oldest man ever elected president. He turned seventy a few days after becoming president and was almost seventy-eight when he left office.

Ronald Wilson Reagan was born in Tampico, Illinois, on February 6, 1911. His father, John Reagan, was a shoe salesman who drank too much and who was not always employed. At seventeen Reagan won a partial scholarship to Eureka College, a small college near Peoria, Illinois, and graduated in 1932 at the height of the great depression when jobs were scarce. Out of gratitude to FDR for the New Deal welfare efforts, Reagan became a Democrat and remained a Democrat until the early 1960's.

Reagan eventually landed a job as a radio sports announcer. In 1937 he took a screen test which won him a Hollywood contract, and over the next two decades he appeared in fifty-three films. In 1940 he married Sarah Jane Fulks, the actress Jane Wyman. They had two children but were divorced in 1948. In 1952 he married Nancy Davis, also an actress, and by her also had two children.

As president of the Screen Actor's Guild, Reagan acquired hard political experience, shifting his personal political views from liberal to conservative during the battles that raged over the issue of communism within the film industry.

When Ronald Reagan reached his forties and became too old to play romantic leads, he had the great good sense to seek other employment and turned naturally to politics. He had become widely known to the public through radio, television, public relations appearances, and television reruns of his old films, and he could expound party lines with force and clarity.

In 1966 the popular, articulate and experienced governor of California, Democrat Pat Brown, was challenged by Republican gubernatorial nominee Ronald Reagan. Brown made the mistake of treating Reagan's candidacy as a joke, regarding Reagan as a middle-aged, washed-up, B-movie actor who had no governmental or political expertise and who merely parroted lines written for him by others. Reagan did in fact run an uneven campaign and exhibited naivete and ignorance in some areas. His simplistic platform entailed a reduction in government spending and the glorification of private enterprise. However, to the abject horror of liberals throughout the land, Reagan won and was even reelected in 1970 to a second four-year term. He was henceforth a popular figure in California and left office more popular than when he was elected.

After unsuccessful attempts in 1968 and 1976, Reagan won the Republican presidential nomination in 1980, choosing former Texas congressman and U.N. Ambassador George Bush as his vice-presidential running mate. In a backlash vote against the Carter administration, inflation and the hostage crisis, Reagan soundly defeated Carter with 489 electoral votes to only 49 for Carter.

Jan. 18.

Dear Miss Onyx

I enjoyed reading your story very much but as I feared, it contains so much of the general flavor of the one we did (The Iron Silence) that I couldn't get it past the rest of our people. This plus the fact that any story would have to replace something already in the mill as we have purchased our full quota for the year.

You certainly do have an area heretofore un-tapped by TV as a series idea and this together with the possibility of European production should increase the potential interest. As I told you I'm prejudiced in favor of the "pilot" selling method. In that regard I wonder if you shouldn't develope one "beginning" story where you set the stage — introduce your characters etc. "The Wolf & The Lamb" is more of a story to take place after a series is under way. We did the original show on T.S. that

Interesting entertainment content Reagan pre-gubernatorial content Autograph Letter Signed, circa 1960.

became "Bachelor Father". In our single story we used the very beginning incident in which our "Bachelor" was handed a "teen age ward" — the series took off from there.

Again my thanks to you & I certainly wish you all the best —

Sincerely

Ronald Reagan

Verso of Reagan Autograph Letter Signed, circa 1960.

Reagan's inaugural address pledged to restore "the great confident roar of American progress and growth and optimism." Two months after taking office, however, Reagan was shot in an assassination attempt. Fortunately, he quickly recovered and resumed his presidential duties.

Reagan was quite skillful in his dealings with Congress, and quickly obtained the passage of legislation intended to stimulate economic growth, increase employment, and strengthen the national defense.

When Reagan ran for reelection in 1984 there had been a strong business recovery, unemployment had decreased, and there was generally more confidence in the nation. Consequently, Reagan defeated the Democratic Mondale-Ferraro ticket with a record number of electoral votes.

In Reagan's second term he continued to seek reductions in the cost of government, and in 1986 he obtained the passage of a massive overhaul of the income tax laws.

Reagan achieved improved relations with the Soviet Union and had two summit meetings with the new Soviet leader, Mikhail Gorbachev. In other areas Reagan began significant multinational trade negotiations and joined the European democracies in taking strong action against terrorism.

Although the Iran-Contra scandal cast a pall over the last two years of his administration, Reagan's personal popularity remained high.

Happily for collectors, Reagan is the sole exception among presidents in the last seventy-five years in that, while not common, he is at least obtainable in A.Ls.S. He wrote quite a number of handwritten letters between his terms as governor of California and his presidential election. Also, as governor he handwrote drafts of letters which he gave to his secretary to type. His secretary wisely retained his drafts, many of which he signed "Ron" or "R.R." In recent years, many of these drafts, which are technically A.Ls.S., have come on the market. They are normally written on plain 8vo paper and usually have a

Authentically signed Reagan presidential Typed Letter Signed with patriotic content written from the California White House.

diagonal line through the text, probably indicating they had been typed. Many of these drafts have excellent content and are more desirable than the typed letters Reagan actually sent out because they are, of course, entirely in Reagan's handwriting. The Reagan A.L.S. drafts normally have very good content, as they are invariably written to important or influential people, close personal friends, or concern important questions or statements of position. For example, a Reagan draft A.L.S acquired by the authors concerns Reagan's first abortive effort to capture the Republican presidential nomination in 1968.

Reagan writes a very legible, backward-slanting hand which has changed very little throughout his adult life. His writing is so devoid of ornamentation and so copy-book legible that at first glance it appears almost to have been written by a child. Reagan carefully connects the individual letters in all words. One of the few peculiarities in Reagan's script is the way he forms capital "T's," making them look almost like the numeral nine. Reagan generally seems to prefer heavy-nibbed pens, and has a passion for felt-tipped pens.

Surprisingly, Reagan's early or vintage material from his Hollywood days is quite scarce, as most of it was signed by studio employees or secretaries, one of whom for a time was his mother. As with many of Reagan's movie contemporaries, much of his early movie material is signed with green ink. Although Reagan personally signed his fan mail, most of his other movie material, including fan-club cards, is secretarial. Happily, even though Reagan's signature is one of the easiest to imitate, most of his secretaries were rather inept and their forgeries can be spotted fairly easily by the trained eye.

As with our other modern presidents since Eisenhower, almost all of Reagan's material during his political career is autopen or secretarial. In Reagan's particular case his material seems to have been signed primarily by autopens. Numerous autopen patterns from his presidency have been identified, and in all likelihood more will be identified. Although at this writing it is still too early to know with certainty about his post-presidential material, it should be assumed that he will continue using autopens to aid in answering his heavy volume of mail.

In terms of content Reagan is one of the few modern presidents to be an excellent letter writer. His letters are direct and candid, and he appears willing to state his views quite frankly and honestly. His letters are unfailingly polite and exude his innate good will and friendliness. We have never seen an angry or unkind Reagan letter.

After Reagan became president and before he became bogged down by the cares and burdens of the presidency, he made great efforts to accommodate autograph collectors with personally signed and inscribed photographs and other items. For a short period of time, courteous letters from serious collectors were rewarded with genuinely signed Reagan White House cards which, although not great in numbers, are at least obtainable, unlike those of most of the other presidents after Eisenhower.

Autograph Letter Signed referring to Reagan's first abortive attempt to capture the presidential nomination. This is a handwritten draft from which Reagan's secretary typed a letter and is, technically, and Autograph Letter Signed.

41. GEORGE HERBERT WALKER BUSH

June 12, 1924 -

Forty-first President
January 20, 1988 -

Republican

Highlights in Office:
U.S. Invasion of Panama

George Herbert Walker Bush was born at Milton, Massachusetts, on June 12, 1924, the second son of Prescott Sheldon Bush, who was a Republican U.S. senator from Connecticut (1952-63). He attended Phillips Academy in Andover, Massachusetts, and Yale University from which he received a bachelor's degree in economics in 1948. He served in World War II as a naval carrier pilot and was awarded the Distinguished Flying Cross. After the war he moved to Texas and engaged successfully in the oil business.

In 1964 he received the Republican nomination for the U.S. Senate but was handily defeated by the well-respected Texas veteran Senator Ralph W. Yarborough. In 1966 Bush was elected to the U.S. House of Representatives from Houston on the Republican ticket and was reelected to that office in 1968. In 1970 he was again an unsuccessful candidate for the U.S. Senate, defeated by Lloyd Bentsen who was to become the unsuccessful Democratic vice-presidential nominee on the Dukakis-Bentsen ticket in 1988.

In 1970 President Nixon appointed Bush as ambassador to the United Nations, in which capacity he served until 1973.

In 1973-74 Bush served as chairman of the Republican National Committee; from 1974-76 he served as chief of the important U.S. liaison office in Peking, and from 1976-77 he served as director of the controversial and trouble-ridden Central Intelligence Agency under President Ford.

In 1980 and again in 1984, Ronald Reagan chose Bush to be his vice-presidential running mate. The Reagan-Bush tickets handily defeated their Democratic op-

ponents in both presidential elections. Bush was one of the most highly visible vice presidents in our history, using the office as a springboard to the presidency in 1988, winning by a wide margin of both the popular and electoral votes.

At present it is far too early to make any assessment of the Bush administration. His presidency got off to a floundering start by his unfortunate nomination of John Tower of Texas as his secretary of defense. Tower ran into trouble on Capitol Hill almost from the start, and Bush's dogged support and defense of Tower in the lengthy confirmation fight probably impaired, at least temporarily, his effectiveness with Congress. One Texan wryly observed after the Tower fiasco that "it is doubtful that Bush could now pass a dose of salts through the Congress." This, of course, remains to be seen, and the Bush administration record is still tabula rasa.

With respect to Bush's autographic material, it would

Thanks for your
letter — George Bush

GEORGE BUSH

710 NORTH POST OAK ROAD
SUITE 208
HOUSTON, TEXAS 77024   713/467-1980

Autograph Note Signed by George Bush on his
pre-presidential business card, circa 1978.

appear that, like his immediate predecessors, he has availed himself of secretaries and autopens during his entire public career, including his vice presidency and presidency. Although it is still too early to identify his presidential autopens, collectors should assume that all Bush material, especially presidential, is autopen unless proven otherwise. He is currently using facsimile signature cards in response to collectors' requests.

Paradoxically, as vice president, Bush seems to have taken pains to personally respond to serious collector requests, often replying with brief A.Ls.S. on his vice presidential correspondence cards. Although much additional study is needed on Bush material, it would appear that he will not be as scarce in authentic material, particularly A.Ls.S., as are some of his predecessors.

We have yet to see a fine-content Bush letter, although some are certain to exist.

Bush's handwriting is semi-cursive and could pass for an illegible version of Jimmy Carter's. His signature is perhaps the most illegible of any president except John F. Kennedy but, unlike Kennedy's, the appearance of Bush's signature is consistent.

Bush writes his signature simply as "George Bush" or as "George" to intimates. Along with James A. Garfield, Harry S. Truman, and Gerald R. Ford, Bush is left handed. Full signatures are rare.

The Vice President
of the United States of America

Dear David —
Glad to sign it!
sincerely, Geo Bush

Embossed vice presidential correspondence card with Bush Autograph Note Signed.

The President
of the United States of America

Geo Bush

Presidential correspondence card introduced by Bush and signed with an autopen signature.

APPENDIX A

Recommended Reading List

Benjamin, Mary A. *Autographs: A Key to Collecting.* 1963.

Cahoon, Herbert; Lange, Thomas V.; and Ryskamp, Charles. *American Literary Autographs from Washington Irving to Henry James. 1977.*

Hamilton, Charles. *American Autographs.* Vol II: *Presidents. 1983.*

_____. *American Autographs; Signers of the Declaration of Independence, Revolutionary War Leaders, & Presidents. 1983.*

_____. *Auction Madness. 1981.*

_____. *Autographs of the Third Reich. 1982.*

_____. *Big Name Hunting: A Beginner's Guide to Autograph Collecting. 1973.*

_____. *The Book of Autographs. 1978.*

_____. *Collecting Autographs and Manuscripts. , 1961.*

_____. *Great Forgers and Famous Fakes. 1980.*

_____. *The Illustrated Letter. 1987.*

_____. *In Search of Shakespeare, A Reconnaissance into the Poet's Life and Handwriting. 1985*

_____. *The Robot That Helped to Make a President: A Reconnaissance into the Mysteries of John F. Kennedy's Signature.1965.*

_____. *Scribblers and Scoundrels. 1968.*

_____. *The Signature of America. 1979.*

Madigan, Thomas F. *Word Shadows of the Great. 1930.*

Manuscript Society. *Autographs and Manuscripts: A Collector's Manual. 1978.*

_____. *Manuscripts: The First Twenty Years. 1984.*

Muns, J.B. *Musical Autographs, A Comparative Guide. 1989.*

Rawlins, Ray. *Four Hundred Years of British Autographs. 1970.*

_____. *The Stein and Day Book of World Autographs. 1978.*

Reese, Michael II. *Autographs of the Confederacy. 1981.*

Sanders, George; Sanders, Helen; and Roberts, Ralph. *The Price Guide to Autographs. 1988.*

Searle, Charles and Searle, Pat. *From the Inkwells of Hollywood* (3vols)., 1989.

Seale, William. *The President's House: A History.* Vols. I & II. 1986.

Stern, Edward. Supplement to the History of the "Free Franking" of Mail in the United States: *Franking Privileges of the Presidents' Widows. 1944.*

Taylor, John M. *From the White House Inkwell. 1968.*

APPENDIX B

Pricing Guide

The following retail prices for various forms of presidential autographs are broad approximations based on the authors' knowledge and experience, as well as on their consultation of the catalogs of most major auction houses and dealers. The reader should be aware, however, that all autographs are unique, and that the price of an item may be drastically more or less as affected by factors such as content and condition. In general, the most valuable form of a president's autographic material is that which was written or signed while he held the presidential office.

	Signature Only	Ls.S. or Ds.s.	A.Ls.s.	Signed Photograph
Washington, George	3,000	12,500	15,000	
Adams, John	1,250	1,950	6,500	
Jefferson, Thomas	1,750	5,000	7,500	
Madison, James	395	1,250	3,000	
Monroe, James	350	650	3,000	
Adams, John Quincy	295	595	1,250	3,500 (engraving)
Jackson, Andrew	395	1,000	3,500	
Van Buren, Martin	295	595	1,000	6,500
Harrison, Wm. H.	495	750	2,500	
Tyler, John	295	495	1,250	
Polk, James K.	595	1,250	3,500	
Taylor, Zachary	650	1,350	5,000	
Fillmore, Millard	195	495	795	7,000
Pierce, Franklin	250	650	1,250	5,000
Buchanan, James	275	595	1,250	5,000
Lincoln, Abraham	2,250	3,000	5,000	10,000
Johnson, Andrew	350	750	6,000	5,000
Grant, Ulysses S.	250	595	1,500	2,000
Hayes, R.B.	175	495	1,200	3,000
Garfield, James A.	195	595	795	2,500
Arthur, Chester A.	295	795	1,500	3,500
Cleveland, Grover	195	395	195	595
Harrison, Benjamin	250	495	1,250	2,500
McKinley, William	295	450	1,250	1,500
Roosevelt, Theodore	250	450	1,250	850
Taft, Wm. Howard	175	295	1,000	450

	Signature Only	Ls.S. or Ds.s.	A.Ls.s.	Signed Photograph
Wilson, Woodrow	250	450	2,500	650
Harding, Warren G.	195	395	2,500	475
Coolidge, Calvin	175	350	2,000	450
Hoover, Herbert	75	175	4,000	450
Roosevelt, F.D.	295	395	2,500	750
Truman, Harry S.	150	395	4,000	350
Eisenhower, D.D.	250	395	5,000	450
Kennedy, John F.	900	1,250	7,500	2,500
Johnson, Lyndon B.	350	595	10,000	750
Nixon, Richard M.	150	295	7,000	250
Ford, Gerald R.	95	195	2,500	195
Carter, Jimmy	95	275	1,500	195
Reagan, Ronald	175	250	1,750	275
Bush, George	250	350	3,500	295

APPENDIX C

Recommended Collector Organizations and Publications

The Manuscript Society
David R. Smith, Executive Director
350 N. Niagara St.
Burbank, California 91505

An international society founded in 1948 whose members include dealers, private collectors, scholars, authors, librarians, archivists, and curators. The Society publishes a quarterly journal, *Manuscripts*, and a newsletter. *Manuscripts* has an established reputation for excellent articles reflecting the diverse interests within the autograph field.

The Autograph Collector's Magazine
Joe Kraus, Editor
P.O. Box 55328
Stockton, California 95205-8828
(202) 473-0570

This is a general-interest autograph publication that covers everything from historical documents and letters to sports and entertainment. *The Autograph Collector's Magazine* announces the major autograph auctions and trade shows throughout the world. It includes news and feature articles on various aspects of the hobby, and also advertising from all the major dealers. Currently published eight times each year, plans are to go to ten issues annually starting in January, 1991. *The Autograph Collector's Magazine* has approximately five thousand subscribers in all fifty states and about forty foreign countries.

Universal Autograph Collector's Club
Bob Erickson, President
1313 Vermont Ave. N.W. #14
Washington, D.C. 20005

The U.A.C.C. was founded in 1965 and has two thousand members in over thirty countries. Collectors of all ages and interests are members. The U.A.C.C. publishes a bimonthly journal, *The Pen And Quill*, which is sent to all members. The journal contains articles in many collecting areas.

APPENDIX D

LYNDON B. JOHNSON:

THE SURPRISING MODERN PRESIDENTIAL "BUTTON GWINETT"*

Lyndon Baines Johnson (1908-1973), 36th president of the United States (1963-1969), may be the "Button Gwinnett" of American presidents for autographic material in general, and is without question in certain forms such as autograph letters signed (A.Ls.S.), of which only a handful are known to exist.

Johnson, who was one of the most brilliant, complex, paradoxical, enigmatic and colorful men ever to occupy the White House, was also one of our hardest-working presidents—possibly *the* hardest working. His grueling schedule put the hard-working James K. Polk to shame. Polk at least required a normal amount of sleep, while Johnson never seemed to rest and averaged only three to four hours of sleep at night. Johnson was also infamous for his early hours telephone calls—he once awakened a powerful and crusty congressman at 3:00 A.M. to discuss a piece of pending legislation. When the sleepy congressman came on the line, Johnson asked him: "Were you asleep?" The congressman, obviously a quick thinker, replied: "No, Mr. President, I was just lying here hoping you'd call!" Johnson was, without question, a legislative genius, widely known among congressmen and senators for the now legendary "Johnson treatment."

Johnson was nothing if not vain. A friend of his once remarked that it required a very large ego for anyone to aspire to the presidency, but that "Lyndon was double dipped!" And so he was. It has been said with some truth that Johnson "wanted to be the bride at every wedding and the corpse at every funeral." He could never be described as dull, colorless, or uninteresting.

The pragmatic Johnson seems to have made the decision early in his career that personally signing or handwriting letters was a waste of time, and he delegated this task to others. Wasting time was the unforgivable sin to Johnson.

His public career spanned thirty-seven years, and it was mistakenly assumed until very recently that his autographic material was common in all forms. It has now become apparent to most dealers and other experts that Lyndon Johnson personally signed relatively little throughout his long public career.

There are only two of his A.Ls.S. in the Lyndon Baines Johnson Library, and these were written to his grandmother and mother during his college and school teaching days. There is also allegedly a cache of holographic love letters he wrote to Mrs. Johnson which are sealed until after her death and which will not, of course, ever come on the market. We are aware of only three presidential A.Ls.S., one of which is signed with his initials on an oblong octavo correspondence card sent to a secretary wishing her a speedy recovery. Strangely, Johnson may be rarer in presidential date A.Ls.S. than even William Henry Harrison, who served but a month and of whose presidential letters only five are known! There are several other presidents who are equally rare in presidential-date A.Ls.S.: Andrew Johnson of whom no such example is known to the authors, and both Hoover and Eisenhower but, unlike Lyndon Johnson, these presidents are common in other forms of material from non-presidential periods. Although they are rare in A.Ls.S. of non-presidential date, they are, unlike Johnson, at least obtainable.

Inscriptions on photographs and in books represent virtually the only obtainable authentic examples of Johnson's script—and almost all of these, with few exceptions which will be discussed, were secretarially or

---

* Button Gwinett (1735-1777) was a signer of the Declaration of Independence who died at age forty-two from complications of a wound received in a duel, only ten months after signing the Declaration of Independence . Because of his obscurity and early death, very little of his autographic material exists and he is the scarcest and most expensive of all the signers. His rare signature alone is worth approximately $150,000.

autopen signed.

Johnson is extremely rare for all periods in authentically signed letters. The relatively few which do exist were usually signed either "Lyndon" or "LBJ." Letters of any date which are authentically signed with his full signature are rare and virtually impossible to obtain, particularly from the presidential period when almost all were signed by autopens or secretaries. Authentically signed letters from his vice-presidential period are even scarcer, if possible, than those of presidential date. Even his vice-presidential oath of office is reputed to have been signed with an autopen!

After leaving office Johnson personally signed few letters but, paradoxically, to the knowledge of the authors, he authentically signed those few, usually with his initials. Virtually the only source of authentic full Johnson signatures are the bookplates for his memoirs. The authors have, however, seen several bookplates signed with his initials. As Johnson lived slightly less than four years after leaving office, his post-presidential material is also rare. At least one reason why most of Johnson's post-presidential material is signed only with his initials is because his health and heart condition had deteriorated so rapidly after leaving office that signing with his initials conserved both energy and time.

Johnson wrote an angular, legible and attractive hand which changed little throughout his adult life, although the size of both his handwriting and signature diminished in size over time. His signature became more illegible with ill-defined letters, particularly of presidential date, with the "nson" of Johnson represented merely by a short, straight, upwardly slanting line. The appearance of Johnson's signature was once compared, with some truth, to an electrocardiogram! A hallmark of authenticity of Johnson's signature from the beginning of his senatorial career (1948) is the presence of a period after his middle initial, which was normally placed far below the "B" and to the left of the lower loop of the "J" in Johnson. However, the period sometimes appears on the right side of the lower loop or on another letter, making its detection difficult. The period seems to always be present in authentic Johnson signatures from and after approximately 1948. There is an exception even to this cardinal rule: Johnson sometimes deleted the "magic period" from carefully written presentation signatures. We have seen senatorial-date signatures, sans period, following unquestionably authentic inscriptions in books. However, even without the period, these signatures are distinguishable from secretarial examples from the same time frame.

Interestingly, the period does not always appear in his early signatures, being absent more often than not. The period is absent in most of his secretarial signatures, although some of his better imitators, notably Bruce Thomas, became savvy to the presence of the "magic period" and started adding it. Their placement of the period, however, was neither as low nor as erratic as on authentic signatures.

Lyndon Johnson enjoyed autographing photographs of himself, particularly while the intended recipient was still in his office. He also liked having his photograph taken, and his presidential administration is one of the most photographically complete of all presidents. The authors were told by a former high official who was frequently at political odds with Johnson that when he was in a group photograph with Johnson, who was considerably taller than the official, Johnson would suddenly and deliberately "point" to something across the room at the moment the photograph was taken, with the intended effect of covering the official's face with his arm or hand in the photograph. The former official said that for the aforementioned reason his face was always covered in newspaper photographs with Johnson!

Many people who had presidential appointments with Johnson were photographed with him and later received handsome, large, calligraphically inscribed photographs. The signatures on these photographs should be regarded with suspicion until more of Johnson's presidential autopen examples are known. Presidential-date photographs of Johnson which are personally inscribed and signed by him are extremely desirable and rare, with only two such examples having ever crossed our desk. Johnson never dated signed photographs and their approximate date must be determined independently by cover letters or the photograph itself. Many of Johnson's presidential photographs are self-identifying as they were taken in the oval office or have other identifiable White House landmarks in them. As with all modern presidents, routine photograph requests were filled by the Johnson White House with secretarial or autopen-signed photographs, many of which came with cover letters from aides stating the photographs were signed by the president.

Johnson wrote several books, including *My Hope for America* (1964), *This America* (1966), *A More Beautiful America* (1964), *No Retreat From Tomorrow: President Lyndon B. Johnson's Message to the 90th Congress* (1967), *To Heal and To Build, The Programs of President Lyndon B. Johnson* edited by James MacGregor Burns (1968), and his 1971 memoirs, *The Vantage Point: Perspectives of the Presidency (1963-1969)*. In 1965 Johnson also wrote the foreword to a charming small book written about his ancestors by his mother, Rebekah Baines Johnson, appropriately entitled *A Family Album*, which he had published after becoming president. With the possible exception of his mother's book and his memoirs, which were an apologia of his administration, all his books were probably written primarily for political reasons and were distributed, with secretarial or autopen inscriptions, in large numbers by both the White House and the Democratic National Committee. We have not seen any authentically signed copies of his first four books, and have seen only a few authentically signed copies of *A Family Album*. Although by no means common, Johnson is obtainable in signed copies of certain laudatory biographies of himself, including *The Professional: Lyndon B. Johnson* by William S. White (1964) which had at least five printings. This book, widely distributed during Johnson's 1964 presidential reelection campaign by the Democratic National Committee and the White House, bore an autopen inscription of a secretarially written and signed sentiment: "With best wishes, Lyndon B. Johnson" (see illustration on page 150.). We have personally seen only one authentically signed copy of this book, and even it was post-presidentially signed. Other favored biographies, copies of which Johnson sometimes signed, are *The Lyndon Johnson Story* by Booth Mooney (1956), and *Lyndon Baines Johnson: The Formative Years* by Pool, Craddock, and Conrad (1965).

Those books which Johnson did authentically sign for an individual were either both inscribed and signed, or signed only. Johnson seems never to have dated either books or photographs, making presidentially signed material difficult to document.

During his presidency, Johnson used a handsome bookplate which had the presidential seal and "Lyndon Baines Johnson, President of the United States of America" embossed in gold. Almost all of these presidential bookplates were calligraphically inscribed and autopen or secretarially signed. We have personally seen only one such bookplate which, in our opinion, was authentically signed.

The only book by or about Johnson which commonly bears an authentic signature is his post-presidential memoirs, usually bearing one of his beautiful bookplates embossed in gold with the presidential seal and his initials (see illustration on page 162). Johnson signed these bookplates with full, bold, black-ink signatures which are virtually the only known source of Johnson's authentic full signature. However, we have seen bookplates in his memoirs with long inscriptions signed both in full and with initials. The few which are also dated seem to have been Christmas gifts, and some also bore Mrs. Johnson's signature. Such examples are very rare and desirable.

On occasion, Johnson even signed some of Mrs. Johnson's bookplates used in her memoirs, *A White House Diary* (1970). On these bookplates, Johnson usually signed with his initials beneath Mrs. Johnson's signature (see illustration on page 162). Very scarce and desirable, too, are copies of Johnson's memoirs inscribed and signed, or signed only, on a fly leaf of the book itself. After Johnson's memoirs were published he kept copies, which he had previously signed on the fly leaf, in his automobile, giving them to friends and admirers with whom he came in contact or who visited the ranch. We were fortunate to acquire the last few copies of his memoirs, all of which were signed on a blank end paper. At the time of his death they were found in his famous Lincoln convertible, the same car for which he received wide criticism during his presidency for driving at high rates of speed while drinking beer!

While president, Johnson had a limited number of his favorite books, by or about himself, bound in handsome and costly red or blue morocco with gold lettering. He gave these beautiful and rare volumes as gifts, usually unsigned, to foreign dignitaries as well as to both friends and foes. Two titles which he had bound in red morocco were *Formative Years* and *A Family Album*. His book *My Hope for America* was issued both in a handsome, blue-morocco edition with blue marbled end papers, and a boxed, red-morocco edition. Few authentically signed copies of any of these beautiful, morocco-covered books are known to exist or to have ever come on the market.

It is interesting and enlightening to note that Johnson even played politics with his books. The previously mentioned former high official, who served in Congress throughout Johnson's presidency and who had frequent adversarial dealings with him, told us an amusing story about Johnson's books while showing us approximately thirty books in his personal library, by or about Johnson, which Johnson had given him over the years. We noticed that there were as many as five copies of the same book, all inscribed to him and signed. When we inquired about the multiplicity of some of the same volumes, he explained that Johnson knew he was a book collector and that, any time Johnson had to refuse a request or they were at odds politically, Johnson would grab a copy of one of his books and write a lengthy, glowing, and intimate inscription to him in a effort to "assuage, massage, convert, or otherwise mollify" him. We also noticed that the signatures in some of the books were obviously autopen or secretarial. When questioned as to the provenance of these copies, he said that all of these had been mailed to him bearing either a solitary signature or inscribed "With best wishes, Lyndon B. Johnson," but none of these had been inscribed personally. In short, only those books personally inscribed and given to him in person were genuine, and none of these was dated.

Johnson loved giving gifts and among his favorites were the books by or about himself, or large, faux, bronze or marble busts of himself, a liberal supply of which he took to Texas when he left the White House. In 1967 when Johnson made his famous whirlwind trip around the world to, among the many stops, Viet Nam and Australia, shortly before Christmas he stopped at the Vatican on the return leg of the trip and presented an amazed and bewildered Pope Paul VI with a large faux-marble bust of himself! To the knowledge of the authors no one has ever seen LBJ's bust displayed in the Vatican, nor is the papal library known to contain any Johnson books, autographed or otherwise.

Much more research is needed on the autographic material of Lyndon B. Johnson, but indications are that Johnson will ultimately prove to be the scarcest of all presidents in most forms of authentic material, particularly from his presidential and vice-presidential periods. Although he is rare in authentically signed books and photographs, he is more obtainable in these forms than in letters. He is more common in books signed before and after his presidency, and in autographed pre-presidential photographs, but he is rare in post-presidentially signed photographs. The authors personally know of only one White House card which bears an unquestionably authentic signature (see illustration on page 158). The brief presidential notes, often earthy and witty, which Johnson wrote to aides either on the bottoms of their memoranda to him or on plain note paper, were normally written in pencil and unsigned except, occasionally, with the single initial "L." Even these brief holographic notes, virtually the only substitutes for a Johnson A.L.S., are virtually unobtainable and command extremely high prices.

A major difficulty for historians and collectors is that even if more of Johnson's material, particularly letters, is authentic than now appears to be the case, in most cases it is impossible to authenticate, particularly for the presidential period, until more autopen patterns and secretaries are identified. Holographic postscripts on letters which he sometimes wrote remain the safest way to authenticate his letters.

With few exceptions, all autographic material purportedly signed by Lyndon B. Johnson should be regarded as not being genuine until proven otherwise. More study is needed.

Pre-presidential (secretarial)

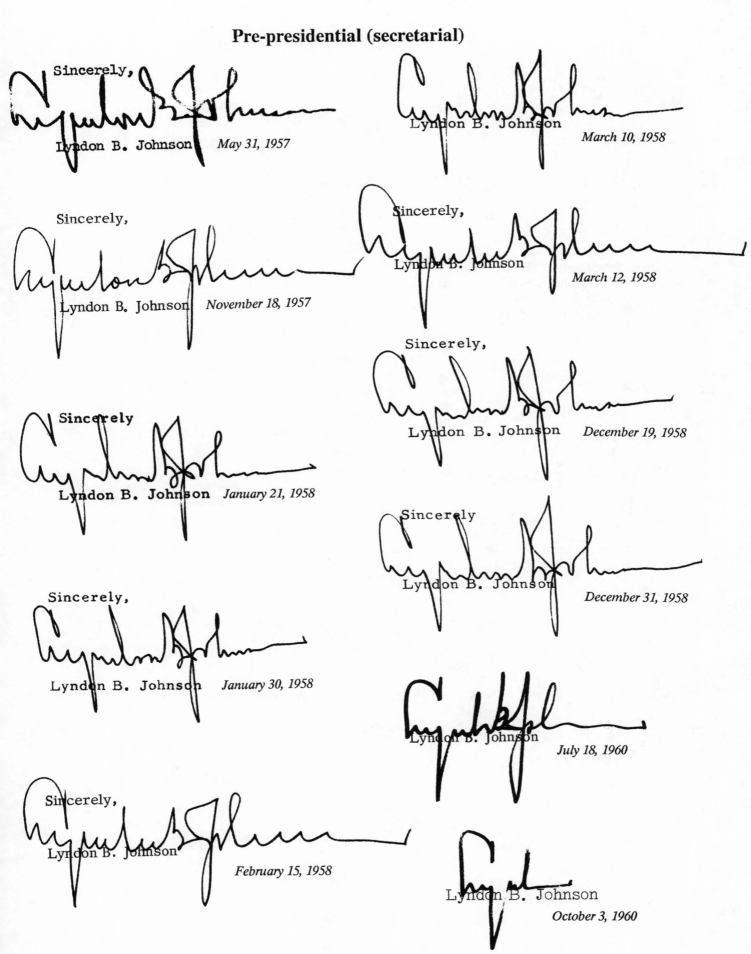

Sincerely,

Lyndon B. Johnson   *May 31, 1957*

Lyndon B. Johnson   *March 10, 1958*

Sincerely,

Lyndon B. Johnson   *November 18, 1957*

Sincerely,

Lyndon B. Johnson   *March 12, 1958*

Sincerely

Lyndon B. Johnson   *January 21, 1958*

Sincerely,

Lyndon B. Johnson   *December 19, 1958*

Sincerely,

Lyndon B. Johnson   *January 30, 1958*

Sincerely

Lyndon B. Johnson   *December 31, 1958*

Lyndon B. Johnson   *July 18, 1960*

Sincerely,

Lyndon B. Johnson   *February 15, 1958*

Lyndon B. Johnson   *October 3, 1960*

Presidential (autopen/secretarial)

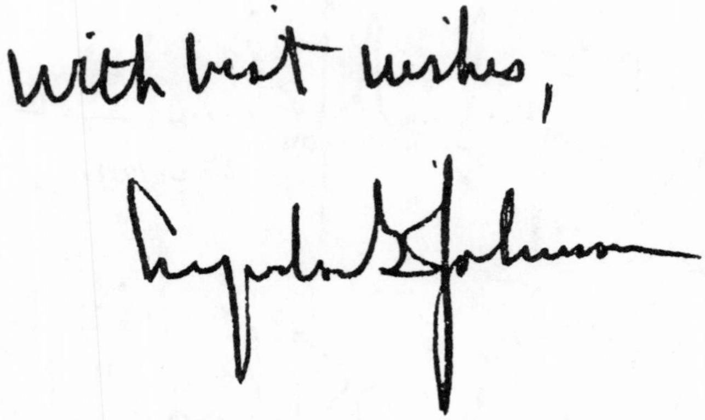

With best wishes,

Lyndon B. Johnson

Autopen inscription and signature of a secretarial inscription and signature by Bruce Thomas. This autopenned inscription appeared in thousands of copies of The Professional.

THE WHITE HOUSE
WASHINGTON

Lady Bird and

Lyndon B. Johnson

THE WHITE HOUSE
WASHINGTON

Lyndon B. Johnson

Secretarial signature on a White House card, written by Bruce Thomas.

Lady Bird and

Lyndon B. Johnson

Secretarial signatures on White House cards written by Bruce Thomas. Interestingly, the signatures of Mrs. Johnson are autopens.

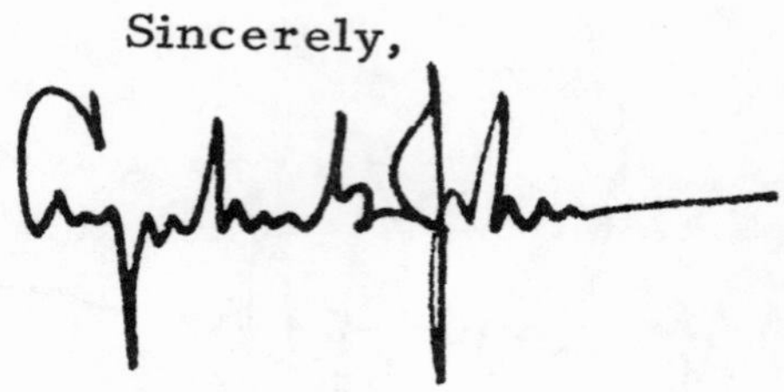

THE WHITE HOUSE
WASHINGTON

with best wishes —

Lyndon B. Johnson

Secretarial inscription and signature on White House card signed by Bruce Thomas.

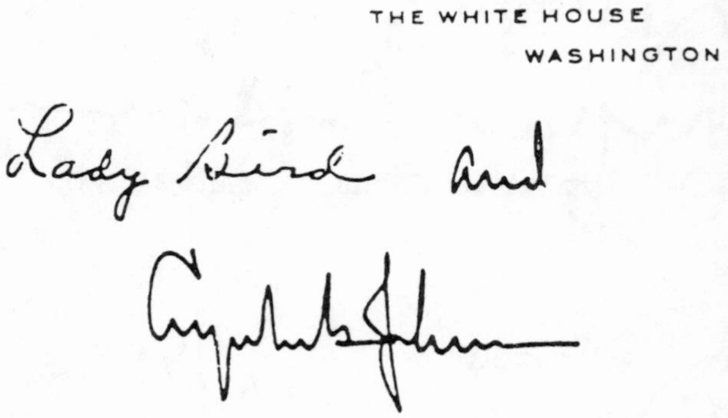

Sincerely,

Lyndon B. Johnson

Secretarial signature on a presidential letter, signed by Bruce Thomas, 1966.

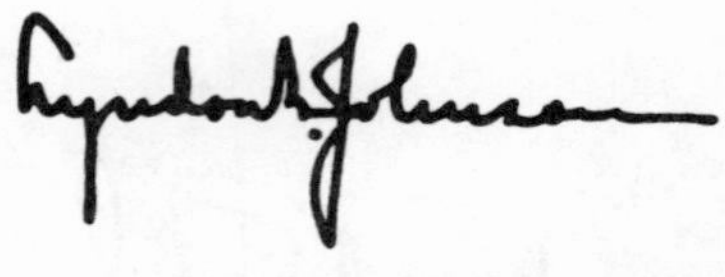

Lyndon B. Johnson

Fascimile signature on an engraved Christmas greeting, 1966.

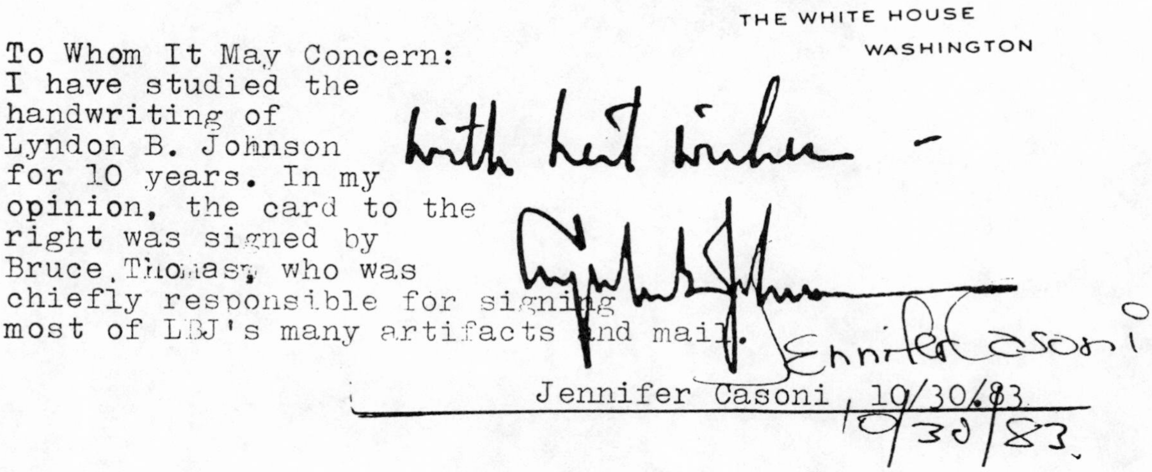

To Whom It May Concern:
I have studied the
handwriting of
Lyndon B. Johnson
for 10 years. In my
opinion, the card to the
right was signed by
Bruce Thomas, who was
chiefly responsible for signing
most of LBJ's many artifacts and mail.

THE WHITE HOUSE
WASHINGTON

with best wishes —

Jennifer Casoni, 10/30/83

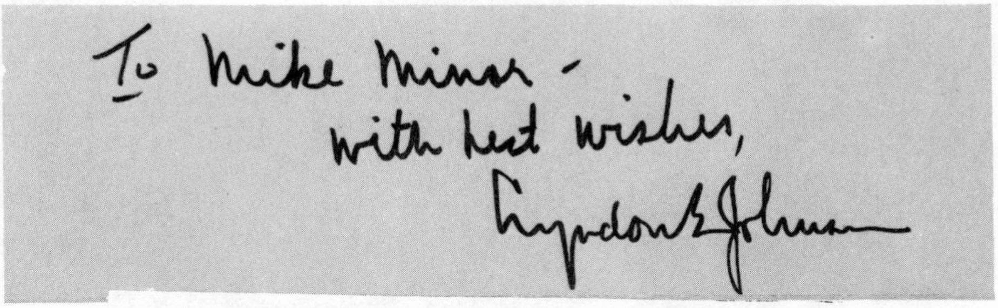

To Mike Minor —
with best wishes,
Lyndon B. Johnson

Secretarial inscription and signature on a presidential photograph (1965). Ironically, the secretary iminated Johnson's handwriting better than his signature.

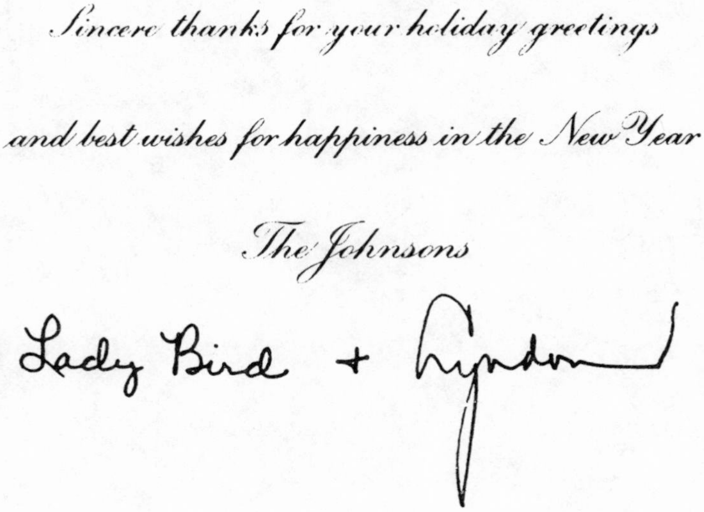

Sincere thanks for your holiday greetings

and best wishes for happiness in the New Year

The Johnsons

Lady Bird + Lyndon

Secretarial signatures of President and Mrs. Johnson on a Christmas greeting.

Early authentically inscribed and signed photograph, 1946.

Pre-presidential (authentic)

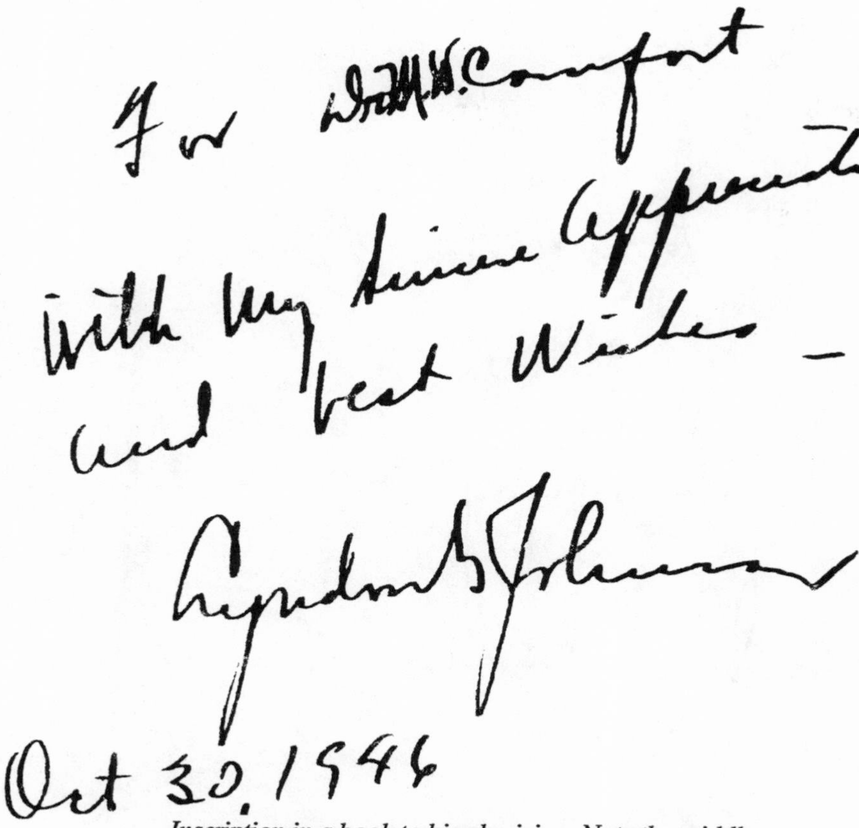

For [illegible]Comfort

with my sincere appreciation and best wishes –

Lyndon B Johnson

Oct 30, 1946

Inscription in a book to his physician. Note the middle
initial "B" is disconnected from the "J" of Johnson.

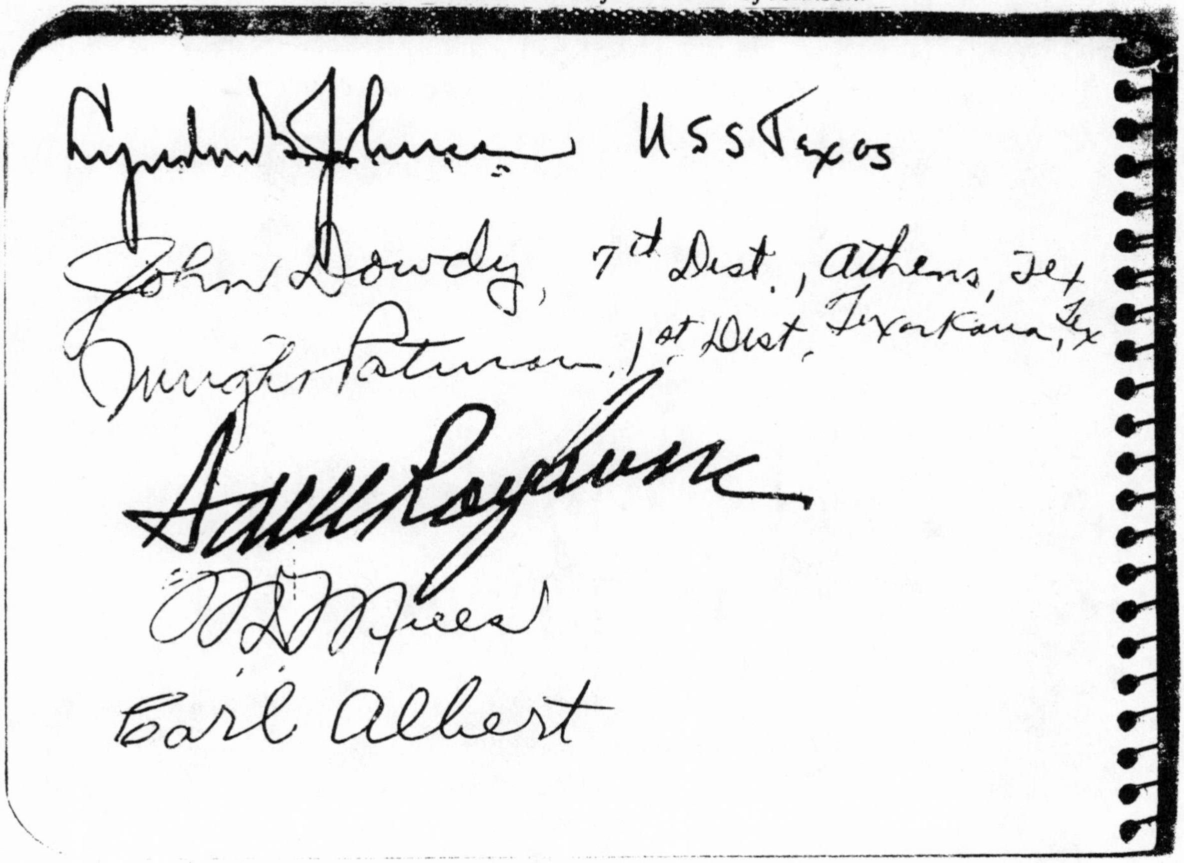

Lyndon B Johnson   U S S Texas

John Dowdy, 7th Dist., Athens, Tex
Wright Patman, 1st Dist, Texarkana, Tex

Sam Rayburn

W D Mills

Carl Albert

In person signature of Johnson in autograph album, 1957

Pre-presidential (authentic)

To Grover Sellers
With my gratitude
and admiration
Lyndon B. Johnson

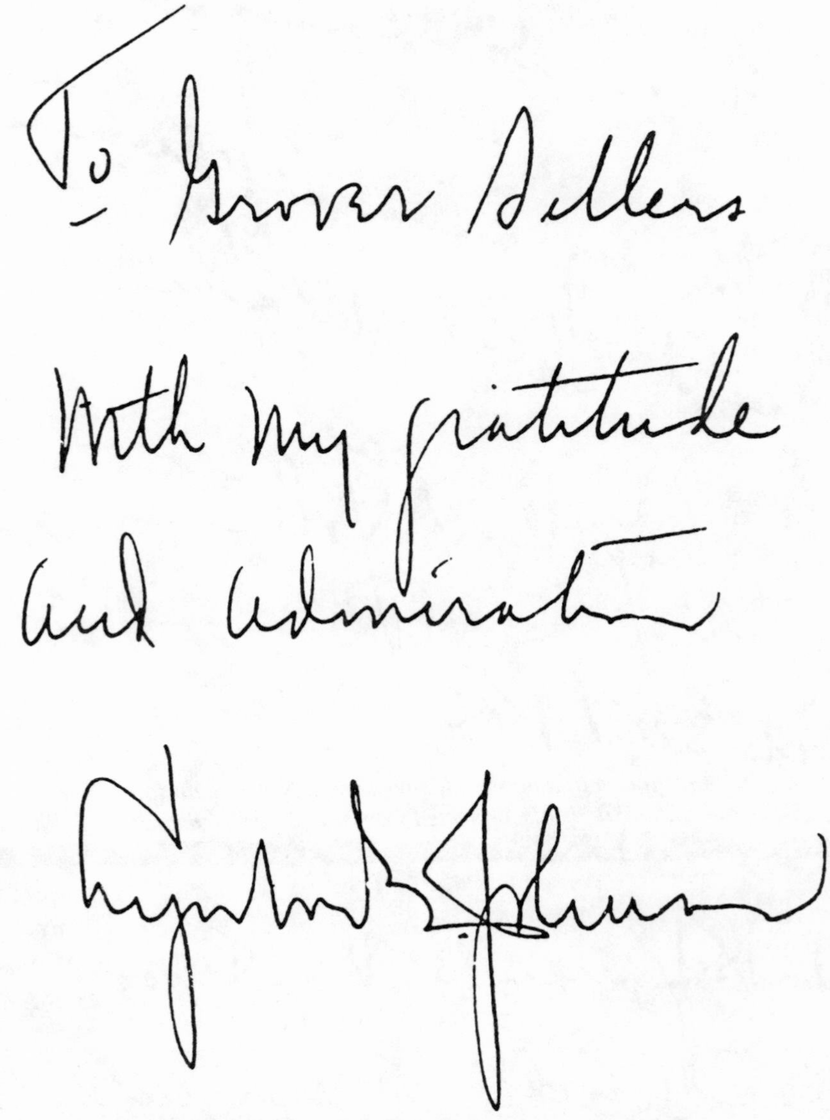

Inscription in book to a former attorney general of Texas, 1955.

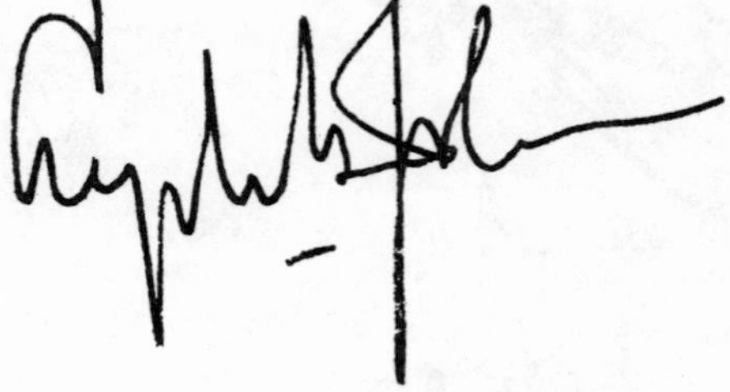

Lyndon B. Johnson

In person signature, Spring 1959

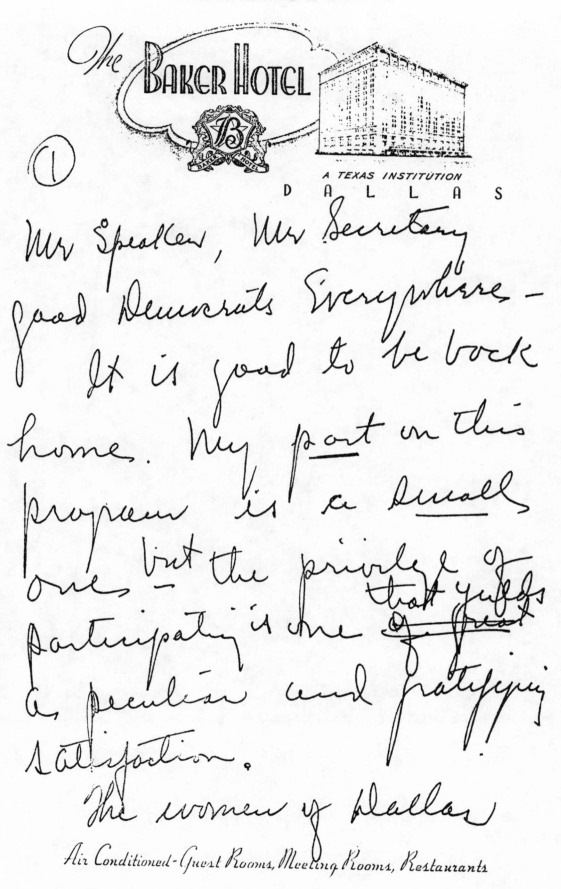

The Baker Hotel

A TEXAS INSTITUTION
DALLAS

① Mr Speaker, Mr Secretary good Democrats Everywhere —

It is good to be back home. My part on this program is a small one — but the privilege of participating is one that yields a peculiar and gratifying satisfaction.

The women of Dallas

Air Conditioned - Guest Rooms, Meeting Rooms, Restaurants

Page from a handwritten speech by Johnson, 1945.

155

Inscribed and signed photograph, 1957.

Presidential (authentic)

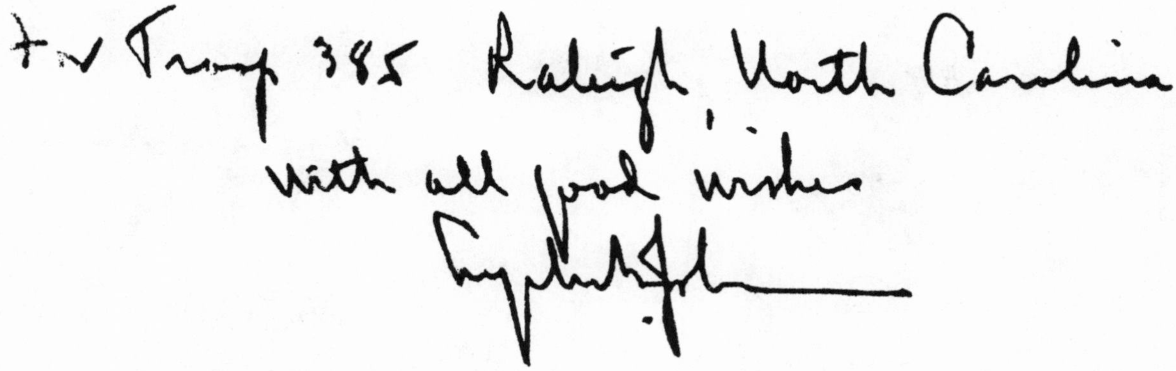

For Troop 385 Raleigh, North Carolina with all good wishes

Authentic inscription and signature on a presidential photograph, 1967

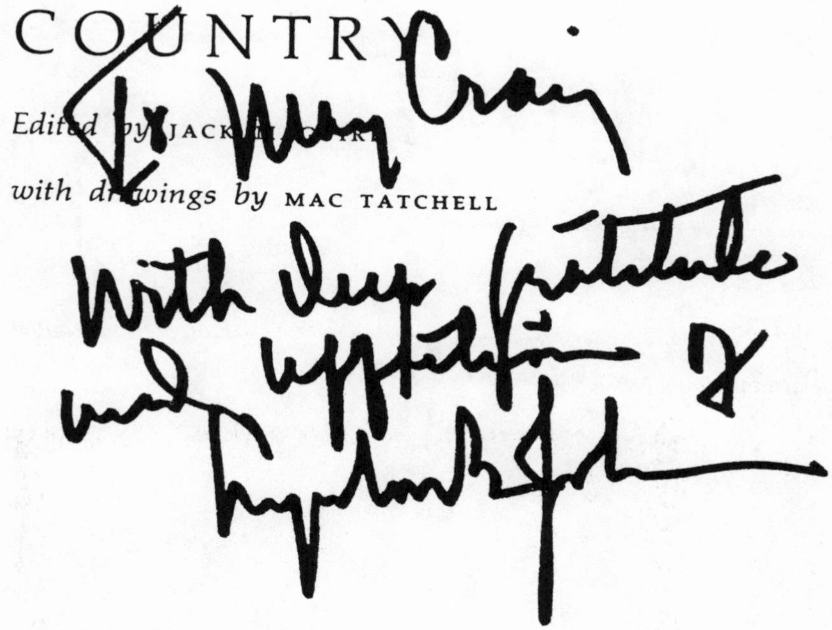

COUNTRY

Edited by JACK...

For May Craig

with drawings by MAC TATCHELL

With deep gratitude and appreciation

Rare presidential inscription to a White House correspondent, 1964.

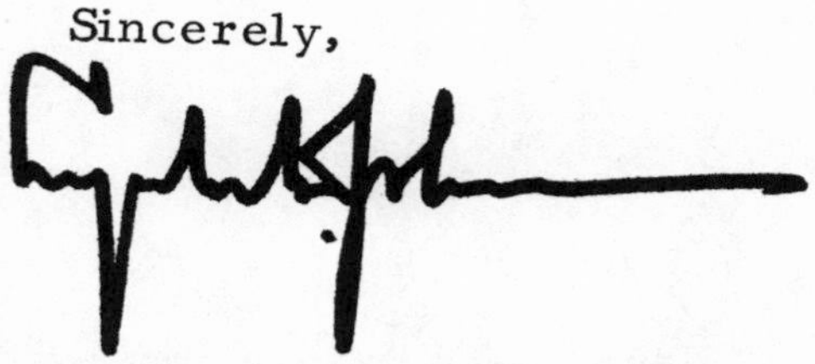

Sincerely,

Authentic signature on a presidential letter

157

To

Herbert Sultenfuss

With my
best wishes

Lyndon Baines Johnson
President of the United States of America

Authentic signature on a rare presidential bookplate.

Sincerely,

Authentic signature on a presidential letter

THE WHITE HOUSE
WASHINGTON

Extremely rare authentic signature on a White House card. (Courtesy of Bob Erickson)

Post Presidential (authentic)

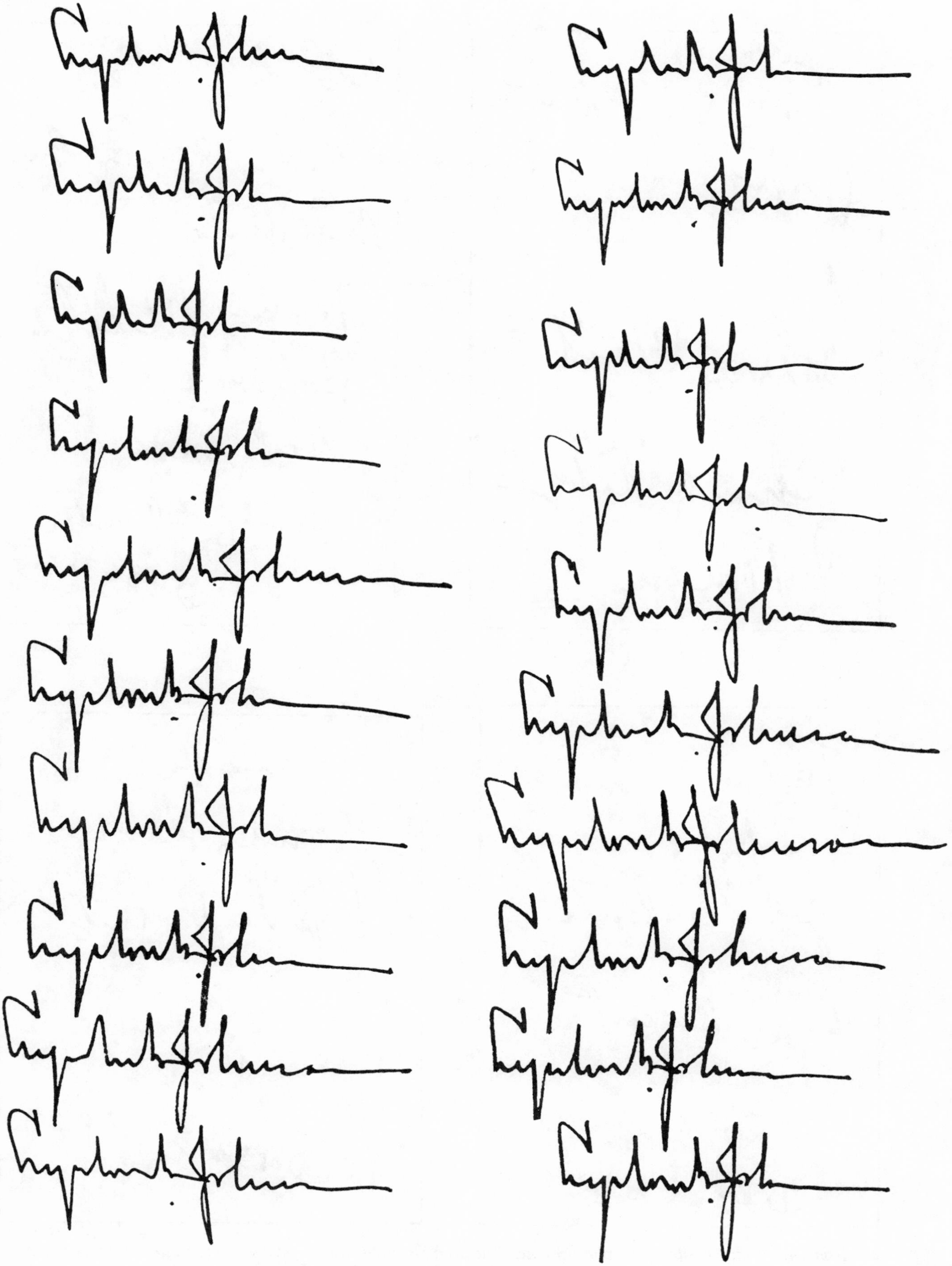

Post Presidential (authentic)

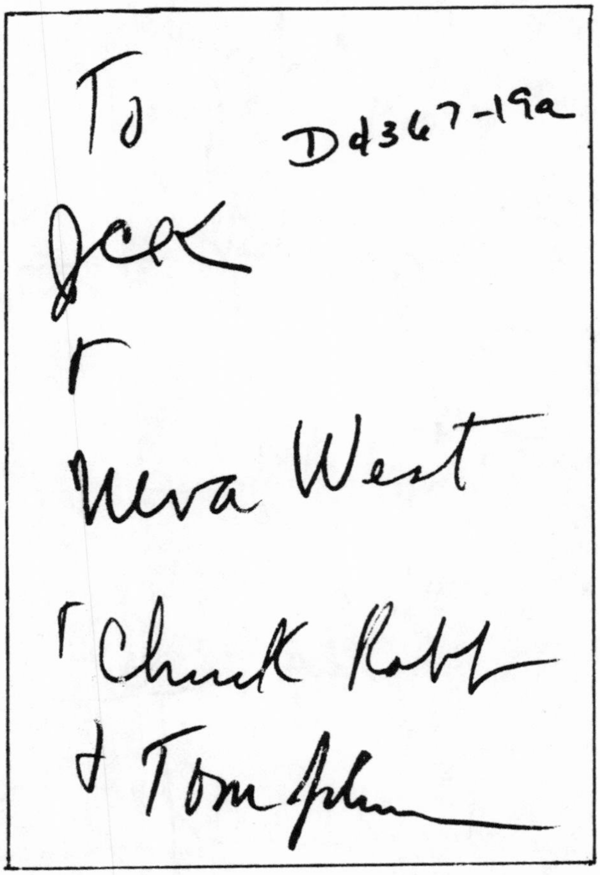

To
Jack
&
Neva West

┌ Chuck Robb
└ Tom Johnson

D4367-19a

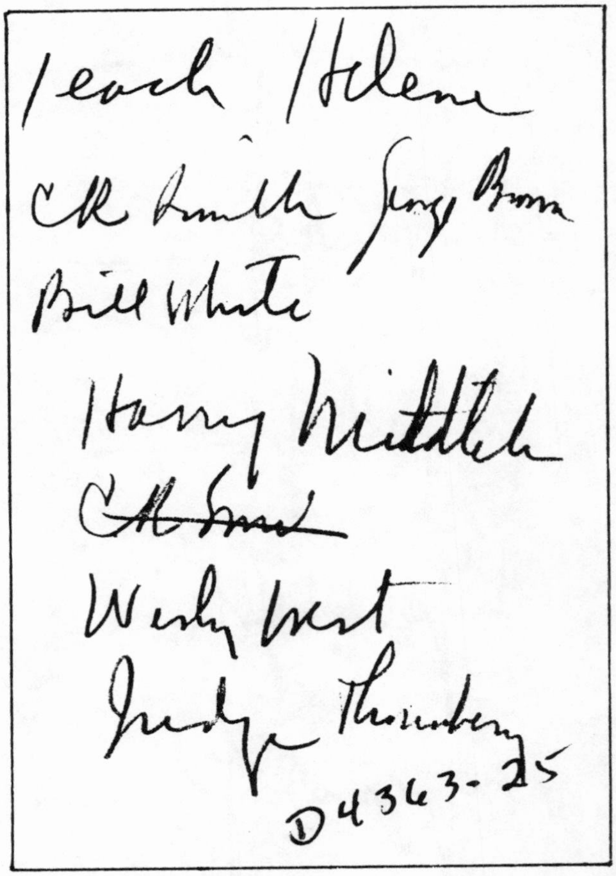

1 each / Helene
CK Smith   George Brown
Bill White

Harry Middleton
CA Smith
Wesley West
Judge Thornberry

D4363-25

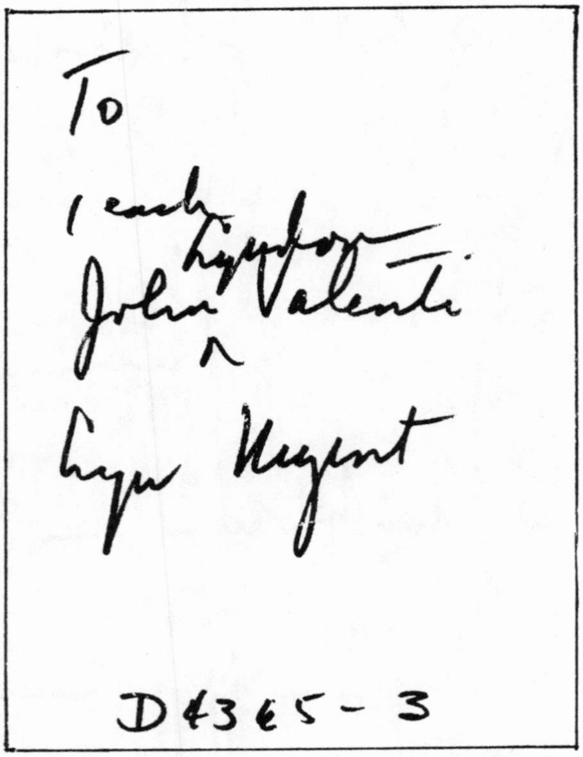

To
1 each   Lyndon
John Valenti
        ^
Lynn Nugent

D4365-3

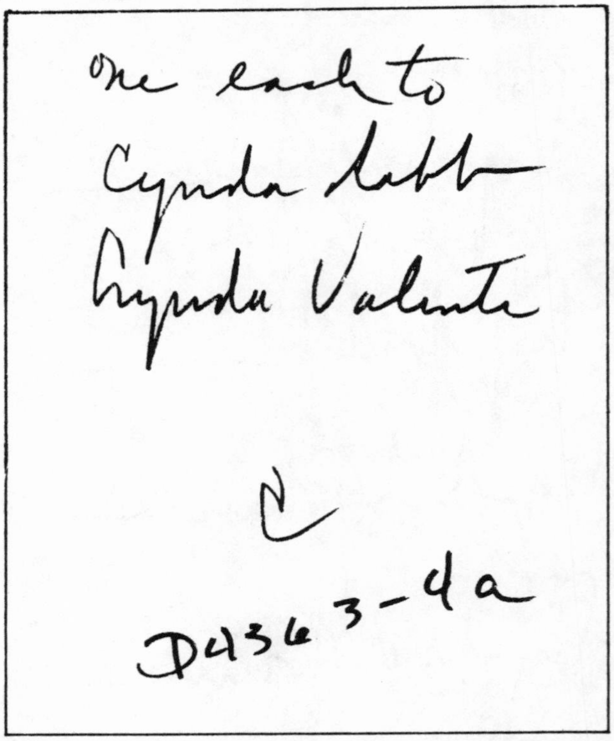

One each to
Cynda Robb
Lynda Valenti

L

D4363-4a

Johnson's handwritten notes to his photographer. The example in the lower right corner is signed with his signle initial "L", as was his custom on inter-office memoranda. Circa 1970.

Post Presidential (authentic)

Sincerely,

March 12, 1969

Sincerely,

March 8, 1970

Sincerely,

December 30, 1971

Sincerely,

December 22, 1970

For Mrs. Edwin Goff—

with pleasant memories
of your visit to our
ranch.

Aug. 6, '70

Extremely rare Autograph Note Signed on 12 mo stationery.

Sincerely,

September 16, 1970

To Jeff
Best wishes

LBJ Ranch

Stonewall, Texas

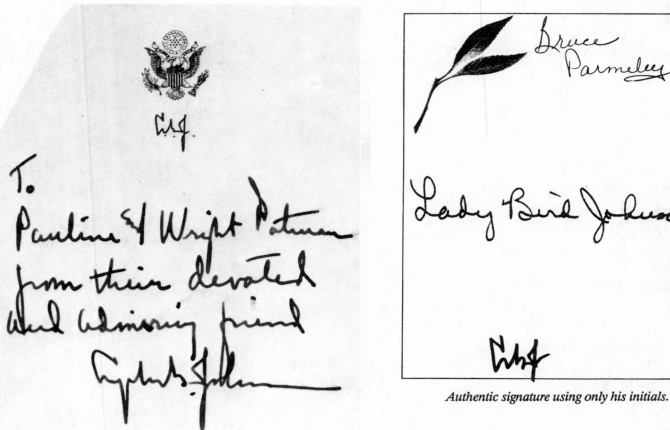

Inscription on bookplate to veteran Texas Congressman and Mrs. Wright Patman.

Authentic signature using only his initials.

Inscription to author, circa 1972.

Post Presidential (authentic)

AUSTIN, TEXAS

Dear Mr. and Mrs. Heffelfinger:

The days preceding and immediately following
the Inauguration brought with them a flood of
letters and telegrams. Mrs. Johnson and I looked
forward to the opportunity to look them over more
closely and we wanted to say thank you again for
your kind message.

You were thoughtful to remember us in such a
nive way. We value your friendship and we
appreciate your good wishes.

Sincerely,

Mr. and Mrs. Peavey Heffelfinger
Route 2
Wayzata, Minnesota 55391

March 12, 1969

Letter signed with Johnson's scarce full post presidential signature.

GLOSSARY OF TERMS

A.D.S., A.Ds.S.	Autograph Document(s) Signed	I	Inscribed
A.L.S., A.Ls.S.	Autograph Letter(s) Signed	L.S., Ls.S.	Letter(s) Signed
A.Ms.S.	Autograph Manuscript Signed	Ms.L.S., Ms.Ls.S.	Manuscript Letter(s) Signed
A.N.S., A.Ns.S.	Autograph Note(s) Signed	n.d.	no date
A.Q.S., A.Qs.S.	Autograph Quotation(s) Signed	n.p.	no place
cabinet	Photograph approximately 5" x 7"	n.y.	no year
c.d.v.	carte de visite	S.P.	Signed Photo
D.S., Ds.S.	Document(s) Signed	T.L.S., T.Ls.S.	Typed Letter(s) Signed
F.D.C.	First Day Cover	4to	approximately 8" x 10"
Folio	approximately legal size	8vo	approximately 8" x 6"
Holographic	A document or letter entirely in the handwriting of the writer.	12mo	approximately 4" x 3"